Never has a darkening world more needed tactics of reconciliation and of its handmaiden, forgiveness. This fine and welcome book does the ultimate: it tells us HOW it can be done and has been done in history. A big Thank You to Michael Henderson again!

—**Georgie Anne Geyer**, *Syndicated Columnist, Universal Press Syndicate*

This is a timely and necessary book from the pens of distinguished public figures and writers. Showing clearly that there is no military solution to the many problems we face, it is a humane and thoughtful guidebook to the troubled times we live in.

—**Martin Bell OBE**, *UNICEF UK Ambassador*

These beautifully written and sensitively told stories of forgiveness and peace should provide inspiration and hope for many readers.

—**Trudy Govier**, *Associate Professor of Philosophy at University of Lethbridge and Author of* Forgiveness and Revenge *and* Taking Wrongs Seriously

Jesus Christ teaches us all about the power of forgiveness. Michael Henderson's book highlights that power in action.

—**John Sentamu**, *The Archbishop of York*

In his latest trail-blazing book on forgiveness, Michael Henderson takes us to a new level. . . . He capitalizes on the thoughtful reflections of world-class scholars and on insights from important political figures such as the late Benazir Bhutto. Through riveting stories ranging from the heart-breaking massacres of Rwanda and Gujarat to heart-warming quests for forgiveness by the Australians for their past treatment of the Aboriginal people and by the British for their participation in the fire-bombing of Dresden, Henderson takes us on a journey that is both moving and inspiring. This book merits the attention of political leaders and policymakers alike. As the book implies, healing the wounds of history should always take priority over waging war.

—**Douglas M. Johnston**, *President and Founder of the International Center for Religion and Diplomacy*

A book that never evades the terrible reality of suffering and injustice, whose answers burn with honesty. Here is the ... brave, difficult but possible. Read it and be ... hope.

—**Anne Perry**, *British Historical Nov...*

I cannot stress enough the importance of this subject, because without forgiveness there is no future for mankind or for any one of us. Forgiveness is a power available to anyone who truly desires it, both victim and perpetrator. It is the only hope also for nations that have lived in perpetual violence toward each other. Forgiveness is a power that we can decide for, and it can be bestowed on anyone.

>—**Johann Christopher Arnold,** *Pastor and Author of* Seventy
>Times Seven: The Power of Forgiveness

Extraordinary stories you will never forget. . . . Michael Henderson takes us across the globe and shares the remarkable journeys that have led individuals and families to a place of hope and healing. His writing is honest, unambiguous and without sentimentality. With compassion and clarity, Henderson invites us to witness the compelling power of forgiveness and to listen to the voices of people who dared to follow the wisdom of the heart. The book is a careful and serious attempt to shift the emphasis from revenge to forgiveness and reconciliation. Readers will take away a deep appreciation of this fact: justice begins when the freedom to avenge a wrong is questioned. Here, Henderson shows us, where vengeance is arrested, forgiveness will blossom.

>— **Pumla Gobodo-Madikizela,** *Associate Professor of*
>*Psychology, University of Cape Town, author o*f A Human
>Being Died that Night: A South African Story of Forgiveness

Michael Henderson has written an extraordinary, inspirational book based on personal narratives of people, groups, and nations who have taken the initiative to heal destructive conflicts that seemed to have no end. The efforts of these healers are clearly acts of courage given the risks to their reputations and even to their lives. Many of the narratives are so moving that they brought tears to my eyes.

This book is a major contribution toward understanding and implementing these healing processes. This work is an essential counterforce to the destructive tendencies of people and societies.

>—**Aaron Lazare, M.D.,** *Haidak Distinguished Professsor of*
>*Medical Education and Professor of Psychiatry, University of*
>*Massachusetts Medical School, and author of* On Apology

no enemy to conquer

Books by Michael Henderson

From India with Hope

Experiment with Untruth

A Different Accent

On History's Coattails

Hope for a Change

All Her Paths Are Peace

The Forgiveness Factor

Forgiveness: Breaking the Chain of Hate

See You after the Duration

NO eNemy to CONQUeR
FORGIVENESS IN AN UNFORGIVING WORLD

michaeL HeNDeRSON

BAYLOR UNIVERSITY PRESS

Cover Design by Pamela Poll
Book Design by Diane Smith

Library of Congress Cataloging-in-Publication Data

Henderson, Michael, 1932-
  No enemy to conquer : forgiveness in an unforgiving world / Michael Henderson.
       p. cm.
  Includes bibliographical references and index.
  ISBN 978-1-60258-140-1 (pbk. : alk. paper)
  1. Forgiveness. I. Title.

BJ1476.H47 2009
179'.9--dc22
                                2008029508

Printed in the United States of America on acid-free paper.

Dedicated to Lucy Henderson-Thomas

contents

foreword
No Peace without Forgiveness

the daLaI Lama

We humans are social beings. We come into the world as the result of others' actions. We survive here in dependence on others. Whether we like it or not, there is hardly a moment of our lives when we do not benefit from others' activities. For this reason it is hardly surprising that most of our happiness arises in the context of our relationships with others. Nor is it very remarkable that our greatest joy should come when we are motivated by concern for others.

When our news media are regularly filled with reports of violence and crime, we can easily forget that the basic feature of society is kindness; and yet it is only through kindness and compassion, caring for others, that society can succeed. No amount of violent suppression can ensure the cooperation necessary for productive human interaction.

This is why it is important in the face of conflict to adopt a wider perspective, to look at the situation from other angles and use our reason and intelligence to analyze what is going on. That way, we can let go of anger and hatred and develop patience and tolerance; then forgiveness comes naturally.

No matter what atrocities we may have experienced in the past, with the development of patience and tolerance it is possible to let go of the sense of anger and resentment. If we analyze the situation, we come to realize that the past is past. There is no use in continuing to foster anger and hatred, which do nothing to change the situation other than disturbing our own minds and provoking our continued unhappiness. I am not saying that you won't remember what happened. Forgiving and forgetting are two different things. There's nothing wrong with simply remembering what happened, and if you have a sharp mind, you will always remember. But if you can cultivate patience and tolerance, it is possible to let go of the negative feelings associated with terrible events.

In this context, compassion plays a key role because it is both the source and the result of patience, tolerance, forgiveness, and all good qualities. If it is correct that qualities such as love, patience, tolerance, and forgiveness are what happiness consists of, and if it is also correct that compassion is both the source and the fruit of these qualities, then the more we are compassionate, the more we provide for our own happiness.

Thus, any sense that concern for others, though a noble quality, is a matter for our private lives only is simply shortsighted. Compassion belongs to every sphere of human activity.

Compassion and love are not luxuries to be enjoyed when we have the time. As the source both of inner and external peace, they are fundamental to the continued survival of our species. On the one hand, they constitute nonviolence in action. On the other, they are, as I have already said, the source of all spiritual qualities; of forgiveness, tolerance, and all other virtues. What is more, they are the very things that give meaning to our activities and make them constructive. There is nothing particularly amazing about being highly educated or even about being rich. But it is only when the individual has a warm heart that these attributes become worthwhile.

One of the goals of Buddhist practice is to overcome the disturbing emotions that afflict us all, because they are of no use to us. Nowhere is the uselessness of disturbing emotions more obvious than in the case of anger. When we become angry, we cease to be compassionate, loving, generous, forgiving, tolerant, and patient. We deprive ourselves of the very things that happiness consists of. Not only does anger immediately destroy our critical faculties, it tends toward rage, spite, hatred, and malice—each of which is always negative because it is a direct cause of harm toward others. Anger invariably causes suffering.

Take for example our attitude toward punishment. Punishment serves an essential function. However, it cannot be justified if it is inflicted primarily in order to satisfy feelings of hatred and revenge toward an offender by the victims or by society. Although punishment may fulfill an important psychological need for victims and others to feel that justice is being done, the infliction of pain on another person also serves to add to the suffering already done and does not increase the potential for happiness of anyone involved. Instead of revenge, it is the notion of forgiveness that should be encouraged and developed. This is emphasized by most religions and humanist philosophies.

Ultimately, revenge is futile. If the object of your revenge—your enemy—is very weak, revenge amounts to simple bullying. On the other hand, if your enemy is very powerful, you cannot wreak revenge on him. When you think, "He did something bad to me, and I got my own back," revenge is a source of misplaced satisfaction. You may feel pleased with yourself in the short term, but where will it end?

We continually make mistakes because we lack a proper understanding of reality. When an unfortunate and distressing event takes place, we tend to settle on one cause or factor out of many to blame and begin to attribute everything that has happened only to that and act accordingly. Sometimes, we retaliate with force and yet the reality is that for any event to take place there are always many factors involved. When something terrible happens, instead of finding some individual or group to blame, fostering hatred and a desire for revenge, we should try to take a broader view and consider the longer term.

Much more constructive than stoking feelings of resentment and revenge is to forgive and transform the negative event and its consequences into a source of inner strength.

acknowledgments

This book has been very much a team effort. I am most grateful to the many men and women who have permitted me to tell their stories; to the academics who have added their helpful commentaries: Dr. David Smock, Dr. Donna Hicks, Dr. Mohammed Abu-Nimer, Dr. Margaret Smith, Dr. Barry Hart, and Mr. Joseph Montville; to the personalities who have provided their insights: HH The Dalai Lama, for the foreword, Benazir Bhutto, Betty Bigombe, Rajmohan Gandhi, and Archbishop Desmond Tutu and Chief Rabbi Dr. Jonathan Sacks for permitting me to quote from their books *No Future without Forgiveness* and *The Dignity of Difference*. I should also acknowledge the permission given by Manfred Schreyer to quote from my articles on the Web site www.spiritrestoration.org, by Arnicacreative for material from my book *Forgiveness: Breaking the Chain of Hate*, and by Pact Publications for material about Caux in my chapter in *Positive Approaches to Peacebuilding*. Additional publishing assistance was given by many, including Andrew Stallybrass of Caux Books, Hugh Nowell of the International Communications Forum, and—above all—Casey Blaine of Baylor University Press who, out of the blue, asked me if I was planning to do another book—which at the time I wasn't. A special thanks to her for her encouragement and to Richard Ruffin for his steady support and advice that constantly enlarged the concept.

preface

An earlier book of mine, *Forgiveness: Breaking the Chain of Hate*, was launched at a prestigious think tank in Washington, D.C. At the occasion, a pompous young man breezed up to me, announced that he was from the office of a certain high-ranking foreign-policy expert, and asked, rather accusatorily, "Is your approach journalistic or analytical?" A bit taken aback, I failed to point out that journalists could also be analytical. "Journalistic," I simply replied. "Ah," he said, "then you'll tell stories."

He was right. I do not come to the subject from academic study but from hands-on experience and with the benefit of working all my life alongside men and women committed to building bridges between people of differing colors, cultures, and languages on the basis that you start with where you and your own people need to be different rather than pointing the finger of blame. It has indeed been my commitment so to live and it has been my good fortune to tell their stories in several books.

In 2006 I heard BBC Radio news interviewer John Humphreys say that he had spent a lifetime covering humankind at its worst, and he wondered how faith was possible in a world of suffering, much of it arguably caused by religion or religious extremism and to which God seemed to have turned a blind eye: "I believed once (that God existed) but for nearly fifty years I've been a journalist and I've seen perhaps too much suffering, too many children dying, too much wanton savagery to continue to believe it." One reason that I continue to believe it is because of the positive developments in people's lives I have myself witnessed, many in settings similar to those Humphreys described. I have seen humankind at its best, you might say. The readiness of men and women to forgive and ask for forgiveness in the most trying circumstances is awe-inspiring. To tell their stories is a privilege.

I was first introduced to the idea that apology and forgiveness have more than personal ramifications through the example of my mother. My Anglo-Irish family had lived for hundreds of years in Ireland as part of a minority Protestant community lording it over a predominantly Catholic country. But in 1922, at the time of Irish independence, my grandfather was told by ultranationalists to leave the country by week's end or be shot. Our old family home was later burned to the ground. We were all that was unpopular at the time: not only Protestants but from a landowning family that for generations had served in the Royal Irish Constabulary and in the British army.

Many years later, my mother finally faced how deeply hurt she felt about being forced out of Ireland. As a family, in 1947, we attended a conference at the center for reconciliation at Caux, Switzerland. The center had been opened the year before by Swiss who felt that, as their country had been spared the ravages of the war, they should provide a place where the hurts and hates of that war could be healed. One day an Irish Catholic senator, Eleanor Butler, spoke. She was a member of the Council of Europe and spoke of unity. Everything in my mother rebelled against her. Who is this woman talking about unity in Europe, and she chucked me out of my country? But in the spirit of that place, she felt moved to apologize to Senator Butler for the indifference our family had shown to Catholics over many years. She did so, and the two became friends and worked together, becoming part of that great army of women who kept the peace hopes alive.

Soon after that visit to Caux, Senator Butler said, "I come from a nation of good haters. We enjoy feuds and we love fighting, almost for the fun of it. But in these last months, I have had to do something I very much dislike. I have had to make some honest apologies for viewpoints that have divided instead of united me to other nations and other parts of my own nation. In every case, new unity was born between myself and those from whom I had been separated." She went on to be one of the founders of the Glencree Reconciliation Centre.

Both women have since died, but they would have rejoiced at the very tangible progress that has been made in Northern Ireland, touched on later in the book. My mother recognized, as the whole family did, that we in Britain must do more to make amends for the way we treated the Irish people over centuries. It was the start of a journey for all of us.

In 1996 I wrote a book about the fiftieth anniversary of that Caux center. The book traced its work through the laying of foundations for Franco–German reconciliation to efforts to help introduce democratic foundations in the countries of the former Soviet Union, from the dialogue of decolonialization in Africa to the healing of hatreds after the killing fields of Cambodia. Looking through its contents for a possible title, it was clear that the common factor in many of the stories was forgiveness, and so it was called *The Forgiveness Factor.* One result was that another publisher asked me to write *Forgiveness: Breaking the Chain of Hate.*

Now, nearly ten years later, the world has seen 9/11, the bombings in Bali, London, and Madrid, the ongoing conflict in Iraq and Afghanistan, and many other demonstrations of the continuing power of hatred and revenge. They are an ever-present reminder of the need for reconciliation and forgiveness.

I visited a bookstore recently to see where *Forgiveness: Breaking the Chain of Hate* was shelved. I found it, eventually, under "self-help." Indeed, I believe that's precisely what it is—and that this book will be as well. But its intention is far wider and that is to make it clear that "soft" subjects like forgiving and asking for forgiveness, as Nelson Mandela has courageously shown, have great significance in public life. They may be adjuncts to the hard political and developmental commitment required, but without them many good initiatives will be fated to fail. Could anyone imagine that South Africa would have gotten to where it is today without that element? Reconciliation and forgiveness are essential in relations between the West and the Muslim world and in how we look at and treat each other. The building of relationships of trust is surely a priority.

I use the word forgiveness in the broadest sense to encompass a multitude of virtues. For the book is, above all, about journeys:

journeys sometimes taken alone, journeys sometimes taken with others. Forgiveness for some may be the start of that journey; for some it may be the destination at journey's end; for most, it is the decisions—often renewed as we falter—that are made along the way.

The aim of this book is not to define forgiveness or to open a theological discussion of the subject. This book is rather a celebration of men and women at their best, some giving credit to their maker, and others distinctly making clear that as far as they are concerned, religion has nothing to do with it. It is not about theory but about hard-won experience. I hope it helps all who read it to "strengthen their forgiveness muscle." It contains dramatic evidence validating the power of forgiveness and personal reconciliation to affect national life; stories of men and women, of different faiths and no faith, who inspire us by their courage.

~~Michael Henderson
Westward Ho!
North Devon

1

cLasH oR aLLIaNCe?

There will be no lasting peace on earth unless we learn not merely to tolerate but even to respect other faiths as our own.

~~Mahatma Gandhi

As the Prophet stood with a group of Muslims, a funeral procession passed by, and the Prophet stood up to show his respect for the deceased. Surprised, the Muslims informed him that this was a Jew's funeral. The Prophet answered with clarity and dignity. Was this not a human soul?

~~Tariq Ramadan

The biggest weapon of mass destruction is the hate in our souls.

~~Chief Rabbi Jonathan Sacks

Forgiveness has an image problem. It fosters so many misconceptions. Some withhold forgiveness for fear that they might easily become a "doormat" for others; or that justice might not be served, and cruel people will literally get away with murder; or that forgiveness and apology, particularly in terms of injustices of the past, is just the latest caving in to political correctness.

With the help of the many stories in the book as well as the generous contributions of academics and personalities of differing backgrounds, I hope to make it clear that such fears are unjustified. One authority on these matters has urged me to "begin the work of reclaiming and revitalizing both the word and the process of forgiveness in the world."

The stories will show that those who forgive are strong and, as Rajmohan Gandhi puts it, that "the stuff of forgiveness is sterner than suspected." They underline that forgiving and asking for forgiveness are not merely personal or religious actions but can deeply influence national and international affairs. Indeed, Chief Rabbi Jonathan Sacks has written that forgiveness is "the single most important word in conflict resolution."

Precise definitions of forgiveness are limiting because human experiences are so varied and often surprising. But some elements are clear, as formulated by the many fine writers on the subject. They may involve not only turning from revenge but also include a compassion for the other—a recognition of their humanity, even an awareness that, given similar circumstances, we might have behaved just as badly. Henri Nouwen calls forgiveness "love practiced among people who love poorly. It sets us free without wanting anything in return." Philip Yancey says that although forgiveness does not settle all questions of blame and fairness, it does allow relationships to start over. Lew Smedes describes forgiveness as surrendering the right to get even. He writes: "The first and often the only person to be healed is the person who does the forgiveness. When we genuinely forgive, we set the prisoner free and then discover the prisoner we set free was ourselves." He points out that revenge never evens the score, for alienated people never keep score of wrongs by the same mathematics: "Forgiveness is the only way to stop the cycle of unfair pain turning in your memory."

The burden of the past is lifted as individuals, and sometimes whole nations, are prepared to move on. Forgiveness frees the victim and, as significantly, sometimes enables them to be listened to by the victimizer. Spencer Perkins, an African American who worked for racial reconciliation, pointed out that when we can forgive and even accept those who refuse to listen to God's command to do justice, "it allows them to hear God's judgment without feeling a personal judgment from us." Archbishop Desmond Tutu believes that forgiveness enables both to come out of the experience better people.

This book, as mentioned in the preface, is about journeys, journeys that, though intensely personal, may have national or even international repercussions and that also—somewhere along the way—involve forgiveness. It is about brave souls who have been willing to embark on a different, less conventional direction than predicted.

A friend who is involved in building community and particularly in race relations between black and white likes to talk about "salt and pepper" teams. He finds that the kind of society he is working toward is most convincingly expressed by those who mirror what they want to see happen. To any interview or event, his teams will go together, black and white, salt and pepper. The image applies perhaps less well to those whose color is the same, yet when Muslim and Christian, Muslim and Jew, Catholic and Protestant, for instance, are seen to be "walking in each other's moccasins" as Native Americans put it, and taking that journey together, it becomes hard to refute their experience. Much of this book is assembled on that principle.

One aim of this book is to further an appreciation of our brothers and sisters of the Muslim faith. In 2007, in an early phase of the U.S. election campaign, a magazine reported that associates of Senator Hillary Rodham Clinton had unearthed information that another presidential candidate, Senator Barack Obama, had attended a radical Muslim school in Indonesia. CNN sent its senior international correspondent to Jakarta to investigate, and he reported that this was not true. There was no evidence as far as I know that Senator Clinton had anything to do with this allegation. What disturbed me most, however, was not that political dirty tricks are played at election time but rather that involvement with the Muslim faith would be regarded as a handle with which to besmirch a candidate.

I remember telling a friend, twenty-five years earlier, that there were then forty-six countries in the world with a Muslim majority. She exclaimed, "How terrible!" More recently, I was e-mailed by another person who said, "When I passed through Heathrow airport, there seemed to be only Pakistanis. I was so frightened."

Such attitudes toward other countries and different faiths sadden me. An American clergyman, Frank Buchman, founder of Initiatives of Change (formerly known as Moral Re-Armament), years ago introduced me to the importance of valuing other faiths besides my own. He was ahead of his time in appreciating that you did not need to water down what you believed in order to find unity. He was never slow to share his own source of power, but as a Christian, he respected the way God's spirit could work through anyone. Sixty years ago, he envisioned the Muslim world from Indonesia to North Africa being a "girder of unity for all civilization."

I long for people to know more about others who are different from them. I first visited a Muslim country, Pakistan, more than fifty years ago and soon after spent several years in Nigeria. In 1953 a young Muslim friend from the Woking Mosque presented me with a copy of *The Sayings of Muhammad*. I read it and still have it.

Over the years, it has been clear to me that Muslims interact with the demands of their faith as rigorously and often more faithfully than I do as a Christian, whether in trying to ascertain the will of God in difficult circumstances or holding to strict moral standards at a time when these are being constantly lowered. They also dislike it—as I do—when actions with which they disagree are done in the name of their faith.

As an Englishman, I am grateful to the Prince of Wales for his appreciation of the Muslim faith. In a 2006 inaugural paper for a series of essays on the Alliance of Civilization and Interfaith Reconciliation for the University of Maryland, he wrote that some people portray the current tensions as a "clash of civilizations" between Islam and "the West," or worse, between "backwardness" and "modernity." He believes this is a "wrong-headed and dangerously simplistic view": "It is too easy to forget that many of the greatest scientific discoveries that underpin our 'modern' Western world were made by great Islamic scholars. In the Dark Ages, at a time when we Europeans were discarding much of the great works of ancient Greece and Rome, Islamic scholars, sometimes working together with their Jewish and Christian brothers, were preserving and studying them—surely one of history's greatest rescue operations—and on that secured the very foundations of modern Western culture. At the same time, it is worth considering that there are some things that trouble many people about Western modernity as it spreads round the world."

Prince Charles started his paper with a personal note: "I know only too well how one's faith can be challenged, having lost a much-beloved great uncle, Lord Mountbatten, in an IRA[1] terrorist attack in 1979. But I remember how it gradually dawned on me that thoughts of vengeance and hatred would merely prolong the terrible law of cause and effect and continue an unbroken cycle of violence. 'An eye for an eye,' said Mahatma Gandhi, 'and soon the whole world will be blind.'"

A challenge for Christians today is to get to know Muslims individually and to realize that attacks on Muslims are often also an attack on the role of faith in society. Many secular-minded Western-ers, particularly in Europe, have a problem with any religion being taken seriously. For them, the only good Muslim is a nonpracticing one. And there is a refusal to believe that Muslims who believe in their faith and take it seriously can become part of modern demo-cratic society.

A challenge for many Muslims is to know how to contest in the public arena the *jihadists* who speak in the name of their religion—and practice many aspects of it—but ignore the basic command to respect the other. Dr. Juzar Bandukawala, an Indian Muslim and distinguished physicist, does not want Muslims to answer hate with hate. As he says in chapter 3, "It is a tribute to the Muslims of India that we have not responded with the weapon of terrorism, despite the provocation for the same. Osama bin Laden is not the answer to the problems facing Muslims in India. His approach can be suicidal for us. His methods violate the basic precepts of Islam, wherein kill-ing of innocents is an unpardonable sin."

In 2006 the United Nations published an initiative titled *Alliance of Civilizations,* a report by a high-level group that contests "the misguided view that cultures are set on an unavoidable colli-sion course" and claims that "politics, not religion" is at the heart of the growing Muslim–West divide. "The problem is never the faith," said Kofi Annan, then UN secretary-general, receiving the report, "it is the faithful and how they behave toward each other: We should start by reaffirming—and demonstrating—that the problem is not the Quran, the Torah, or the Bible."

The report concludes that an honest look at twentieth-century history shows that "no single group, culture, geographic region, or political orientation has a monopoly on extremism and terrorist acts."

In no one country alone will the issue of the clash of cultures be determined. The issue affects and will be affected by all of us, by our attitudes toward people within our own borders and in our foreign policies. Nigeria is certainly on the front line of that struggle as it faces the problem within its own border. This chapter starts with the story of two Nigerians who would have said a few years ago that clash was inevitable—and even right—but since have found a different approach.

Nigeria: The Pastor and the Imam

Muhammad Nurayn Ashafa, a Muslim imam, was once committed to the total Islamization of Nigeria. James Movel Wuye, a Christian pastor, was just as committed to its total evangelization. They were bitter enemies, determined to kill each other. Today they are friends and joint directors of an NGO,[2] the Interfaith Mediation Centre in Kaduna, one of the most important cities in northern Nigeria. The archbishop of Canterbury, Dr. Rowan Williams, has called their story "a model for Christian–Muslim relations."[3]

In a world that debates whether the future is a clash or an alliance of civilizations, their remarkable journey is a beacon of hope—and not just for Nigeria. I learned from them what had "transformed vengeance into reconciliation."

Between September 2001 and May 2004, nearly fifty-four thousand men and women were killed in three years of ethnic conflict in Nigeria's central plateau.[4] This led in May 2004 to then-President Olusegun Obasanjo declaring a six-month state of emergency for Plateau state, replacing the elected civilian governor with a military administrator. With the largest population in Africa (140 million: half Muslim, half Christian or local African religions) and being the seventh largest oil producer, Nigeria is, according to John Paden, professor of international studies at George Mason University, a key fault line in one of the most strategically important countries in the world, central to global stability.

Dozens of mosques and churches were destroyed in the country's interreligious strife. The reasons for the plateau killings were not just Christian–Muslim conflicts, but also clashes between farmers and local authorities and other issues such as relocation of markets, disputes over access to government posts, "indigene versus settlers syndrome," and the political manipulation of symbols. But as Paden maintains, "Very few religiously mixed communities can afford to ignore the issue of interfaith dialogue and the need for regular mechanics of conflict mediation."

In his book *Muslim Civic Culture and Conflict Resolution*, Paden, who served as an international monitor in the Nigerian presidential elections of 1999 and 2003, draws attention to the example of the Interfaith Mediation Centre in its work to build capacities in conflict prevention and mediation: "The efforts of an evangelical pastor and Muslim imam are a prototype for many of the secondary school and university 'peace committees' already having an impact on conflict resolution efforts in Nigeria." He believes that the cultural capacities of Nigerians—Christian, Muslim, and traditional—to set an example in conflict resolution "will have enormous implications for global society in the years to come."

The work of "the Imam and the Pastor," as Ashafa and Wuye are widely known, is having ramifications way beyond Nigeria, not the least because, for a time, they were at the heart of the problem. The men address a key issue facing people of faith today: how the Christian and Muslim worlds can live and work together without compromising their fundamental religious principles.

I first met the two men at an international conference in 2004. Their witness, standing together, was powerful: two militant religious extremists, now working, as they put it, "for the transformation of society."

They both come out of the heart of the religious teaching of their communities. As a rebellious young man, James Wuye was challenged by a Christian minister. "When he started preaching, it was like somebody told him about me. Pointing his hand at the congregation, it was like he was pointing his hand at me. I kept ducking under the pew to avoid him. I had a conviction in my heart that God was speaking to me and that I needed to change." He became a Pentecostal minister, a passionate evangelist, and vice president of the Christian Youth Association of Nigeria. With community relations strained to a breaking point, he decided to join a Christian militia group. "People were laughing us to scorn, pastors were being killed. My hate for Muslims had no limits."

Imam Muhammad Nurayn Ashafa comes from a strong religious family, a long line of imams. His father was a spiritual leader, and the family felt they were custodians of Islamic heritage. Because of his family's struggle with Western colonial authority, he was not able to get a Western education. "Most of us had nothing to do with the West. We have a zeal of protecting, reviving the reforming spirit, and bringing back to Islam the glory of Islam."

As religious conflict intensified, both young men joined in the struggle, participating on their respective sides. In the early 1990s, the two men had wished to kill each other, during communal riots. Muslim extremists cut off Pastor Wuye's hand when he was defending his church, and Christian extremists killed Ashafa's spiritual teacher, seventy-year-old Ahmad Tijjani, and two of his brothers. "For forty-eight hours," says Ashafa, "we were killing and maiming each other. I was fighting, believing I had to defend my faith community." In May 1995 the two men met for the first time at an event convened by the wife of the military administrator of Kaduna state, under the auspices of the State Women's Commission. James went expecting that Ashafa's men were planning to identify him as a target for possible attack. "By his dress, Ashafa was the embodiment of an Islamic fundamentalist. We saw them as fanatics." They were to write later: "We were both startled by some discoveries. Hidden behind the turbaned imam was a gentle man, not the violent man the pastor had assumed he was; the suited pastor was a bird of the same feather as the imam. We found we had a lot in common."

It was suggested that the men might have a part in bringing healing. They were encouraged to talk, and each began to question the cost of the violence, finding passages in the Bible and the Quran that showed common approaches. The imam says that as they focused on what they could take on together, rather than looking at their differences, there was hope for "a united front against evil." They saw their survival as a sign from God and set up an organization to encourage dialogue. Despite, as they put it, strong tongue-lashing from their respective organizations, they decided to meet together with their executives, not at a church or a mosque but on neutral ground. Out of this encounter came the Muslim Christian Youth Dialogue Forum. The imam was met with disdain when he first came in full regalia to the Christian group, and the pastor was met with suspicion when he first visited the mosque. "I wasn't sure I would come out of the place alive," remembers the pastor. They were labeled as "betrayers" by some of their own people and even accused of being funded, separately, by the Vatican and Israel.

In 1999 the two published a book about their discoveries, *The Pastor and the Imam: Responding to Conflict.* They detailed theological places of agreement in their respective faiths and also points of difference. In it, they pay tribute to Nigerian leaders over the years who worked for religious understanding and write, "If we do not wish our beloved nation to end up like Somalia, Burundi, Liberia, and Rwanda, where ethnic-religious conflicts have threatened their very existence, we must collaborate and work together as a team to check these bad elements that use religion, especially Islam and Christianity, to cause discord within humanity."

They quoted then-Archbishop of Canterbury George Carey: "In most, if not all our traditions, there are things of which we should rightly be ashamed. But there are also things in which we can rejoice. Part of our task is to help people focus on the latter in the faith of others and to speak of those faiths with the respect they deserve."[5] And they quoted Kano Governor Ibrahim Shekarau: "Every good Muslim will like to deal with a good Christian; likewise every good Christian will like to deal with a good Muslim. I did not choose to come from a Muslim family nor do you choose to come from a Christian family; these were accidents of birth. But God chose to create us that way so that we may know each other and live with one another in peace. Who am I to challenge God's wisdom in this respect?"[6]

It was one thing for the two religious figures to talk intellectually. Real friendship, however, was slower to come. "We were programmed to hate one another, to evangelize or Islamize at all costs," says the pastor. "I used to want to have nothing to do with Muslims until I met Ashafa."

A turning point for Imam Ashafa came when he heard another imam preach in the mosque about forgiveness and the example of the Prophet. "At that point, the concepts of forgiveness and mercy were far away from my conviction," he says. You have a right to redress, this imam told them, but the Quran teaches further that it is better to turn evil into something that is good. So therefore, if Muslims refuse to forgive those who persecute them, they are not the true embodiment of Muhammad (PBUH[7]) who in Mecca forgave the people who tried to destroy him. "As the imam spoke, I felt he was looking right at me." Tears flowed down Ashafa's cheeks as he wondered whether he could forgive his enemy. "Muhammad has forgiven, you have to forgive," the preacher said, "and he was looking in my direction. He talked as if he knew what I was thinking in my heart. I was in an ocean of confusion, between my conscience and my desire for revenge. Suddenly he finished his sermon and said, 'Let's pray.' We prayed and after that I started thinking I can really forgive James."

The relationship began to grow. But it took Pastor Wuye three years to overcome his hatred. When they began traveling together, even sharing a room, he was sometimes tempted to carry a pillow to suffocate Ashafa when sleeping. "Each time I wanted to retaliate for my hand."

Seeds of reconciliation were sown when the imam and other community leaders visited the pastor's sick mother in a hospital. "Ashafa was radiating love, but I'd been blinded by hate and pain," he says. A turning point for him was the word of an evangelist: "You cannot preach to someone you hate. If you will truly do this work, you must begin to forgive them for every hurt against you or against anyone you have loved or you love dearly."

As their work expanded, teams of pastors and imams traveled to trouble spots. These teams had much to learn about each others' faith. Christians had to learn to be patient when Muslims went for prayers and likewise Muslims on Sundays when Christians went for theirs. One emphasis of their Interfaith Mediation Centre was on bringing young Christians and Muslims together for conferences and workshops.

Where violence has broken out in northern Nigeria, they have gone together to the streets to calm tempers and find solutions. At one point, Imam Ashafa protected Christian women and children in his home and was threatened with death by militant Muslims, and Pastor Wuye saved a Muslim woman during one particularly violent episode.

At the invitation of the state governor, the International Centre for Reconciliation at Coventry Cathedral was invited to help end the violence in northern Nigeria. When the center's director, Canon Andrew White, came to Nigeria to see how their center could help bring the different faiths together, the Anglican bishop recommended he meet Imam Ashafa and Pastor Wuye. For five months, they worked with the center and with other religious leaders brought together by the imam and pastor to produce a document known as the Kaduna Peace Declaration, which in 2002 was signed, in the presence of some twenty thousand religious leaders and other top dignitaries, by eleven Muslims and eleven Christians, all influential in the community. The document, based on the Alexandria Declaration of Religious Leaders for Peace in the Holy Land, starts this way:

> In the name of God, who is Almighty, Merciful, and Compassionate, we who have gathered as Muslim and Christian religious leaders from Kaduna State pray for peace in our state and declare our commitment to ending the violence and bloodshed, which has marred our recent history. According to our faiths, killing innocent lives in the name of God is a desecration of His Holy Name and defames religions in the World. The violence that has occurred in Kaduna State is an evil that must be opposed by all people of good faith. We seek to live together as neighbours, respecting the integrity of each other's historical and religious heritage. We call upon all to oppose incitement, hatred, and the misrepresentation of one another.

Despite such promising initiatives, Nigeria saw renewed violence in 2002 and twenty-five thousand troops had to be deployed to subdue the unrest. Consequently, what was called the Yelwan Shendam intervention came at the invitation of the Plateau state administrator; the pastor and the imam gathered key leaders for five days of sharing and negotiation. Working through all the issues, they finally made a joint peace affirmation. On 19 February 2005, thousands celebrated the peace agreement, including many who had fled their homes and now felt safe enough to return.

Their story, as David Smock of the U.S. Institute of Peace says, is "a narrative of religious peacemaking." Progress would not have been achieved if the pastor and the imam had not combined both religious exhortations with well-tested conflict-resolution techniques, demonstrating "that even the bloodiest religious conflicts in Nigeria can be addressed creatively." They then turned their attention to comparable religious violence in the Plateau state capital, Jos, and again a peace accord was signed.

Both Pastor Wuye and Imam Ashafa stay faithful to their religion. "I always say I will die as a Christian," says Pastor Wuye, "and I am not compromising one inch on my principles. But we are creating space for one another." Embracing him, the imam said, "He is no more an enemy but a friend." They regard themselves as victims of the situation they had a part in creating. Indeed, the very fact that they were both at the heart of the previous interreligious violence "gives us our credibility," says Wuye. They are able to show themselves as examples because they used to be part of the militias: "We tell them we lost our loved ones, I lost my hand. When you have dialogue, you have peace. We feel in forgiveness there is strength. You are stronger when you forgive someone."

Wuye says, "Presenting Christ does not really mean verbalizing it; you can live it. By living a Christian life, I can influence people positively without saying it out [loud]. I practice my faith vehemently, and he does too, and we are still coexisting and living together." Ashafa adds, "I want Muslims to provide a safe haven for people and the world who are from other faiths and traditions as demonstrated by Prophet Muhammad (PBUH)." "Christians and Muslims can coexist side by side and still go to the heaven we dream of, that is true," concluded Wuye.

In December 2006 a documentary film about their work premiered at the United Nations in New York.[8] Reviewer Bunmi Akpata-ohohe described it in *Africa Today* as "a harrowing and inspiring story of gratuitous violence but also of forgiveness and friendship." She wrote, "It brings a message of hope for the world on the volatile issue of Christian–Muslim relationships. Who says that good things don't come out of the most populous black country in the world—Nigeria? Such people should think again!"

The film begins with the two men praying in Arabic and English at mass graves of people killed in clashes between Christians and Muslims and thanking God for having created a "safe space to dialogue." It ends with the two of them offering a simple statement of belief and their commitment to the idea that though they may differ on some theological issues, they are committed to making the world a safer place. Ashafa says, "I never compromise the principles of Islam. But Islam says, 'create space for others.'" Of Wuye, he says, "Even though he is not a Muslim, I like him. I can give my life to protect his honor and dignity—that is what Islam taught me to do. I live for it and I will die for it." Wuye says of Ashafa: "I love him because I'm told to love my neighbor as myself. I live by that principle."

Lebanon: Militia Enemies Step Back from the Brink

The two militia leaders—Christian and Muslim—are lucky to be alive. In a battle for a seafront hotel during the Lebanese civil war, they were on opposite sides. It was a civil war in which more than 125,000 died and many thousands are still unaccounted for.

Mohieddine Chehab, a fighter in a Sunni leftist militia, led his men up a staircase littered with corpses while Assaad Chaftari, at the time a simple Christian militiaman, may have been on the top floor shooting at anyone who moved. The two men could have been among the numerous combatants who fell that day, but on a visit to the United States they sat together in a Washington, D.C. restaurant and were, one reporter wrote, "completing each other's sentences as they discussed how they had learned to accept their differences and embrace their likenesses."

Today Chehab is an elected public officer of a part of Beirut, and Chaftari is manager of a small company.

The story goes back nearly thirty years when a young Christian lawyer, Ramez Salamé, decided to take stock of his life, putting right what was wrong and accepting a daily discipline of listening for God's guidance. He returned library books he had intended to keep and asked forgiveness from his father for his hatred and from his brother for his jealousy. As he took these steps, he began to get ideas for his country and, in the midst of the civil war, felt that he was not fighting the right battle.

When the war started in Lebanon in 1975, most young men of his age, then 28, bought guns and joined local *ad hoc* militias. His home in Beirut was close to the line that separated the respective predominantly Christian and Muslim quarters. And as he had done military service a few years before, enforced by the Lebanese state, it was not a problem for him to handle guns. "In a moment of prayer, I believed God was telling me that he had a more important role for me to fulfill than to engage in the military fight." He gave up his gun and courageously began having conversations with his Muslim compatriots. As a token of a new approach, he sought out the Mufti, the leader of the Muslim Sunni community, to apologize for the way the Christians had acted to keep the reins of power in their hands, not permitting the Muslims full responsibility for the country. He told the Mufti that he wanted to accept the changes in his own life that would help create a new Lebanon. The Mufti rose and shook his hand: "What you say is one ray of light in the present darkness. Thank you."

Salamé began to bring together groups of Lebanese, wherever possible both Muslims and Christians. "Dialogue is a powerful weapon, which unfortunately is little used," he says. "After our first meeting, we felt joy in our hearts; we saw the beauty in the other person. We saw our enemy had fears like our fears, aspirations like ours. We grew in love and appreciation of each other."

It was at such meetings that Assaad Chaftari began to find a new thinking. Out of these encounters came his decision in February 2000 to apologize through the main Lebanese newspaper *Al-Nahar* for what he did to his Muslim adversaries in the name of Christianity. Charles Sennott, writing in the *Boston Globe*,[9] said that Assaad Chaftari "stunned Lebanon with a statement extraordinary in its simplicity and honesty."

Explaining his action later at an international conference, Chaftari said that he had regarded Muslims as traitors because they looked toward the Arab world and he looked toward the West. "We were conservative, democratic Christians and we felt superior to Muslims and Palestinians." As deputy intelligence director of the Christian militia, he ruled over the fate of captives. "I became the policeman, judge, and executioner. It was up to me if they were killed, exchanged for others, or used to bridge intelligence gaps. If they killed four of us, it was my duty to inflict more harm in our retaliation. I had lost my sense of humanity."

Chaftari said that "after a week full of mischief, I could go to church on Sunday at ease with myself and with God." However, he had come across Salamé's forum for dialogue between Christians and Muslims and recognized the human being in Muslims he had forgotten about through the civil war. "I discovered that my behavior was very far from God, that it was no use trying to change the world if I did not start changing my own life and having God first."

In his apology to his war victims, he asked for forgiveness and promised to try, with God's help, to do any reparation he could. "I decided to get rid of my prejudices, jokes, and contemptuous attitude against the Muslims." He added that he had also forgiven his enemies, some of whom were Christians like him.

As the audience rose in a standing ovation, another Lebanese, Hicham Chehab, came to the platform and embraced him, shouting out, "I am a Muslim who was shooting at his countrymen from the other side of the green line. I also apologize and accept his apology and will help him in any way I can." As a young man, he had been trained to shoot with the admonition, "Imagine there's a Christian in your sights." He had shelled Christian areas and sniped at Christians. But his conscience had told him that political causes were not worth bloodshed. "I pledge to walk hand in hand with Chaftari," he promised.

On the same platform a year later, Mohieddine Chehab apologized for atrocities he had committed when he had a responsible post in the Muslim militia in the civil war. He had been known by his men as a staunch foot soldier who led them with cunning through the fiercest battles. But once in a while he had been forced to ask existential questions. "We once drove the Christian militias from a neighborhood after a bloody battle, and we found a dead old man tied on a chair and riddled with bullets. Obviously, the Christian militia eliminated him before they pulled out. I stood in front of the dead body that seemed to be gazing at me with glassy eyes. I felt that he was talking to me. I wondered about the purpose of life, God, and death. It was the first time I cared for a dead body. I untied it and called a military ambulance to take it decently to a morgue. Such experiences stuck in my conscience, but I could not change myself. I was afraid that my comrades would consider it cowardice and mock me."

When the fighting stopped, he started visiting Christian villages. He would get into conversations, hoping Christians would say negative things about Muslims so that he could justify his past actions. But this rarely happened. "We were so deluded. I have met such decent people who have feelings, fears, nagging worries like us. I looked at my children. I knew what happened to us, but what about them? I found out that the Christians are human beings like us. Some were rich, others were poor, and some had the same stereotypes we had about them. They were only different in being Christians. Right then my reconciliation walk started."

Together with Hicham Chehab, who is his cousin, he founded a social committee to spread the idea of dialogue and overcoming hate. Harsh criticism of their activities, even physical attacks, only increased their determination. In municipal elections, they decided to do what was good for both Christians and Muslims in their district. They took a Christian candidate on their ticket, though no Muslim was willing to vote for a Christian. "We wanted our ticket to be a model of coexistence for all Lebanon and to show that our country is like a bird that can only fly with two wings, the Christians and the Muslims. We won the elections. It showed that our efforts to spread tolerance had started to bear fruit."

Women, too, are taking a lead in reaching out to "the other." Marie Chaftari, a Maronite Christian and wife of Assaad, had enlisted in the Lebanese forces in the civil war. She would have liked to see all Muslims leave Lebanon, and to her, the only good Christians were those who shared her beliefs. In attending the meetings initiated by Ramez Salamé, she found two ideas that enlightened her path: the greatest cause one should serve is love, and you either choose to be a victim or take responsibility. She asked herself whether she had made the effort to reach out to the other side and to understand their fears and concerns. She realized that deep down she wanted them to be more like her and that if they weren't, they were wrong.

At one of these encounters, she met a Muslim Lebanese, Lina Charafeddine, from a well-known Shia family. "Lina was there with her heart wide open, and I took one step in her direction. She had stronger moral qualities than I, as a Christian. She was as deeply Lebanese as I was. She was scared, too, yet she always welcomed my suggestion to try and deepen the dialogue between us." Their friendship survived many difficulties including political developments and opposition from their families. Lina says, "We don't interact with other people, but with the idea of who they are. This is often a misrepresentation of the truth that justifies our negative feelings toward others—while boosting our own ego. We end up fearing this misrepresentation that we, ourselves, originated."

In the summer of 2005, Marie Chaftari and Lina Charafeddine created a group called *Linaltaki* ("let us meet") to provide a framework for meetings between women from various religious and cultural backgrounds. They wanted to reconcile differences on the life experience of participants rather than on interfaith dialogue. "We realized," says Chaftari, "that we had similar goals and concerns. We all fear for the future of our children. It is this fear of hardships to come that has brought us together, after we admitted our own mistakes." Charafeddine says, "Religious diversity must be a driving force for civilization, not an obstacle."

The women regarded the conflict in the summer of 2006 as a litmus test. They were afraid that *Linaltaki* would not survive. They stayed in touch daily. Chaftari says that as Christian women, they could not sit on their hands while the Shia community was suffering, so they brought snacks for the children and cooked food for the Shia populations that sought refuge in the Christian-inhabited areas where they lived. This was another opportunity to talk with them.

Charafeddine says she has learned to step into the shoes of her Christian friends, to see the beauty in things whenever they see it, to share their joy and grief, to find a spiritual connection that is based on faith. She learned to follow her heart and common sense. She thanks Chaftari for supporting her that summer even though she was the cause of her hardships: "She taught me to stretch myself and keep walking the path, no matter what."

In Beirut, there is a garden of forgiveness. It is a symbol of this growing readiness on the part of Lebanese to take an honest look at the past as a preparation for the future. In November 2005, Assaad Chaftari and Mohieddine Chehab were invited by the initiator of the garden, Alexandra Asseily, to meet in her home with New York women who had lost family members in the 9/11 attacks.

Both men told their remarkable and often horrifying stories. Chehab described how in 1983 he was about to kill two American prisoners after the *New Jersey*, a U.S. ship, shelled west Beirut with a horrific bombardment and he saw his mother terrified and shaking. His mother pleaded with him not to do it. He did not do so and exchanged them for Lebanese prisoners instead.

An American CEO, one of seven who accompanied the women, afterward said to Chehab, "I was stationed aboard one of the U.S. Navy ships off the coast. I want to ask your forgiveness—not for my hate, but for my indifference at that time to the suffering of your mother and the people of Beirut." An American woman who had lost her son, a New York fireman, also came up to him in tears, hugged him, and told him, "Now, I am able to really forgive."

It has been a long journey for these two Lebanese to move from hatred and prejudice to working together to address Lebanon's problems. Already well known within the country—particularly

Assaad Chaftari because of his open letter to his victims—the men are called on to speak, especially at times of crisis in the country. They say that they are sustained by the realization that they went too far in violent and unjust actions during the war. In a spirit of repentance, they wish to repair the wrongs of those past deeds and contribute to a sane society. Their words give hope that fruitful dialogue is possible. "Asking for forgiveness is difficult," says Chaftari, "and forgiving seems impossible but is essential for the reconstruction of a country. The Lebanese people are making peace with themselves. They have been slowly walking back from the brink. That's what I did."

Jewish–Muslim Dialogue: Honoring Daniel Pearl

Professor Judea Pearl, father of murdered journalist Daniel Pearl, is forthright. Among his first words to me were "I'm a soldier rather than a forgiver. My mission is dialogue toward Muslim–Jewish understanding, not forgiveness." He was understandably hesitant at first to have his experiences included in a book with forgiveness in the title.

Certainly his public dialogues with Dr. Akbar Ahmed, a Muslim professor and former diplomat from Pakistan, have opened minds wherever they have been held and perhaps opened some hearts to a forgiveness of others that was not there before. Pearl put it plainly to Abigail Cuker of the *Canadian Jewish News:* "Our mission is not to embrace each other with full understanding, but mainly to listen to each other, to hear two narratives side by side. To acknowledge each other's narrative."

"In the Jewish tradition," he told me, "forgiveness is inextricably tied to the notions of atonement, responsibility, and change in behavior; until this materializes, one cannot genuinely forgive. Rather, I am fighting the hatred that took Danny's life, and dialogue is my weapon."

"It could be expected his father would want revenge," wrote Cuker. "But what is Judea Pearl's idea of revenge? Eradicate the hatred that took his son."

It was an especially gruesome murder. Videos of it were sent round the world. The hostage was decapitated and, because the film camera missed the picture, the action was repeated.

This was the murder in Pakistan in February 2002 of Daniel Pearl, a Jewish twelve-year veteran reporter from the *Wall Street Journal* who was known for being particularly sensitive to feelings in the Islamic world and committed to explaining them to readers in the West.

The three-minute, thirty-second video showed not only Pearl's last moments but also the bodies of dead Muslims, U.S. President Bush shaking hands with Israeli Prime Minister Ariel Sharon, and a list of demands of the Pakistani hostage takers against a background of severed heads and captives at Guantanamo Bay.

Pearl's body, cut into ten pieces, was found in a shallow grave on the outskirts of Karachi. His wife, Mariane, a French citizen and a Buddhist, was expecting their first child when he died. Their son was born four months later.

To further the ideals that inspired his life and work, Daniel's parents set up the Daniel Pearl Foundation to "continue Danny's mission of dialogue and friendship and to address the root causes of his murder" by promoting cross-cultural understanding through journalism, music, and dialogue.

The idea was inspired by a concert that took place in Tel Aviv on 22 February 2002, a day after the world heard Danny had been murdered. That night, George Pehlivanian, Danny's neighbor and friend from Paris, was scheduled to lead the Israeli Philharmonic Orchestra as a guest conductor. Deeply troubled by the news, he was reluctant to perform but, at the last moment, decided to defy the perpetrators by proudly dedicating the concert to Danny. "As the orchestra played Tchaikovsky's Symphony no. 5, I finally understood the triumph of hope over despair," said Pehlivanian. It was an emotional and triumphant concert, ending with fifteen minutes of sustained applause. "The idea spread like a forest fire," says Ruth Pearl, Danny's mother. "Evidently the fuel of goodwill around the globe was merely waiting for the right spark."

Daniel Pearl was an accomplished violinist, and on 2 October 2002, which would have been his thirty-ninth birthday, the foundation launched the first Daniel Pearl World Music Days, which over the next years were to include thousands of performances in sixty countries, all dedicated to tolerance and humanity. Other foundation initiatives include PEARL, an acronym for Prepare and Educate

Aspiring Reporters for Leadership, which provides internships, a Web-based news service and other youth-oriented programs, and Daniel Pearl fellowships and a lecture series at UCLA and Stanford. The news service, working with the Education and Resources Network, is linked with twenty thousand high schools in a hundred and nine countries.

Judea Pearl, professor of computer sciences at UCLA and editor of *I Am Jewish: Personal Reflections Inspired by the Last Words of Daniel Pearl*, is president of the foundation. His public dialogues with Dr. Akbar Ahmed, chair of Islamic studies at American University and former Pakistan high commissioner to Great Britain, have focused on divisions between Muslims and the West and between Jews and Muslims. "Dialogue brings respect," says Ahmed, "respect brings friendship, and with friendship, you can talk about difficult issues."

Pearl was inspired to reach out to the Pakistani professor because of his writings, which he knew and appreciated, "Ahmed was the only Muslim author I read who had expressed empathy for the sense of siege Israelis feel. Empathy is the essence of understanding and prerequisite to dialogue." Akbar responds, "In Pearl, I saw great compassion. Here is a man whose son has been killed in the most brutal of ways, and through this tragedy he saw a need for the bridges of dialogue."

The two men find these dialogues an appropriate way both to honor Daniel Pearl and to address vital issues affecting their nations. In undertaking them, they have become friends.

Akbar is no stranger to conflicts in South Asia. He has vivid memories, from age four, of the uprooting of his family and a frightening train journey as, with twenty-four hours' notice, his family moved from India to Pakistan during the 1947 partition. After years of interfaith activity in Britain, after leaving his diplomatic post and resigning from the civil service, he accepted an offer to teach at American University—and arrived in the U.S. capital weeks before September 11, 2001. "Since then until today," he says, "I don't think I've had a peaceful twenty-four hours."

The two men quote polls that show that about 75 percent of Americans say they know nothing about Islam or are hostile to it and that the figures in the Muslim world are equally alarming, with anti-Americanism and anti-Semitism rampant and widespread.

Akbar believes that because of September 11, the twenty-first century will be the century of Islam but that "the hijackers of the four American planes not only killed thousands of innocent people, but also created one of the greatest paradoxes of the twenty-first century: Islam, which sees itself as a religion of peace, is now associated with murder and mayhem."

Akbar underlines the significance of the Muslim world to the United States. He notes that the Muslim population is one of the fastest growing, with about 1.3 billion Muslims living in fifty-seven countries and one-third of the world's Muslims living in non-Muslim countries, with 7 million in the United States and 2 million in the United Kingdom. On his Web site, Akbar points out that Muslim nations are indispensable for American foreign policy. Of the nine "pivotal" states—identified by foreign-policy experts—on whom the United States bases its foreign policy, five are Muslim. The main terrorists on America's wanted list are Muslim—Osama bin Laden and Al Qaeda and Taliban leaders such as Mullah Omar; but so are America's main allies in the war on terror—former President Pervez Musharraf of Pakistan, President Karzai of Afghanistan, and King Abdullah of Jordan. "Therefore, if both implacable opponents and close allies are Muslims, it is imperative to begin to understand Islam."

Akbar writes, "If we are to prevent the world from lurching toward one crisis after another, one flashpoint to another, then we all need to radically rethink the relationship between our religion and other religions; a radical reassessment of one another. The West must send serious signals to the ordinary Muslim people—via the media, through seminars, conferences, meetings—that it does not consider Islam to be the enemy, however much it may disagree with certain aspects of Muslim behavior."

The first dialogue between Pearl and Akbar, organized by the American Jewish Committee and held at the University of Pittsburgh, took place two years after Daniel Pearl's murder. Four hundred people turned up for it. There was frank talk, but there were also the foundations laid for a bridge. "Hatred took the life of my son," said Pearl, "and hatred I will fight to the end of my life." There were questions, and members of the audience spoke out against religious hatred. The secretary-general of the Pakistani American Congress, Faizan Haq, and a member of Pakistan's Parliament,

Umar Ghuman, both asked forgiveness of Pearl for his son's death. "On behalf of the people of Pakistan," said Ghuman, "I beg for forgiveness for the murder of your son." Pearl responded, "I am grateful to these brave officials for making public statements which to me represent sincere commitment to educate people toward tolerance and acceptance." David Shtulman, executive director of the American Jewish Committee, said that people had a chance to speak but also to listen: "People heard each other through Akbar and Judea in a way they normally are unable to hear one another."

A second dialogue took place three months later at the University of Pennsylvania in Philadelphia. The audience was larger and enjoyed greater community support, with more dignitaries from the Jewish and Muslim communities present. The two men shared what they had learned from their first encounter. Pearl said, "I learned that the overwhelming majority of Muslims are more religious than I imagined and that they genuinely feel under siege, something that might seem absurd considering their numbers and the fact that they control such vast amounts of energy resources."

Both men must contend with critics who do not like to see such dialogue. "How can you shake the hands of the rabbi whose hands are dripping with blood?" a Muslim journalist wrote to Akbar when he learned that he had agreed to take part in an interfaith dialogue organized by the Washington (D.C.) Hebrew Congregation. Akbar wrote back that such stereotypes were not only inaccurate but plainly anti-Semitic. He was then accused of sounding like a representative of the Israeli embassy. "Not an encouraging start for my first visit to a synagogue," says Akbar. "However, the friendship and knowledge of the rabbi, whose hands were certainly not dripping with anyone's blood, made up for the discouraging note—discouraging, because the Jewish and Muslim communities in the United States now have a historic opportunity to lead the dialogue between their great faiths."

It was supposed to be a one-time event in Pittsburgh, until the participants grasped that a lot of people wanted to hear what Daniel Pearl's father had to say to a Muslim intellectual who grew up in the city where his son died—and vice versa. Now, every few weeks, the two men travel to another city for a public dialogue. Their theme is "Toward Interfaith Understanding: A Journey through Dialogue." Although they've learned that merely sharing a stage is a controversial act in some quarters, their public conversation continues. They have been to the United Kingdom, Canada, and across America, invited by organizations or universities who see a need to ease tensions between Muslim and Jewish communities.

Daniel's widow, Mariane, believes that "dialogue is the ultimate act of courage, far more courageous than killing someone." At the same time, she says that forgiveness must rest on a firm foundation of justice. Indeed, she called for the death penalty for his killer not out of revenge but because it represents society punishing someone for murder and would have been in Pakistan a strong political statement against terrorism. In her view, there is a huge difference between taking revenge into your own hands and leaving it up to the law.

But even if the murderer suffered the death penalty, it would not have made her feel any better. "Revenge," she says, "is a basic human instinct, the animal part of man, and it gets us nowhere. Not to retaliate doesn't mean you're weak. In fact, being able to rise above your instincts is a sign of strength—far more heroic than bombing another country or planning a suicide mission."

She believes that you have to win some sort of victory over the people who have hurt you, and you can only do that by denying the terrorists their goal. "They try to kill everything in you—initiative, hope, confidence, dialogue. The only way to oppose them is by demonstrating the strength they think they have taken from you. That strength is to keep on living, to keep on valuing life. So now it's up to me to create something of my life." She told President George W. Bush that if she let bitterness overcome her she would lose her soul "and if I lost my soul, I would also lose Danny's. This is my biggest battle."

Thousands of people wrote from all over the world to Mariane, to her son Adam, to Danny's parents, and to his colleagues, and e-mails flooded in to the *Wall Street Journal* and to American consulates asking to be forwarded. "After this excruciating ordeal, there was nothing I needed more than to be reassured about human nature . . . those letters have been the rope that, word by word, allowed me to raise my hopes again and see the light at last, . . . I am convinced that if we ultimately overcome terrorism and the spread of hatred, it will be because there are millions more on this earth like those who wrote to me. We call them ordinary people. To me, each one is extraordinary."

Mariane wrote a moving memoir, *A Mighty Heart,* in tribute to her husband and their son. In May 2007, a film based on the book and dedicated to Adam premiered at the Cannes Film Festival; a month earlier Daniel Pearl's name was added to the Holocaust Memorial Wall, the first time that a non-Holocaust victim has been so remembered. Mariane's prologue to her book starts: "I write this book for you, Danny, because you had the courage of this most solitary act: to die with your hands in chains but your heart undefeated. I write this book to do justice to you and to tell the truth. I write this book to show that you were right: The task of changing a hate-filled world belongs to each one of us."

Speaking about the foundation's work at a gala dinner of the Council of Christians and Jews in London, Judea Pearl explained that his son was a bridge builder who communicated joy, humor, and understanding. That, he said, was the challenge before guests that evening. They too were looking evil in the eye as they looked at world events today. "This," he told them, "is what my son Danny did, in a dark dungeon in Karachi in the midst of great madness." He said, "We do not have the resources to move armies or conquer territories, but we do have the goodwill of millions of principled people around the world—Christians, Jews, and Muslims; Pakistanis, Europeans, Americans, Israelis, and Palestinians; journalists and musicians—who are determined to form a coalition of the decent and restore this planet to an orbit of sanity."[10]

The Process of Forgiveness
Dr. David Smock
Vice President, U.S. Institute of Peace

Reverend David Smock directs the U.S. Institute of Peace (USIP) Religion and Peacemaking Program. He has held positions with the Ford Foundation, the Institute of International Education, International Voluntary Services, and the United Church of Christ, and is author or editor of nine books including *Interfaith Dialogue and Peacebuilding* and *Religious Perspectives on War.*

The notion of forgiveness often is used in vague and imprecise ways. This is partly the consequence of a Christian heritage in which the injunction to forgive is so frequently invoked. The imprecision of our usage masks the fact that forgiveness means different things in different contexts. To forgive someone for not greeting you is quite different from forgiving someone for killing your child. In addition, to forgive an individual offense is quite different from forgiving a community or nation for committing societal offenses, for instance in initiating an attack or a war. When we analyze forgiveness, we must be clear about the context in which we use it and the particular kind of offense.

The defining characteristic of forgiveness is preparedness to forswear revenge and hatred. Donald Shriver describes this as the "conquest of enmity."[11] This requires the careful management of one's anger. Gandhi's quote repeated in the preceding chapter asserts that "an eye for an eye, and soon the whole world will be blind." Judea Pearl is taking "revenge" at his son's murder by trying to eliminate the hatred that motivated the murder. He has chosen dialogue as his "weapon." He recognizes, as Martha Minow has stated, that vengeance can generate a downward spiral that creates cycles of revenge and escalation.[12]

Empathy toward the perpetrator is another key to forgiveness. Empathy is distinct from sympathy and does not necessarily entail warm feelings. It requires openness to the humanity of the other, to hearing his or her stories. It requires seeing the other as a person and not simply an object. It may enable the victim and perpetrator to build a new relationship that permits a shared future. Judea Pearl is quoted as saying, "Empathy is the essence of understanding and the prerequisite to dialogue."

Sometimes empathy enables the victim to recognize the perpetrator as also being a victim. Ramez Salamé says that after the Lebanese dialogues: "We saw that our enemy had fears like our fears, aspirations like ours" and Mohieddine Chehab said, "I have met such decent people who have feelings, fears, nagging worries like us." Lina Charafeddine said she was finally able to step into the shoes of the Lebanese Christians with whom she was interacting. Akbar Ahmed says that in his dialogue with Judea Pearl, "Our mission is not to embrace each other with full understanding, but mainly to listen to each other, to hear two narratives side by side, to acknowledge each other's narrative."

For meaningful forgiveness to be offered, it is helpful if the facts of the situation are fully understood. Was the offense accidental or intentional? Was the offense a case of retaliation for an offense that was committed previously? What was the motive for the offense? What kind of person committed the offense, and does this person have any redeeming virtues? To ask someone, or a community, to forgive without knowing the facts is an unreasonable expectation.

Shared understanding between the offender and the offended about what actually happened permits a greater likelihood of forgiveness. When the facts of what happened remain in dispute, forgiveness and reconciliation are more difficult. Communities with historical grievances against each other are likely to shape the "facts" in their favor, which only drives the parties farther apart. If the offender admits to the offense, it usually is easier for the offended party to come to terms with it.

Establishing the truth may go beyond identifying the facts and the motive for the offense. Yassin Malik was a leader of a Kashmiri force fighting for an independent Kashmir, motivated by hatred for Indian oppression and India's Hindu majority. But when Hindu doctors treated him with compassion and professionalism at the time he needed life-saving surgery, Malik revised his opinion of Hindus. He abandoned his violent agenda and turned to peaceful resistance. When Imam Ashafa recognized that Pastor James was a gentle person despite his Christian militancy, Ashafa reevaluated how he should relate to James and to Christians in general. When both James and Ashafa recognized that the Bible and the Quran advocated peace, they modified their assessments of the other faith.

Mohieddine Chehab and Assaad Chaftari had been engaged in armed combat against each other in Lebanon. But after they met and "saw the beauty in the other person," they "grew in love and appreciation of each other." After engaging in Christian–Muslim dialogue, Assaad recognized that Muslims are human and that his attacks on Muslims were contrary to his Christian faith. Through dialogue with Akbar Ahmed, Judea Pearl realized that Muslims are much more religious than he had understood and that they feel themselves to be under siege by Israel and the Western world. This enabled him to reassess the relationship between Muslims and the Western world.

Forgiveness does not require forgetting. An evil offense should neither be forgotten nor excused. In fact, forgetting or repressing memories can inflict terrible psychic damage that could undermine true forgiveness. Denial of past injury will likely result in later re-emergence of the pain experienced. Donald Shriver has recognized the importance of memory in stating, "Pain can sear the human memory in two crippling ways: with forgetfulness of the past or imprisonment in it. The mind that insulates the traumatic past from conscious memory plants a live bomb in the depths of the psyche. . . . But the mind that fixes on pain risks getting trapped by it. Too horrible to remember, too horrible to forget; down either path lies little health for the human sufferers of evil."[13] William Faulkner once wrote that "the past is never dead; it's not even past."[14] In undertaking dialogue with Akbar Ahmed, Judea Pearl is honoring the memory of his murdered son Daniel.

A serious obstacle to forgiveness is "remembering" distorted versions of past atrocities. Political actors trying to build animosity toward the enemy often distort history and memory to mobilize their supporters to seek revenge. A Serbian soldier responded to the question "Why are you fighting this war?" by stating "Because of what they did to us at Kosovo [in 1389]." Exaggerated charges against a community or a person are more difficult to come to terms with than reality. Courageous peacemakers can identify the distortions and set the record straight. They also can identify strands of a common history between the communities that will demonstrate that animosity is not the only thing they share.

Forgiveness should not rule out justice.[15] What is inconsistent with forgiveness is revenge and using the legal system simply to inflict retaliation. While a victim might be willing to forgo punishment of the perpetrator, justice may be necessary for societal healing. Moreover, a victim may be better able to forgive once the legal system has dealt with the perpetrator. Amnesty for the perpetrators of atrocities is often a component of a peace agreement reached to end a civil war. But it rarely provides the basis for true forgiveness and often leaves much about history unsettled and unsettling. Mariane Pearl, Daniel's widow, believes that forgiveness must rest on a firm foundation of justice, but that justice must be meted out by the legal system, not by the victim or the victim's family.

The best way to promote healing is a form of restorative justice that does not merely punish but seeks to rebuild relationships. The process of restorative justice can be used to reintegrate the perpetrator back into society. This is the approach that Archbishop Desmond Tutu and other South Africans have termed *Ubuntu*, from a Bantu word for "humanness."

Justice, in another of its meanings, also can be a central component of forgiveness. Crimes may be committed because of structural injustices in a society, as in apartheid South Africa. Forgiveness could depend on these structural injustices being remedied. The black theologians who authored the Kairos Document during the struggle against apartheid insisted that the system must be dismantled before the victims of apartheid could consider genuinely forgiving its architects. Forgiveness cannot condone evil. Forgiveness does not absolve the perpetrator of responsibility.

Nor is forgiveness dependent upon the denial or suppression of suffering. As Geraldine Smyth has written, one's suffering needs to be acknowledged in order for there to be a "letting go of the grief or anger that new awareness may evoke."[16] She quotes Dorothee Soelle in noting that suffering may need to go beyond "mute pain" to find its voice in a "language of lament, of crying, of pain, a language that at least says what the situation is."[17] To forgive does not remove the awareness of one's woundedness.

All the foregoing makes clear that "cheap forgiveness" is neither healthy psychologically nor effective as a means of promoting interpersonal healing and societal peace.

At the same time, one must avoid wallowing in victimhood. Victims wallowing in victimhood develop a conviction of their own superiority that leads them to withhold recognition of the humanity of the perpetrators permanently, even when the perpetrators apologize and make amends for their deeds.

Genuine forgiveness, as Audrey Chapman has pointed out, is not merely a spoken word but consists of actions performed and commitment to a new way of life and revitalized relationships.[18] Thus, forgiveness is a *process* that often extends over a period of time, as we learn from Pastor James and Imam Ashafa as well as from Mohieddine Chehab.

Overcoming resentment and bitterness can open the way for renewed psychic and spiritual health, as well as the transformation of relationships. Pastor James and Imam Ashafa describe the lengthy process during which they achieved the management of their anger and the conquest of hatred in their relationship. Mariane Pearl is quoted as saying that if she let bitterness overcome her, she would lose her soul.

The relationship between apology and forgiveness is multifaceted. Apology by the perpetrator unquestionably facilitates forgiveness. Some would argue that true forgiveness is dependent upon a prior apology or repentance. The Kairos Document mentioned above states that one is under no obligation to forgive an unrepentant sinner, with specific reference to the architects of apartheid. Donald Shriver has asserted that forgiveness requires the reality or at least the prospect of repentance. "Conversely, repentance may require the possibility or likelihood of forgiveness."[19] Apology might come as words, deeds, gestures, or a combination of these. Some kind of restitution is the most sincere form of apology. It took Assaad Chaftari ten years to gain the courage to apologize to Lebanese Muslims for his prior aggression against them. He finally did so in a letter published in Lebanon's leading newspaper. The secretary-general of the Pakistani American Congress apologized to Judea Pearl for the murder of his son, Daniel, at the hands of Pakistani terrorists. This does not carry the same weight as would an apology directly from the murderers, but it most likely helped Judea Pearl avoid hating Pakistanis.

Forgiveness is possible without apology, but it is much more difficult and may not be as deeply felt.

Forgiveness has been described as the "boundary between exclusion and embrace."[20] Geiko Muller-Fahrenholz urges us not to focus on repairing the past but instead on covenanting for a better way forward. He "understands forgiveness as entailing liberation from the bondage of the past. At its core, it is based on mutuality in which the perpetrator asks for forgiveness, the victim grants it, and both sides are changed by the encounter."[21] Past losses cannot be recovered, but new relationships that move us toward reconciliation provide some compensation and comfort. Reconciliation can be solidified through joint action to address jointly perceived injustices. Pastor Wuye and Imam Ashafa have accomplished this in Nigeria through their campaign to end religious violence there. Their theological differences remain, but they share a commitment to making the world a safer place. Marie Chaftari joined with other Christians and Muslims to provide aid to Shia Muslims displaced by the war between Israel and Hezbollah in the summer of 2006.

Religious discourse, and particularly Christian discourse, often is weighted heavily with injunctions to forgive our enemies. But exhortation to forgive often is ineffective and may be even counterproductive. Making someone or a community feel guilty for not forgiving may lead to cheap forgiveness, based upon either superficial forgiveness or a denial of one's suffering. As discussed already, this may implant psychic damage and a later urge to retaliate.

There are more effective ways than exhortation or the invocation of moral injunctions to facilitate and encourage forgiveness. Opportunities can be created for the parties to express their grief, share and mourn their losses, and express fears about the future. Space and time can be provided for personal storytelling of loss and injury. Each side can be given the opportunity to convince the other that their concerns are understood and their pain is felt. Self-criticism and apology for one's own past shortcomings will help the other side to reciprocate. Akbar Ahmed is quoted in the chapter as saying about his dialogue with Judea Pearl, "Dialogue brings respect, respect brings friendship, and with friendship, you can talk about difficult issues." Observing their dialogue, an official of the American Jewish Committee said that people hear each other through Akbar and Judea in a way they normally are unable to do.

Perspective
A Stunningly Original Strategy
Sir Jonathan Sacks

Jonathan Sacks has been chief rabbi of the United Hebrew Congregations of the Commonwealth since 1991. He is visiting professor at the Hebrew University, Jerusalem, and an honorary fellow of Gonville and Caius College, Cambridge. A writer and broadcaster, his books include *The Dignity of Difference* (2002) and *Radical Then, Radical Now* (2001).

In the late summer of 1999, I visited Kosovo. The NATO action was nearing its end, and the refugees had returned. There was some semblance of normal life, yet the tension was palpable. It was then, standing in the center of Pristina amid the wreckage and rubble of war, that I understood as never before the power of a single word to change the world—the word *forgiveness*. The conflict had started more than six centuries earlier, in the battle of Kosovo of 1389. Both sides retained strong memories of that event. If Serbs and Albanians could forgive one another, they would have a future. If not, they were destined to replay the battle of 1389 until the end of time.

Nothing is more dispiriting than the cycle of revenge that haunts conflict zones and traps their populations into a past that never relaxes its grip. That has been the fate of the Balkans, Northern Ireland, India and Kashmir, and the Middle East. The virus of hate can lie dormant for awhile, but it rarely dies; instead, it mutates. Under a dictatorship, Serbs and Croats had lived together peaceably for fifty years. They had become friends and neighbors. But, as in virtually every other zone of historical conflict, something happens—there is a shift in the power structure; a totalitarian government that had held local populations together by fear disintegrates; an episode occurs in which the members of one side commit an atrocity against the other—and it is as if the years of coexistence had never been. Friends become enemies; neighbors, antagonists. A wall of separation is then the least bad outcome, and even that often fails to end the violence.

Retaliation is the instinctual response to perceived wrong. Historic grievances rarely are forgotten. They become part of a people's collective memory, the narrative parents tell their children, the story from which a group draws its sense of identity. A note of injustice not yet avenged is written into the script, which is then reenacted at moments of crisis.

It is this that makes forgiveness so counterintuitive an idea. It is more than a technique of conflict resolution; it is a stunningly original strategy. In a world without forgiveness, evil begets evil, harm generates harm, and there is no way short of exhaustion or forgetfulness of breaking the sequence. Forgiveness breaks the chain. It introduces into the logic of interpersonal encounter the unpredictability of grace. It represents a decision not to do what instinct and passion urge us to do. It answers hate with a refusal to hate, animosity with generosity. Few more daring ideas have ever entered the human situation. Forgiveness means that we are not destined endlessly to replay the grievances of yesterday. It is the ability to live with the past without being held captive by the past. It would not be an exaggeration to say that forgiveness is the most compelling testimony to human freedom. It is about the action that is not reaction.

It is the refusal to be defined by circumstance. It represents our ability to change course, reframe the narrative of the past, and create an unexpected set of possibilities for the future.

In the face of tragedy, forgiveness is the counternarrative of hope. It is not a moral luxury, an option for saints. At times, it is the only path through the thickets of hate to the open spaces of coexistence. I still can remember my undergraduate days, when I would return after a vacation laden with luggage. In those days, I couldn't afford a taxi so I carried my heavy cases from the station to my college. They were so heavy that still, when I recall those days, I can feel the aching muscles and numb wrists. That is what it is to carry hate, resentment, and a sense of grievance. They weigh us down. They stop us thinking of anything else. We may feel righteous. Indeed there is none so self-righteous as the one who carries the burden of self-perceived victimhood. More than hate destroys the hated, it destroys the hater.

Judaism is often portrayed as a religion of justice rather than of mercy and forgiveness. That is not the case. Justice and forgiveness go hand in hand. Each is an answer to the problem of revenge, and neither is sufficient on its own. Justice takes the sense of wrong and transforms it from personal retaliation—revenge—to the impersonal processes of law—retribution. Forgiveness is the further acknowledgement that justice alone may not be enough to silence the feelings of the afflicted.

It is impossible to understand the force of forgiveness without, at the same time, acknowledging its difficulty. It is hard precisely because it conflicts with our sense of keeping faith with the past. Forgiveness is possible because, once the impartial processes of the law have taken their course, justice done, sentences served, amends made, and apologies expressed, a halt must be made to the otherwise endless voice of implacable grief. Forgiveness does not mean forgetting; nor does it mean abandoning the claims of justice. It does mean, however, an acknowledgement that the past is past and must not be allowed to cast its shadow over the future. Forgiveness heals moral wounds the way the body heals physical wounds. At its height, it is a process of shared mourning between those who commit and those who suffer the consequences of wrong; the former for harm done, the latter for harm suffered—and like all acts of mourning, it is the only bridge from the pain of loss to reintegration with the present and its tasks.

I am a Jew. As a Jew, I carry with me the tears and sufferings of my grandparents and theirs through the generations. The story of my people is a narrative of centuries of exiles and expulsions, persecutions and pogroms, beginning with the First Crusade and culminating in the murder of two-thirds of Europe's Jews, among them more than a million children. For centuries, Jews knew that they or their children risked being murdered simply because they were Jews. Those tears are written into the fabric of Jewish memory, which is to say Jewish identity. How can I let go of that when it is written into my very soul?

And yet I must. For the sake of my children and theirs, not yet born. I cannot build their future on the hatreds of the past, nor can I teach them to love God more by loving people less. Asking God to forgive me, I hear, in the very process of making that request, his demand of me that I forgive others. I forgive because I have a duty to my children as well as to my ancestors. The duty I owe my ancestors who died because of their faith is to build a world in which people no longer die because of their faith. I honor the past not by repeating it but by learning from it—by refusing to add pain to pain, grief to grief. That is why we must answer hatred with love, violence with peace, resentment with generosity of spirit, and conflict with reconciliation.

* An extract from *The Dignity of Difference* by Dr. Jonathan Sacks. Reprinted with the permission of the author.

2

reaching out to "the other"

C. S. Lewis, in a letter to his brother, mentioned that he prayed every night for the people he was most tempted to hate, with Hitler, Stalin, and Mussolini heading the list. In another letter, he wrote that as he prayed for them, he meditated on how his own cruelty might have blossomed into something like theirs. He remembered that Christ died for them as much as for him and that he himself was not "so different from these ghastly creatures."

~~Philip Yancey, author of *Prayer*

It was very repugnant to think that we could sit down and talk with those people, but we had to subject our plan to our brains and to say, "without these enemies of ours, we can never bring about a peaceful transformation to this country." And that is what we did. The reason why the world has opened its arms to South Africans is because we are able to sit down with our enemies and to say, "Let us stop slaughtering one another. Let's talk peace."

~~Nelson Mandela[1]

Too often, we judge ourselves by our ideals and others by their actions. We do it with our nations as well as with our lives. As the Scottish poet Robert Burns wrote, "Oh wad some power the giftie gie us to see oursels as others see us!" He went on, in words rarely remembered but no less appropriate, "It wad frae monie a blunder free us, an' foolish notion."[2]

Consider also Jesus' words: "Why beholdest thou the mote that is in thy brother's eye, but considerest not the beam that is in thine own eye?" and the challenge that followed: "Thou hypocrite first cast out the beam out of thine own eye."

Foolish notions of "the other" are fed by much of what we read, by gossipy e-mails, by tabloids, and by sources of misinformation now infinitely magnified on the Internet. Too many of us are brought up on historic pictures of "the other" that have been exaggerated in the telling.

We need to listen to wiser voices.

Archbishop Rowan Williams, passing through an Israeli barrier on his way to Bethlehem while on a Christmas pilgrimage in 2006, referred to "fear of the other and the stranger, which keeps all of us in one or another kind of prison" and in May 2007 said of Muslims and Christians: "We must keep our bridges in good repair." Rajmohan Gandhi, who has used his intellect, his research and writing skills, and his heritage as a grandson of the Mahatma to shed light on the subject, says, "If we blame Muslims for being Muslim, or Jews for being Jews, or Americans for being American, we are condemning them for their birth, for their blood, for their DNA. Condemning people for being born to their parents is not a new thought for human beings. The world knows that it led to the horrors of the Holocaust, the shame of slavery, and the crime of untouchability."

Gandhi says that after 9/11 we seem to have been willing once again to target a section of human beings for being who they are, for being Muslims, or Brits, or Americans, or Jews, or whatever: "All humans are flawed, and many are vulnerable before poisonous winds. When such winds blow, the wise fortify the structures around them and allow an inflow of healthy air."

In this chapter we meet courageous people who are providing some healthy air as they reach out to and walk with "the other." Sometimes forgiveness has come into the equation, sometimes not.

That "other" may belong to a different race, class, gender, or religion.

As mentioned in the preface, the "other" for my Church of Ireland mother was the Catholic majority in Ireland.

Mari Fitzduff, a southern Irish Catholic married to a descendant of the Protestant settler community, directs the international master's of arts degree program in Coexistence and Conflict at Brandeis University and is a former chief executive of the Northern Ireland Community Relations Council. A Northern Ireland resident, she notes that research has shown that Northern Irish children, before their teenage years, learn thirty-two ways to discern an enemy, that is, a Protestant or a Catholic—and this in a country where almost all the population are white and Christian. She has seen her husband's business blown up three times: once by loyalists and twice by nationalists. Thirty of their neighbors had lost their lives, and she had felt there had to be another way. She started to study conflict resolution and mediation. Half of her first class knew so little about the subject that they thought they were coming to a class on meditation!

Mari points out that this need to have a conversation with "the other" is paramount in a world that is increasingly one and where all wars are global and connected: "Forty percent of New Yorkers are foreign born, and in the attack on the Twin Towers, people from eighty nationalities lost their lives: All our countries are struggling with problems of ethnicity, different cultures, and languages. We must learn to respect and validate diversity."

We like our enemies and our beliefs to be simple, she says, and there is a tendency toward fundamentalism in all of us. For a time, her feminism had convinced her that the true enemy was the male half of humanity. Others blame America, or Britain, or capitalism. Weapons and aggression rarely change the perspectives of our enemies. Where there are structural and cultural issues to be addressed, the conversation with "the other" has to be strong enough to deal with issues of equity and exclusion.

This chapter begins with Northern Ireland, where there has been tangible progress in recent years. Suspicions and reservations still run deep, but an overwhelming majority wants peace to continue, and there is little appetite for a return to violence. This has been helped considerably by southern Ireland's economic boom and the increase of profitable joint enterprises. There is a proliferation of men and women on all sides, individually or in groups, who are working for reconciliation—often very quietly and after much suffering. More than ever, there is a reaching out to the other, with clergy on both sides praying for the other and working together.

Attitudes from the past, which were thought to be unchangeable, have responded to the war weariness of the province as new ways to end conflict are being pursued.

One of the most interesting developments for me concerns the police. My family served for three generations in the Royal Irish Constabulary. My great, great, great grandfather was deputy inspector-general and one of the founders of modern policing. I am proud of the fact that he was knighted for his service to the Crown. Perhaps I shouldn't be. He helped thwart an important nationalist uprising, and I am well aware of the terrible things my country did in Ireland over several centuries, such as the way we used Ireland for our convenience, beginning with the planting of Protestant colonists in a Gaelic Catholic Ireland. "Who can doubt," as Donald Shriver [3] writes, "that the apology of Prime Minister Tony Blair for British irresponsibility in the 1840s over the Irish Famine was another increment of the healing of memories between the two peoples." Shriver has described the Irish as possibly rivaling the peoples of the Balkans as "the world's superspecialists in memory."

It was exciting at the start of 2007[4] to see Gerry Adams, president of Sinn Féin, the political wing of the Republican movement in Northern Ireland and the main architect of the peace process from the Republican side, make what one commentator said was "the most important speech of his political career." In it, he directed his party to support the very policing and justice services that their military wing, the Provisional Irish Republican Army (IRA), had spent forty years trying to destroy. The long-term aim of both is still a united Ireland, but the vitally important factor is that all main parties now accept that any changes to the constitutional situation should occur by the consent of all concerned—which thereby ends any justification for armed struggle.

Four years earlier, another psychological building block was laid, this time by Protestants when, under the terms of the Good Friday Peace Accord, the Royal Ulster Constabulary was renamed the "Police Service of Northern Ireland." The baggage of the past was being shed. Even as someone whose family is long removed from the Irish scene, I can still sense the psychological importance of such change. My affection for the old names and uniforms underlines for me how difficult it has been for present-day Irish nationalists to have anything to do with the Police Service of Northern

Ireland, just as it has been hard for many Protestants in the north to see that rather dull name replace "Royal Ulster Constabulary."

Just as one never expected Sinn Féin to recognize the police, one would never have predicted another stepping-stone on the path to peace taken two months later. The *Times* of London called it "history in the making" and underlined its significance with the front-page headline "Old enemies agree to share the future."[5] The paper's story began: "The words that nobody thought they would ever hear from the mouth of the Rev. Ian Paisley came at 12 minutes past noon. 'We have agreed with Sinn Féin.'" Paisley, the leader of the Protestant Democratic Unionists, who had sworn "never, never, never" to share power with Sinn Féin, had reversed a forty-year policy of "never sitting down with terrorists." He said, "We must not allow our justified loathing of the horrors and tragedies of the past to become a barrier to creating a better and more stable future. In looking to that future, we must never forget those who have suffered during the dark period from which we are, please God, emerging." The *New York Times* wrote, "It took a few centuries, but Ireland's biggest chasm was bridged on Monday." And, a few weeks later, after the formal acceptance of power by Ian Paisley as first minister and Martin McGuinness as deputy first minister of Northern Ireland, the London *Times* editorialized, "The past cannot be allowed to become a ball and chain on the future. So Mr. Paisley and Mr. McGuinness were each wise to pay tribute to those who have suffered—and to conclude that the proper memorial is their cooperation."

If that is not enough welcome surprises from Ireland, here's another, concerning a rugby game between it and England: as BBC News reported, "When the English squad's preparation includes a history lesson, you know that this is no ordinary rugby international."

Croke Park in Dublin is home of the Gaelic Athletic Association, which has often been defined less by the sports played there than by its hatred of the British. Before 1971, Gaelic footballers and hurlers could be suspended from their organizations not only for playing "foreign games" like football (soccer) or rugby but even for attending a dance organized by a football or rugby club. When the ban was lifted, little thought was given to the fact that one day England might play at Croke Park, and its national anthem would be sung.

But Croke Park is much more than a sporting facility. It is also the site of the first Irish "Bloody Sunday," where British auxiliary police, the "black and tans" as they were known from their uniforms, fired on the crowd in 1920, killing twelve people—with two others trampled to death—in retaliation for the murder that morning of twelve British agents in their beds. One who was shot was Michael Hogan, a Gaelic footballer after whom its main stand is named. Croke Park is a nationalist shrine.

In February 2007, this particular England–Ireland game was played there because Lansdowne Road, Dublin's traditional rugby ground, was being rebuilt. "Every patriotic Irishman should feel ashamed if 'God Save the Queen' is sung at the beginning of the match," said one Irishman, son of one of the most successful Gaelic footballers of earlier times.

But, despite the predictions, of many, the spirit was quite otherwise.

The *Times* of London had a headline: "The day hatred went missing."[6] The national anthems of both countries were sung—without incident. Simon Barnes, the paper's chief sportswriter, wrote that although a million anticipatory words were written about it on both sides of the water, "it was an occasion that had all the furniture of hate, but hatred itself went missing." The singing of the British national anthem was "preceded by a silence that was almost reverent—not in respect of the sentiments of that terse and tuneless ditty but because freeing oneself from the shackles of history is worth a moment's savouring. Afterwards there was not a whistle or a catcall or a boo. . . . Then, extraordinarily, a round of applause that the end of an era was being celebrated."

The English team played its part convincingly by being soundly beaten by a superb Irish team "and the Irish went away with rather more than victory over England; they also had victory over the past and a celebration of Ireland as a prosperous, effective, forward-looking nation. Freed from Britain, now freed from history."

John Inverdale wrote in the *Daily Telegraph*, "It was one of the most joyous sporting occasions it has ever been my privilege to attend, and when all the revellers woke on Sunday morning (or probably afternoon) it was time to put the hangover of history to bed and embrace the future."[7] The Irish *Sunday Independent* called the match "a milestone in the growth of a nation."

A rugby match, a historic sitting down of two opposites, a recognition of the police should not be underestimated. The profound changes in Northern Ireland have not been achieved principally through forgiveness or repentance but rather through dramatic changes of attitude in hard-line Protestants and Catholics, substantial economic packages and development, political initiatives, plus persistence from the American, Irish, and British governments. However, the political advances, if they are to be sustained, will need undergirding by men and women who can build relationships that contribute to trust between the communities and heal the deep bitternesses of the past that remain.

The major challenge for all sides has been how to move forward to a modern Ireland while keeping faith with the past, in other words, without dishonoring one's ancestors. This challenge recalls the words of Canadian historian Michael Ignatieff: "Reconciliation can stop the cycle of vengeance as a form of respect for the dead." This chapter begins with a remarkable story of two who are working to put the notion of "the other" behind them.

Northern Ireland: Journey without a Map

At 2:35 a.m., 12 October 1984, the IRA detonated a massive bomb at England's Grand Hotel, Brighton, in an attempt to murder the whole British cabinet. The BBC called it the "most outrageous crime in their history" and said that not since Guy Fawkes, who tried to blow up the House of Parliament in 1605, had "such an audacious crime been attempted in the name of politics." Five people died and more than thirty were injured. Prime Minister Margaret Thatcher, who narrowly escaped death, told the Conservative Party conference the next day "This government will not weaken, this nation will meet the challenge, democracy will prevail." The IRA released a statement: "Today we were unlucky, but remember we only have to be lucky once; you will have to be lucky always."

Patrick Magee, the IRA's chief explosives officer, planned the attack and reconnoitered the building before setting the bomb. Already having served time in a British prison, his aim was "to get the Brits out of Ireland."

Two months after the attack, the police knew Magee was the main suspect. He was identified by a fingerprint taken when he was stopped for a teenage driving offense years before. After a wide manhunt, he was caught and was given eight life sentences in 1986. The judge sentenced him to a minimum of thirty-five years behind bars and called him a "man of exceptional cruelty and inhumanity." Magee lifted his clenched fist and shouted in Gaelic *Tiochfaidh ar La*—"our day will come."

Magee was released under the 1998 Good Friday Peace Accord, having served only fourteen years. One of the provisions of this accord, signed by British and Irish governments and endorsed by the people of Northern Ireland and of the Republic, was the early release of political prisoners. The government's official spokesman described his release as "very hard to stomach," a view shared by most in Britain.

Since the IRA's ceasefire in 1994, Magee has claimed that the fatal blast paved the way for peace. He believes that the awareness that it could have been worse gave the IRA more leverage than if they had actually killed Mrs. Thatcher: "If half of the British government had been killed, it might have been impossible for a generation in the British establishment to come to terms with us."

Sir Anthony Berry, a Conservative member of Parliament, former treasurer of the Queen's household, and Princess Diana's uncle, was killed that fateful day; the only means of identifying him was his signet ring.

Sir Anthony's daughter, Joanna (Jo), says, "That day didn't only kill my Dad but it also changed me forever. Within the next few days, I had the sense that however traumatized I was feeling and in shock, that I wanted to bring something positive out of the trauma. I suddenly felt that that conflict in Northern Ireland was mine. The me that existed could no longer exist. I could no longer just travel around the world without any sense of responsibility." Two days after the blast, she prayed in her church, Saint James', Piccadilly, "Please, somehow, could I find a way to deal with my pain and also end up with a way to help." She had a choice, she believes, "to stay a victim, blaming others for my pain, or to go on a journey of healing and understanding."

Her journey has inspired many, and worried some, because it involves Patrick Magee.

A man whose name to this day Jo does not know set her on her extraordinary path. A few months after her father's death, she found herself sharing a taxi with a man from Republican West Belfast. His brother had been in the IRA and had been killed by the British army. She told the man who she was. "We should have been enemies," she says. "We should have been sitting there going 'It's all your fault.' But we didn't. We shared a vision of how there could be a world where violence wasn't a way to sort out conflict." As she left the taxi, she felt that a bridge had been built, and it gave her hope that there was something she could do. "I knew I didn't want to blame. If I blamed, I was going to end up bitter and closed down. Yet the need in me to blame was immense."

Over the next months and years, she met people who had been terrorized by the British army and began to understand some of the stories of people who had been unjustly treated, even that of a senior Sinn Féin leader she had to meet in secret, who apologized to her for her father's death. "It was all part of my learning, of my healing." But she also got out of her depth, even into dangerous situations. Often in tears, she realized she still hadn't dealt with the emotional legacy of the bombing.

In 1999 Patrick Magee was released from prison. While behind bars, he had gained two academic degrees and, based on his Ph.D. thesis, wrote a book *Gangsters or Guerrillas? Representations of Irish Republicans in "Troubles Fiction."* When he was released, Jo relived the Brighton bomb experience and realized that there was still a lot of repressed pain and trauma in her life. In January 2000, she attended a conference on forgiveness at Findhorn, a spiritual community in Scotland. Although shy, she spoke about wanting to meet and forgive the man who had killed her father; she wanted to hear his story. Suddenly, she says, it was like a door being opened in her heart. "I had been living in a desert, not communicating with anyone in Northern Ireland; I had been on my own." She met people, including some from there, who had been through similar experiences and felt ready to address her trauma. One man who responded was Colin Parry, whose twelve-year-old son had been killed in an IRA blast in Warrington. He invited her to take part in a project at the Glencree Reconciliation Centre in the Republic of Ireland, a place where all victims of the Northern Ireland conflict were invited. "It was the first time I met victims from England, or any victim, and I knew that through meeting these victims I was going to be able to get the support I needed. I knew it was safe to share my story, as no one would be scared of my pain. I later met ex-prisoners who knew Patrick, which was an important preparation for meeting him."

However, the interaction with more Republican ex-prisoners broke all the rules of emotional safety and preparation she later learned were important. She was again upset and wondering whether she was betraying her father.

A reconciliation charity, Seeds of Hope, arranged an introduction to Patrick. Seeds of Hope was founded by Anne Gallagher, a Belfast nurse whose father and three brothers were interned by the British. She says, "We encourage people not to judge others. There's healing in that. The idea is that when you hear my story, and I hear your story, it becomes our story, and seeds of hope are sown."

Jo was terrified at the idea of meeting Patrick. As she went over to Ireland in the ferry, she wondered if he would even turn up. Meanwhile Patrick, who knew nothing about Jo, did not know what to expect. Someone had even said to him, "She might kill you."

Wanting to reassure him, she went up to him and said, "Thank you for being here." "No, no, it's you I want to thank," he responded. And the two of them talked for three hours without stopping. "I discovered that his need to meet me was the same as my need to meet him. I regard that now as a miracle." He was amazed at her willingness to listen to him and said, "I want to hear your pain, your anger, your story." This was just the beginning.

Back home she wondered if she had gone too far: "I was on a journey without a map."

Two weeks later, and over the months, they met again; their encounters, though very private, were filmed for reconciliation purposes. They found themselves supporting each other, as neither had support elsewhere. The BBC approached them to do a documentary. "I was scared because of the other victims of Brighton; my family knew nothing about it; my stepmother had been badly injured; my family's lives had gone through so much, I didn't want to make it worse for them." But she felt she should participate, as it would help reconciliation. Before it aired, she wrote to all the Brighton victims and to her family, preparing them for it.

She says, "If we can talk and hear each other's stories and see each other as human beings, then maybe that can help others. It has been so important for me to see Pat's humanity and to see him as a real human being rather than this demonized IRA terrorist that was portrayed in the media. Through seeing his humanity, it has also helped me to re-find mine. Victims of terrorist violence do lose some of their humanity, and also those that take up violence do. Part of the journey is reclaiming that."

Over the years, she and Patrick have continued to learn and to use their lessons for others, sometimes speaking together of their journey and doing workshops. Jo is starting a charity called "Building Bridges for Peace," which she sees as "a vehicle for looking at the roots of conflict and developing alternative ways to end violence." The two have linked up with other groups working for reconciliation and trying to turn tragedy into something positive: for instance, at a Basque peace conference that included victims of the Madrid bombings, in Turkey at a Palestinian and Israeli peace conference, and with a group of Americans who lost loved ones on 9/11, as well as working for the Forgiveness Project and on restorative justice initiatives. She is chair of an international network for peace, comprising groups and individuals working for peace who have been affected by violence. "I just feel that everyone is worthy of their dignity, of having their stories heard, being listened to," she says.

Twenty years after the Brighton bombing, she still is faced with challenges, is not always at peace, and sometimes has doubts. But she is encouraged by the people who have heard them both speak. One fourteen-year-old told her that she now knew what she wanted to do with her life—to make a contribution to peace—and that she was going to heal a damaged relationship in her family. A worker for reconciliation in Israel e-mailed her: "You give us hope."

Jo says, "Forgiveness is a word that I know very little about. What I feel I can do is to make a choice, to open my heart enough to hear Pat's story or anyone else's stories that have hurt me. I don't want to actually forgive Pat because I feel that if I've forgiven him I'm not allowed to be angry anymore. Maybe the only person I can forgive is me, because I'm sure, given any situation where I feel my rights have been taken away, I also could make decisions to be violent."

As I heard her say in a public meeting in Coventry, "Through his opening up I have come to understand that I could have made the same decision. That understanding is more important than forgiveness."

She feels that, at first, she used the word *forgiveness* too easily. Now, she doesn't talk about it. To say "I forgive you" she feels is almost condescending, locking you into an "us and them" scenario, keeping me right and you wrong. "Sometimes when I have met with Pat, I've had such a clear understanding of his life that there's nothing to forgive."

Patrick e-mailed me in 2004 after I met him at the Forgiveness Project's F-word exhibition in London: "The concept of forgiveness is pretty well redundant in terms of our experiences; forgiveness seemingly can't be codified. And yet the first question, nigh on invariably put, is 'has the perpetrator shown remorse, and has the victim forgiven?' Jo is brilliant at articulating why the term is of little use to her personally. Jo says that the purpose of such meetings is to gain an understanding of the other's motivations, experiences; to forgive could rob her of many emotions she is entitled to, such as anger, because to forgive—and then for anger to resurface—suggests the opposite of the closure sought. This has met a need in Jo to be able to put her loss into some meaningful context. Forgiveness may eventually ensue, but should it occur, then it's a point of arrival, not the beginning of a journey. This is our lesson from the journey."

In many ways, the basic issue in Northern Ireland—or anywhere that has historic grievances—is how you best honor your ancestors. Jo says that when she first used the word *forgiveness* on television, she received a death threat from a man who said that she had betrayed her father and her country. Pat wrestles with the question of how he best honors the commitment of the Irish nationalists who came before him. If you admit that a course of action is wrong, are you then betraying your heroes? Do new situations allow you to adopt new truths? Are we condemned to follow the past, or can we make a break with it? Neither Pat nor Jo is comfortable with the word *forgiveness,* but they are on a journey that shouts the word out whatever the outcome.

Pat has gone so far as to say that he is sorry that he killed Jo's father. *Guardian* writer Simon Hatterstone asked Pat whether he worried that some day one of his victims would persuade him that what he did was wrong. "Well, you have to allow for that possibility. All the participants are on their own separate journey. And I'm not at the end of that process yet."[8]

As one looks at the sometimes stuttering but inevitable progress in finding a settlement to centuries of division in Ireland, Patrick may find that "the day" he defiantly called for at his sentencing is coming but in a different manner than expected, and Jo has found a way—as she prayed—to help, a way to draw meaning from tragedy.

South Africa: After the Heidelberg Tavern Massacre

The Heidelberg Tavern massacre was described by the Amnesty Committee of South Africa's Truth and Reconciliation Commission (TRC) as "brutal." On New Year's Eve 1993, the Azanian People's Liberation Army (APLA), the armed wing of the Pan Africanist Congress (PAC), carried out this attack on a Cape Town restaurant on the orders of APLA's director of operations, Letlapa Mphahlele, now PAC president. Many were particularly shocked as it happened at a time when the date for democratic elections had already been set for April 1994.

One of the four people killed was twenty-three-year-old white student, Lyndi Fourie, who was just finishing her civil engineering degree. Her mother, Ginn, a university lecturer, says of Mphahlele, "If I had met him then, I could have killed him with my bare hands."

Yet today Ginn Fourie and Letlapa Mphahlele share platforms in South Africa and around the world, speaking of reconciliation after tragedy through the Lyndi Fourie Foundation.

In 1978 Mphahlele, incensed by apartheid and oppressed by poverty, crossed the border to Botswana to enlist as a soldier to fight white people. He was seventeen. "Since God seemed unwilling to solve the issues for which I had prayed, I would take the liberation into my own hands." Several times in Botswana and Lesotho, he was thrown into jail. His brightness and commitment meant that he quickly rose in the leadership of the PAC's armed wing. In 1993 he slipped back into South Africa and was dubbed its most wanted terrorist. "I ordered the killing of white civilians," he says. "I thought that I would bomb them out of their cocoons of indifference to the country's reality. I believed that terror had to be answered with terror."

In July that year, armed APLA cadres under his command stormed into Saint James' Church in Cape Town during a service and killed eleven people. He had issued an order suspending attacks on civilian targets but waived the order after some black civilians had been killed in Umtata. He wanted to show that APLA had the capacity to retaliate and that no more were blacks going to be killed and massacred with impunity. At year's end, he targeted the Heidelberg Tavern.

Within a week, the three APLA soldiers involved in the attack were caught and sent for trial. Ginn Fourie attended the trial. "At the trial, I was confronted by my own feelings of anger and sadness but somehow I could engender no hate. I felt an unexplained empathy and sadness for them." She sent a message to them that she forgave them. Still, she was relieved when all three were convicted of murder and sent to prison for an average of twenty-five years each. "I was comfortable forgiving them at that point because, as a Christian, I had the role model before me of Christ forgiving his murderers, yet at the same time I depended on the law to avenge my loss."

Meanwhile, the Truth and Reconciliation Commission was set up. This commission, which was getting at the truth of what was done on all sides during the anti-apartheid struggle, had the authority to grant immunity to those who had committed crimes if they disclosed what they had done. Fourie heard that the three killers might be granted amnesty and was not against it.

At the end of the hearings, the three men asked to speak to her. They thanked her and said, whether they received amnesty or not, they would take her message of forgiveness and hope to their communities and to their grave.

Mphahlele was urged to appear before the commission to make a full disclosure of his crimes. He accepted at first but then withdrew as he did not like the way the hearings were conducted and insisted that he had waged a just war that shouldn't be treated as a crime. He was charged in the Supreme Court but acquitted on a technicality.

In 1998 Mphahlele, with the help of journalists, met Charl van Wyk, a survivor of the tavern attack and an ex-soldier who had been carrying a gun and had returned fire. They shook hands before TV cameras and shared their respective experiences. "It was the beginning of an exciting journey I was to travel," Mphahlele says. "I had to face the fact that people were killed and harmed because of my orders and that I had to sit down with those who were prepared to do so and pour out our hearts to each other."

Van Wyk, a devout Christian, invited Mphahlele to his church. Mphahlele was an avowed atheist, but for van Wyk's sake he said he would come. Van Wyk joked about it being a "spiritual ambush." Afterward, they went to the prison to visit Gcinikhaya Makoma, who had taken part in the attack on Saint James' Church. At the entrance, warders asked Letlapa if they were carrying guns. Letlapa said no, as he didn't expect people to emerge from a church service with a gun. But van Wyk was indeed carrying the gun he had used to defend against the attack in the Saint James' Church.

Mphahlele teased, "I guess you will be armed at heaven's gate."

"Yes," said van Wyk, "of course, you never know. There may be APLA hanging around the gates, and one would have to defend heaven."

"I don't think God would give a poor shot like you the task of defending heaven's gate. APLA would overrun them!" responded Mphahlele.

They laughed.

In Letlapa's autobiography, *Child of This Soil,* he described his life's journey and included this interaction with van Wyk. Ginn Fourie heard him interviewed about the book on the radio. With a "sense of anger and righteous indignation," she attended a book signing and publicly asked him, "Did you not trivialize the TRC by not participating?" She was surprised and impressed by the integrity of his response: "You could see it that way, but I felt that if the truth was sought, why were lawyers there to tell people what to say? Furthermore, my cadres were treated as common criminals, [whereas members of] the South African Defence Force remained in the army when they had clearly committed more and worse atrocities." He came from the podium to where she was sitting and said, "I'll do anything if you will meet me this week." She saw remorse in his eyes and body language. "It would have been so much easier if he'd been a monster with horns and a tail—if there was something to hate."

He offered to meet her in private—and so began their remarkable journey of reconciliation. "I did not ask for forgiveness," he says, "but she forgave me. It was the most important gift that one can receive from another human being." Ginn Fourie says, "It's not that I don't feel a great sadness of losing my daughter, but forgiving her killer has made it bearable and given me a creative way forward. Letlapa has told me that in forgiving him I have restored his humanity."

In an interview on South African radio, a commentator asked, "One wonders why she could forgive what many others found impossible. Is it because she is a Christian or that she has grappled with her own role in the country's history? Perhaps it is because she has been writing her doctoral thesis on forgiveness. Or is it all of this and the mission statement she wrote two years before her daughter died (in which she wrote she had to extend God's grace to everyone she had ever met)?"

Many, including some of her own family, could not accept her forgiveness of Lyndi's killers, but she says, "As a Christian, I cherished the role model of Christ for forgiving murderers. I have come to understand forgiveness as a process that involves the principled decision to give up one's justifiable right to revenge."

Not everyone affected by the attacks has accepted the hand extended by Mphahlele. "Some people have decided not to forgive me for what I have done," he says. "I know it's not easy to forgive and I understand them. But to those who do forgive me, it is the start of rebuilding our communities."

Letlapa had been in exile for many years. In 2003 his homecoming was formally celebrated in his village of Seleteng. Guests of honor—two of the few white people present at the occasion—were Ginn Fourie and Charl van Wyk. Fourie was invited to speak to the crowd. "Your comrade's bullets killed my daughter," she said. "That terrible pain will always be with me. But I have forgiven this man who gave the command." She spoke of her sorrow about the 350 years of oppression by her people. "It has been a long and healing journey," she said, "but now I know there is work for us to do."

"I asked," she says, "that they teach us to dance the rhythm of Africa by sharing what we are feeling, particularly fear of each other, anger, or sadness. Vulnerable feelings when expressed to each other have the potential to establish lasting bonds and may overcome the violence and corruption that oppresses us all at the moment."

Mphahlele responded, "In the past, apartheid divided us racially and ethnically. Generations that lie ahead won't forgive us if we continue to stay apart out of our own choice." Turning to Fourie and van Wyk, "people who had every reason to hate but who chose to understand and forgive," he said. "Thank you for your gift of forgiveness." He read a poem he had written the year before for Lyndi:

> Forgive our idiocy
> Our Souls retuned

To heed prophecy
By the graveside of the Prophet
Whose blood we spilt
Whose teachings we ridicule
While he walked among us.

Fourie's was "the most moving speech of the day" according to Mphahlele. "She also got the loudest applause, longer than I got after nearly two decades in exile."

In July that year, Fourie and Mphahlele were invited to the Grahamstown Festival to participate in a conciliation march from Rhodes University to the cathedral. Extending what she had said to the Africans about the need for her people to face up to the past, she asked Afrikaners present to forgive her British ancestors for the shame and humiliation brought upon them by the Anglo-Boer War. "No Truth and Reconciliation Commission or conciliation, the ghosts of the past still haunt us, in the pain and violence enacted by many."

In the succeeding years, Fourie and Mphahlele have spoken together at many forums in different countries. Mphahlele, who in 2005 toured British schools to talk about his experiences, says, "The fuel that keeps me running now is community involvement. Out of the gift of forgiveness, which so many black and white people have given me, I am regenerating community development."

He visited thirty-six British schools and interacted with their senior students, as well as speaking in homes or doing interviews. He had to respond to many probing questions, ranging from whether in similar circumstances he would make the same decisions to what it was that turned the struggle for a new society in South Africa. "I have changed since then and I no longer believe that you should meet violence with violence," he says. "The key to change in South Africa was when the ordinary people lost their fear."

He made it clear that injustice needs to be confronted and that there is a price to pay for that. But there was also a price to pay in self-worth if you did nothing.

Young people pursued many angles on the question of forgiveness. Mphahlele told one group that the dropping of charges did nothing for his spirit after the years of hassle that he had experienced with legal proceedings. But when Fourie forgave him, *that* reached something deep within and restored his humanity.

A woman of Jamaican heritage asked, "How can you as a black man forgive what whites have done to your people?" He replied, "Forgiveness does not rule out the need for justice. But unless we forgive, we destroy ourselves." One girl asked, "What is your biggest fear in coming to speak to us?" He replied, "If you all sit there and say nothing."

In 2006 the National Prosecuting Authority (NPA), whose task is post-TRC prosecutions of those who were denied or refused to apply for amnesty, was investigating Mphahlele, and Fourie was asked to help. She inquired what would happen if she did not cooperate and was told she would be subpoenaed. She then agreed to write an affidavit making it clear that Mphahlele was passionate about bridge building and reconciliation. She told the NPA that she would trust Mphahlele with her life, "which is not something I could say about you." Because of her response, she was derided by them as being "infinitely naive."

Today Fourie says, "We are good friends, not enemies," and Mphahlele, who once said, "My proudest moment was when I saw whites being killed on the battlefield," has been called by the *Cape Argus* "a peacemaker of international renown." "You can't legislate for or against forgiveness," Mphahlele is quoted in the *Mail and Guardian*: "It is an individual choice. My involvement with the people who were hurt because of my orders has no cutoff date—it is an unfolding process. I think it is the right thing to do because after hurting each other, we must become agents of healing, spiritually and practically."

Israel and Palestine: Parents Circle–Families Forum

A 2002 misconnection in the Middle East has led to an interconnectedness. An Israeli woman dialed a wrong number and found herself put through to a Palestinian. Instead of hanging up, the two began a dialogue about Middle East politics and the Israeli–Palestinian conflict. Word of this unusual interchange reached a group of Israelis who had lost family members in the conflict and were looking for ways to reach out to Palestinians similarly affected. They knew that most Israelis were unaware of the extent of Palestinian suffering just as most Palestinians were oblivious to the level of Israeli anxiety.

The two peoples had seen each other as subhuman. Why not use computer technology to facilitate dialogue, they thought.

The result: "Hello Peace, Hello Shalom, Hello Salaam." In its first few years, more than a million families have taken advantage of the toll-free telephone service set up by Parents Circle–Families Forum and financed by the European Community. Arabs and Jews are picking up the phone daily and talking to people "on the other side."

Friendships have been created. Calls are made to ensure friends are okay after attacks. One Palestinian asked a Jewish Israeli to speak to his children. He wanted them to learn that Jews were not monsters. Another told a correspondent from the New York *Daily News* that he thought that Israelis didn't care when innocent Palestinians suffered or were killed. "Now, I know that that they do care and I have hope that there can be peace."

The organization that seized on the potential of the wrong number was Parents Circle–Families Forum, which now numbers more than five hundred Israeli and Palestinian bereaved families. Their aim, they say, is "to strive to offer a breakthrough in people's frame of mind, to allow a change of perception, a chance to reconsider one's views and attitudes toward the conflict and the other side." They have experienced the truth, as Archbishop Tutu wrote in a message to them, that "peace is possible when we allow ourselves to be vulnerable." In fact, they see hurt as their common ground. They may well have set a precedent in having bereaved families, victims from both sides, embark on a joint reconciliation mission while the conflict is still active.

Parents Circle was set up in 1995 by Yitzhak Frankenthal after his son, Arik, was kidnapped and killed by Hamas. After his son died, life changed drastically for Frankenthal, as he told Iris Makler for *Religion Report:* "Once it was very important for me to live in a nice house, but today I don't care about it." Parents Circle is trying to transform bereavement into a tool to move their society.

Frankenthal, an Orthodox Jew who fought in the Yom Kippur War in 1973, has found that working for peace by reaching out to Palestinians has cost him friends. In a synagogue, for instance, when he needed ten men to say a prayer for his son, as required by Jewish law, his friends walked out in order to prevent him from mourning his son as required by his faith. Makler concluded her report about his work, saying, "In the Middle East, blood is easily spilt, and it justifies the spilling of more. But these parents are seeking an alternate path, one that gives hope that the murderous cycle here can be broken."

Shortly after his son's death, Frankenthal, speaking at a public rally, urged security forces not to seek revenge. By all means, he said, bring his son's murderer before an Israeli court, but prevent injuries to innocent civilians: "It is unethical to kill innocent Israeli or Palestinian women and children. It is also unethical to control another nation and to lead it to lose its humaneness. It is patently unethical to drop a bomb that kills innocent Palestinians. It is blatantly unethical to wreak vengeance upon innocent bystanders. It is, on the other hand, supremely ethical to prevent the death of any human being. But if such prevention causes the futile death of others, the ethical foundation for such prevention is lost.

"Arik's killer was born into an appalling occupation, into a moral chaos. Had my son been born in his stead, he may have ended up doing the same. Had I myself been born into the political and ethical chaos that is the Palestinians' daily reality, I would certainly have tried to kill and hurt the occupier; had I not, I would have betrayed my essence as a free man."

One of the first to respond to Frankenthal was Roni Hirshenzon, who has lost two sons to the conflict. He is now assistant manager of the Parents Circle–Families Forum. Hirshenzon e-mailed me: "I and others like myself will never forgive but are ready to reconcile. Working for ending the conflict between Israelis and Palestinians, that's what I do day by day."

A prominent member from the Palestinian side is Ali Abu-Awad, who was arrested for resisting Israeli occupation in the first Intifada, as was his mother. He was released after the signing of the Oslo Accords. During the second Intifada, he was shot in the leg by a settler, and his brother was killed.

He met Frankenthal and Hirshenzon and, along with his mother and brother, joined the Parents Forum, which he describes as "a means of helping yourself in addition to being a means of resistance, a different kind of revolution for my people." He is active in spreading a message of reconciliation and nonviolence. "Through our lectures, we try to explain the reasons for the hatred and misunderstanding and convey that the people on the other side aren't animals, they are humans. We don't belong to any political party;

our message is a humanitarian one. We try to enable people to live with their pain. From the pain, we extract the good and that is a very hard thing to do. Because of the Forum, when I wake in the morning, I have a feeling there is something I can do."

The members of Parents Circle support each other in their losses and act together "to prevent further bereavement threatening all peoples of the region as a result of the conflict." Their slogan: "It will never end until we talk." They would like to see a political settlement achieved through reconciliation and communication between the two peoples "through mutual consideration and respect of each others' national and legitimate aspirations."

Forum members meet with governmental representatives and decision makers to get their message across. As well as the telephone calls, they have organized lectures—Israelis and Palestinians together when the security situation permits—and conferences, have staged coffin displays, each covered by flags representing an Israeli or a Palestinian who has been killed, and have arranged blood donations—Israeli to Palestinian and Palestinian to Israeli—with the theme "One blood, one pain, one future." Projects include dialogue meetings in high schools, where they reach some forty thousand students each year; reconciliation workshops in the community, attended by thousands of adults in Israel and the Palestinian Authority; and *Kol Hashalom*, a bilingual radio program produced by two young members of the Forum "All for Peace" radio station. With the theme "Knowing Is the Beginning," members of the Forum are researching their family histories with the aim of understanding one another better and becoming more effective in what they do together. They hope eventually to turn these histories into books or films so that the public, too, can better understand the causes of the conflict.

In 2006 *Encounter Point,* a documentary about four Israelis and four Palestinians from Parents Circle, was shown at the Tribeca Film Festival and has since been seen widely in the United States, Canada, and the Middle East. It had its British premiere in November 2007 at the UK Jewish Film Festival at Swiss Cottage, London. Two of those featured are Ali Abu-Awad and Robi Damelin. Damelin came to Israel from South Africa in 1967 to "do whatever is needed to support Israel" and has never left. Her son, David, was killed by a sniper's bullet. Joshua David Stein reviewed the film on the *Huffington Post* blog. He described the participants as having "overcome prejudices, seen through their anger, and work together to find a peaceful solution." He wrote, "Hatred is not a subtle emotion, grief is rarely rational, and rage, like war, is total. Yet Damelin and Awad, and five hundred other Israeli and Palestinian families, have managed to moderate the political absolutism that often follows loss and tread a line that, though meandering and indirect, might be the only path to peace. . . . Bereaved Families Forum, the organization in which Damelin and Awad are both active, operates on the assumption that one bereaved mother can sit down with another and that the body of grief between them will bridge them together, that a grief so personal must also be universal."

Robi Damelin told me in June 2007 that she had written to the family of the sniper who killed her son and is now in prison. She described to them her son's and her commitment to peace and the efforts to stop the cycle of violence and work for dialogue that can lead to reconciliation. She told them she hoped they would show her letter to their son and that one day they could meet. "Writing and having the letter delivered," she says, "was like removing a stone from my heart. It brought a sense of relief and freedom from being a victim. Each person goes through their own personal path to forgiving."

Former President Bill Clinton believes that "better than anyone, these families understand the cost of the continuing violence in the Middle East and they work to end the fighting through peaceful means."[9]

Israel and Palestine: Combatants for Peace

Bassam Aramin, a Palestinian who lives just outside Jerusalem, is one of thousands of Israelis and Palestinians who know firsthand about suffering. But there is a certain difference about him. He will not seek vengeance.

His ten-year-old daughter, Abir, was shot in the head as she left school, caught in an altercation between Israeli border guards and other children who may have been throwing rocks at them. The Israeli army said first that Abir was among the rock throwers and then said that "something" blew up in her hands. Her older sister saw otherwise, and Abir's hands were undamaged. Aramin was unsurprised by the allegations but anguished by fabrications that meant that Abir's name and innocence were desecrated.

"It would be easy, so easy, to hate," he says. "To seek revenge, find my own rifle, and kill three or four soldiers in my daughter's name. That's the way Israelis and Palestinians have run things for a long time. Every dead child—and everyone is someone's child—is another reason to keep killing. I know. I used to be part of the cycle. I once spent seven years in an Israeli jail for helping to plan an armed attack against Israeli soldiers. At the time, I was disappointed that none of the soldiers was hurt. But as I served out my sentence, I talked with many of my guards. I learned about the Jewish people's history. I learned about the Holocaust. And eventually I came to understand. On both sides, we have been made instruments of war. On both sides, there is pain, and grieving, and endless loss. And the only way to make it stop is to stop it ourselves."

As his daughter Abir lay dying, "her small face chalk white, her eyes forever closed," a group of Israeli men came to support and comfort them. Every one of the group was a former combat soldier whom he has come to love as brothers. "Men who know my past and who share it; men who, like me, were trained to hate and to kill but who now also believe that we must find a way to live with our former enemies."

Aramin will not rest until the soldier responsible for his daughter's death is put on trial and made to face what he has done. "But I will not seek vengeance. No, I will continue the work I have undertaken with my Israeli brothers. I will fight with all that I have within me to see that Abir's name, Abir's blood, becomes the bridge that finally closes the gap between us, the bridge that allows Israelis and Palestinians to finally, *inshallah,* live in peace. If I could tell my daughter anything, I would make her that promise. And I would tell her that I love her very, very much."

Aramin is part of a group of some three hundred Palestinians and Israelis called Combatants for Peace (C4P) who were once on the front lines of combat and who say they shot, bombed, and killed, believing it was the only way to serve their cause. Palestinian Sulaiman Al Hamri is a cofounder of C4P and its international and foreign affairs coordinator. His family has spent a total of twenty-five years in Israeli prisons. He started his own struggle at the age of sixteen, spent four and a half years in prison, and is still angry about it. In prison, however, he met senior Israeli military who were interested in solving the conflict "in another way." "We have paid the price in the conflict," Al Hamri says, "yet I remain committed to peace." He sees it as a duty to retaliate against an occupation, whether from national or religious motives. His grandfather had done so against British occupation, and his father had done so against the Israelis, as he also had done when he was arrested in the 1980s after an Israeli soldier was stabbed. "But it is also a duty to do so peacefully."

Zohar Shapira, who served in the Israeli forces for fifteen years, got C4P started on the Israeli side when he left the army. He felt that its actions in Palestinian territories were "immoral" and managed to contact some Palestinian Fatah fighters, who were at first fearful and suspicious. Their organization was conceived in a number of clandestine meetings in 2005 and went public in April 2006 in a program "to raise the consciousness" in both Israeli and Palestinian societies of the aspirations and fears of "the other side." "Initially," he says, "we were full of fear about meeting the other side." But they learned that they were all human and could talk together.

The Israeli coordinator of C4P is Elik Elhanan, who from 1995 to 1998 served in the Israeli army. In 1997 his sister was killed by a Palestinian suicide bombing in Jerusalem. "I have seen the damage the violence can cause," he says, "and I decided not to take part in that cycle any more."

He and Al Hamri and others have traveled together in the United States, speaking in public forums of their experiences. Indeed, one of their stated aims is to implement an educational lecture series, which will be given jointly by an Israeli and a Palestinian veteran.

On one occasion, Al Hamri traveled to the United States with Shimon Katz, a former elite Israeli soldier who had refused to serve in the Palestinian territories, risking a court martial and possible jail time. Katz says, "I believe that as an Israeli citizen, I am obliged to go to the army just like I am obliged to pay taxes. So I work to find a middle path that will allow me to remain true to my values." The two men told an audience at Seattle University that they were not politicians or professors; their aim was to demonstrate the existence of Palestinians and Israelis who could be partners toward a negotiated settlement. Both supported a two-state solution, believing that the history of bloodshed required a vigorous separation of their two peoples. "We are not starting a love story," said Al Hamri, to laughter from the audience and his counterpart. "We are starting an ugly divorce. We are still combatants, still fighters, but using nonviolent ways to solve the problems of the two people."

Despite opposition on both sides of the struggle, C4P is committed to meetings of combatants "which allow each side to understand the other's narrative via the approach of reconciliation rather than conflict."

Men who had previously seen each other only through weapon sights now believe that by joining forces they will be able to end the cycle of violence, the bloodshed, and the occupation and oppression of the Palestinian people. They state, "We no longer believe that it is possible to resolve the conflict between the two peoples through violent means; therefore, we declare that we refuse to take part any more in the mutual bloodletting. We will act only by nonviolent means so that each side will come to understand the national aspirations of the other side. We see dialogue and reconciliation as the only way to act in order to terminate the Israeli occupation, to halt the settlement project, and to establish a Palestinian state with its capital in East Jerusalem, alongside the state of Israel."

At an early meeting in 2005, one participant was Chen Alon, a former major in the Israeli armed forces, who, as he said, had never spoken in front of Palestinians, particularly ones he may have fired at. In his last night in the occupied territories, he demolished a house and saw in the village young girls who were just like his own daughters. "It was then that I decided that I will no longer take part in this situation, no matter what price I would have to pay. I believe our voice can make a difference in our societies. I hope that we may be able to turn all those incidents in which we crossed the lines and carried out forbidden actions into means for finally ending the occupation before it ends our societies and leads to their total collapsing."

Also present was Suliman Al Chatib, from north Jerusalem, sitting, as he put it, with people possibly harmed by his actions. He had long felt that the only possible solution was a military one, joining the Fatah movement at age twelve, involving himself by throwing stones, writing slogans, and preparing Molotov cocktails. At age fourteen, he and a friend stabbed Israeli soldiers. He was sentenced to fifteen years in jail. He told the gathering that he had acquired his entire education in jail and constructed his worldview there.

Through the jail library and learning groups, he learned about the history of the Jewish people. "This is when I started having new thoughts about the conflict and the means for resolving it." When he was released in 1997, he helped establish a peace center. He says, "We believe that combatants, who personally paid a price for their active involvement in the conflict, are the ones who can significantly change the situation."

The C4P logo is powerful and hopeful: it shows two figures tossing away their weapons and walking toward each other with open arms.

Germany: Meeting the "Monsters of My Dreams"

Zella and Helga are best friends. Two middle-aged women, traveling together, talking about children and grandchildren and the pills they take for migraines; all very normal. But should they be doing this? Some have difficulty accepting their friendship.

They are cofounders of an organization called "One by One, Inc." that takes its name from a book about the Holocaust by Judith Miller. Miller wrote, "We must remind ourselves that the Holocaust was not six million. It was one, plus one, plus one. . . . Only in understanding that civilized people must defend the one, by one, by one . . . can the Holocaust, the incomprehensible, be given meaning."

Members of One by One are children of victims of Nazi atrocities, who grew up in the shadow of their parents' suffering and trauma, and descendants of the Nazi era, whose parents or grandparents were perpetrators or bystanders in one of the most evil chapters of human history. They seek out the humanity in each other as they listen with compassion to one another's stories of pain, guilt, anguish, loss, and fear. As the stories resound within them, the women say, the burdens are lightened and the impact of their legacies transformed, offering hope to future generations.

The path of transformation is never easy, and the stories of Zella and Helga are testimony to that.

Zella Brown is the daughter of Wolf and Barbara Kaplansky, two Holocaust survivors. Seventy-five members of her family died in the Holocaust. Wolf survived thirteen concentration camps and felt that the only reason he had been spared was to bear witness to the truth.

Zella, her younger sister Judy, and their brother Ely grew up listening to "those relentless stories that defy description." Wolf's daily reprimand: "Don't ever forget what Hitler did to the Jews," resounded in her ears long after the stories faded into the night. Fearing the children would forget, he would follow this with the command, "Write it down so you don't forget."

Over the years, other Jewish children told her how lucky she was to have parents who spoke to her about their experiences. But at times, she wanted to blurt out, "You call this 'lucky' when every waking hour you try desperately to erase the image of that yellowed photo of the naked dead bodies piled high like cords of wood. *'Kikh, dos is vos zey ongemakht tsu di Yidden'* ('Look, this is what they did to the Jews')." As Wolf spoke these words, he would place the picture inches from her face to make sure she would "never forget."

She wrote it down and has remembered, but at a cost. It took years of therapy, twelve-step recovery programs, and her newfound Buddhist practice to unburden the heavy load. She and sister Judy joined a Boston-based group of child survivors called "One Generation After." One day, a peculiar ad in its monthly newsletter caught their attention: "Descendants of Holocaust survivors wanted for meeting with descendants of Nazis." With her comfortable, middle-class life unraveling because of divorce, the last place she expected to find herself would be in a room full of Germans, whom she called "the monsters of my dreams." Her sister, however, responded to the ad for them both.

So on a beautiful fall day in Boston in September 1992, Zella, who held all Germans responsible for killing her grandparents, aunts, and uncles and for the mental and physical abuse of her parents, and who had done everything she could to avoid meeting them, suddenly found herself sitting with eleven of them. "Suddenly, I found myself facing the enemy, the descendants of the Third Reich, and I was shocked to find that they, too, suffered from Hitler's legacy."

Meanwhile, Helga Mueller, married with two sons and living near Munich, faced a different challenge. She had been born in 1943 in the midst of the war. Her father had been "a good man," an ordinary foot soldier of the Reich, "who had saved lives." At least that was the family lore.

Later in life, dogged by serious psychological problems, she went into psychoanalysis. She was haunted by nightmares filled with images of corpses and skeletons, and her therapist asked her to find out about her father's work in World War II. After a laborious search, she discovered first he had been in an SS unit in White Russia in 1942 and 1943 and then that he actually had been the Gestapo chief in White Russia, responsible for the deaths of forty thousand men, women, Jews, Russians, old people, and children—personally participating in murder.

This discovery, in April 1989, shattered her. "I sank into a deep hole." Frightened of death, she locked herself into her room. For weeks she wouldn't dare go out of the house. She felt that the descendants of her father's victims were pursuing her. Her whole life, she had felt guilt; now she knew why. She felt she was being suffocated by the horrors she had discovered. After what seemed an eternity to her, and the return to a "more normal" life, she needed to find out how to live with this newfound awareness. "When you get divorced, you can get a book on how to do it; and when someone dies, you can get a book on how to deal with it. But there's no book to get on how to deal with a father who is a mass murderer."

Up to this point, she had always shut out World War II from her life. Now, she began to read everything she could lay her hands on about the Holocaust. By fanatically immersing herself in the subject, she felt she was repenting for her father's guilt. She even went to White Russia, now Belarus, where her father had committed his crimes. She felt a growing desire to meet descendants of the victims. "I hoped they would spit on me and clearly express their contempt, that it would lessen my pain if they thrashed me and walked all over me. I wanted to reduce the pain that I, as a daughter of this man, deserved."

While doing research about her father, she found out about a planned study project whereby children of survivors and of perpetrators would have an opportunity to encounter each other. Asked to be one of the eleven German descendants, she prepared to travel to Boston in September of 1992.

As she got ready to encounter her "enemies," she developed an irrational fear of those she was to meet. "I came to Boston alone and lost, stuffed with fear but also with an inner emptiness. It really was like a lamb for the slaughter. I stood in front of the door of the house where the meeting was to take place. My legs were leaden. I wanted to turn and run." A woman asked her whether she had come for the research project; together they found their way to the meeting room.

She saw some strangers. A voice called out, "Honey, can you help me cut some bagels?" An elegant middle-aged woman handed her a plastic knife. "It was my first meeting with a Jew: Zella Brown." Much later, they would laugh together about this first encounter with a plastic knife.

The session began. The twenty-three participants each told their stories. Helga knew little English and had never heard the word *Holocaust* before. "I only understood a fraction of what was talked about and noticed with alarm that my time to talk was getting closer." When it came, she was tongue-tied. "I couldn't get out a word. I didn't know what to say. I was told I could speak in German, and it would be translated. I still couldn't do it." Zella took her hand and she began.

Zella says, "This is how I first met Helga. With fear in her eyes she told us that she hoped she would be safe among us and that she suffered right along with us. Bravely she shared with us how her relentless search for the truth had brought her to this conference. I suddenly felt a release of some kind, an opening of my heart that Helga's display of honesty and raw emotions triggered. I had to tell her, 'Helga, I'm here to say to Hitler, "You failed. You're not going to succeed in getting me to hate Helga any more."' In my wildest dreams, I could never have anticipated her response to me: 'You mean more to me than my mother—and she is still alive—because you said that.'"

"A miraculous bond took place during those five, emotionally draining days in Boston," Zella told me. "The only word that genuinely describes what transpired is healing. Years of therapy were not able to accomplish what this experience was able to do for me and others."

In the next weeks, Zella and Helga continued to get acquainted through an exchange of letters, sharing their innermost thoughts. Six months later, Helga and Zella were invited to another dialogue, this one in Germany, in the Black Forest. Unlike the first one in Boston, all the old and new participants would be staying under one roof, and Zella and Helga were excited to be roommates.

Since 1993 Jewish and German members of One by One have met annually for week-long retreats to tell their stories and face the terrible legacy they share. They now number in the hundreds. "Many of us have a dark, heavy burden from this horrible past, and we need to heal from it and do something positive about it," says One by One board member Rosalie Gerut, a cantor and musician whose parents survived Hitler's death camps.

The members of One by One do not equate dialogue with forgiveness or understanding with excusing. Zella e-mailed me: "The subject of 'forgiveness' is dear to my heart given the long and tedious journey I have had to take as the daughter of two Holocaust survivors. But our organization has avoided the 'forgiveness' topic. For Helga and me, it has never come up. I don't need to forgive her for something she didn't commit. It was a dialogue process that brought us to a place of healing, friendship, and love. Some did have the need to apologize 'for what their ancestors did,' and when I heard such a statement, it was gratifying."

Nor would they ever compare the suffering of the survivors' side with that of the perpetrators. Listening does not blur the differences or what separates them. But listening to descendants of survivors, they say, is an attempt to repair the threads of their common humanity that Nazi Germany sought irrevocably to break, and the dialogues are held in Germany because it is important to reclaim their right to be there in the home of their relatives and ancestors. It gives a chance for many Germans who have never met a Jew to meet one. The first challenge is for facilitators to help everyone feel "safe" so that "their story becomes our story," and all suddenly realize that they could easily have experienced what he or she did if they were born in the other's place.

Helga says that talking about her father's crimes to those whose families suffered under the Nazis has helped her to deal with the guilt and shame that she thought she could never escape. Today, she is not guilty, she says, but she would be if she were to push away history as some Germans have done. "I will never forget the way my Jewish friend has helped me survive this horror. Discovering my father was a mass murderer has produced so much that is positive in the people I have met." Zella finds it "especially heartwarming that, at least for our families, the cycle of hate will end with our children."

In an early exchange of letters, Helga asked Zella, "Don't you think we can both change the world?" Zella replied much later, "Yes, I do believe we can change the world. In fact, I think we already have." She recalled the remarkable teens at Carver High School in Plymouth, Massachusetts, who had bonded with them after their talk and whose teachers begged them never to stop what they were doing; and the congregants from Temple Beth Abraham in nearby Canton who were moved to tears when they told their stories during their Yom Ashoah commemoration. She referred to the grateful soldiers and their families at Fort Sill, Oklahoma, who had formed a receiving line to thank them individually for telling their stories so courageously; and to the time when the entire staff at the Holocaust Museum in Washington, D.C. gave them a standing ovation.

"But Helga," Zella went on, "you will agree that the most memorable and most emotional experience for both of us was in my parents' home in Holbrook, Maine, when my mother approached you as we were leaving: 'Helga, I want you to know that I don't hate you for what your father did. I am just so happy that you, together with my daughter, will tell the world the truth, because it pains me so when I hear people say that it did not happen.' And then she hugged you, gave you a kiss on the cheek, and said, 'Be sure to write, Helga.'"

Dignity for All
Dr. Donna Hicks

Dr. Hicks is an associate at Weatherhead Center for International Affairs and a former deputy director of the Program on International Conflict Analysis and Resolution at Harvard University. She specializes in postconflict reconciliation and is writing a book, *The Power of Dignity*, on the role indignity and dignity play in creating and resolving conflict.

The powerful stories chronicled in this chapter are illustrations of the best that we are capable of under the worst human circumstances. They show us four extraordinary experiences of tragic human loss that end with startling outcomes—the victims of these tragedies end up extending themselves to their perpetrators, dramatically shifting their image of and relationship to "the other."

Michael Henderson admonishes us to "listen to wiser voices" expressed in these stories. The implication is that we use these remarkable stories as models for our own behavior, setting aside our self-centered tendencies to "judge ourselves by our ideals and others by their actions."

Our very human tendency to see clearly the faults of others puts us in the dangerous position of feeling righteously superior to them. This attitude of superiority quite dangerously disconnects us from our own human shortcomings. It's easier to judge negatively the behavior of others than it is to hold the mirror up to ourselves and look at our own human vulnerabilities.

Our blind spots make it difficult to see aspects of ourselves that others see. The irony is that we have so much to learn about ourselves from the other. Martin Luther King Jr. put it this way:

> Here is the true meaning and value of compassion and nonviolence, when it helps us to see the enemy's point of view, to hear his questions, to know his assessment of ourselves. For from his view, we may indeed see the basic weaknesses of our own condition, and if we are mature, we may learn and grow and profit from the wisdom of the brothers who are called the opposition.[10]

Dr. King said that "if we are mature, we may learn and grow and profit from the wisdom of the brothers who are called the opposition." What does maturity look like in our relationship to "the other"? What does it take to heed Henderson's admonition to "listen to wiser voices"? How do we become wiser and more mature in our response to "the other" when he or she has created unspeakable pain and loss for us in a way that feels wrong and unfair, when it feels justified to hate them?

The stories in this chapter are profound examples of victims and perpetrators reconciling under extreme circumstances—clear displays of both wisdom and maturity. What process did they go through? In one case, forgiveness occurred; but in the others, it did not. In those cases where forgiveness did not take place, what else happened that enabled them to reconcile?

I will attempt an answer to these questions by creating a framework other than forgiveness for assessing what happens when victims and perpetrators reconcile after painful loss and conflict.

The overarching goal of reconciliation is the mutual *restoration of humanity,* not forgiveness. It enables us to make a distinction between the process of reconciliation (what people go through, like forgiveness) and the outcome of reconciliation (the restoration of their mutual humanity). This framing creates space for naming and identifying other processes besides forgiveness that can bring about a transformation in the relationship.

Another process that brings about reconciliation is *honoring dignity.*

In both processes, it is helpful for victims and perpetrators first to *grieve the loss they have suffered.* This allows time to experience and express the anger, rage, and frustration of what happened to them, as well as to receive acknowledgment by others of the unfairness of their loss. Bypassing this grieving process by calling for forgiveness or the honoring of dignity before the parties are ready can be retraumatizing, prolonging the individual healing process.

Restoration of Humanity

By framing the goal of reconciliation as the *restoration of humanity,* we make a clear distinction between the *outcome* of being reconnected to "the other" and the *process* it takes to get there. The field of conflict resolution and postconflict reconciliation has suffered by confusing outcome with process. Much of the discourse has focused heavily on the role of forgiveness in bringing about peace and reconciliation. It is certainly one way to reach reconciliation, but it is not the only way. Framing the outcome of reconciliation as the *restoration of humanity* allows for other processes besides forgiveness that may be more appropriate for some people in some circumstances. This framing enables us to address the complicated dynamics of reconciliation in more complex ways.

First, what is meant by "humanity"? When we say, "I saw his humanity," we are usually referring to the "good" aspects of who the person is. Or, when we meet someone who has done something horrible and discover the side of him that is kind, caring, and sensitive, we might say, "I saw him as a human being for the first time."

In dialogues I have conducted with warring parties around the world, I often have heard one side say about the other, "They showed their humanity. They are really good people."

But seeing humanity as something good and desirable is only half of the picture. Our full humanity—something we all share by virtue of being human—includes our capacity not only to be good but also to do harm. Create powerful enough conditions for us, and we can behave like perpetrators and aggressors, hurting others in the process.

Civility is the first thing to go when we feel threatened. We can say and do hurtful things to "the other" that we would never dream of if we didn't feel violated. We'd be horrified to act in such an aggressive way under normal, nonthreatening circumstances. Anyone who has been married or in a committed relationship for any length of time knows this to be true. Intimate relationships bring out the best and worst in us.

Add to this problem the human tendency to ignore those more harmful aspects of ourselves, and we can begin to see why accepting the full range of our humanity is critical in reaching out to "the other." When we deny others their "humanity," we not only see them as all bad but we also see ourselves as all good. If we were able to stay in touch with our own very human capacity to harm others when we feel threatened, we might not judge them with such harshness. We might say, "There but for the grace of God go I."

We feel righteous indignation when someone hurts us, forgetting that we, too, are capable of harm. If we could stay connected to our human vulnerabilities—the same undesirable truth that we all share—we would be more capable of seeing ourselves in the eyes of the other. We'd be more capable of opening our hearts to them, more willing to seek understanding rather than to rush to judgment.

But we are much more skilled at making excuses for our own bad behavior than we are at excusing the wrongdoings of others. If we were able to consider the circumstances that led to the hurtful behavior of others, as we automatically do for ourselves, we may not rush to the conclusion that they are bad, and we are good. In both cases, half of humanity is lost: we lose touch with the half of ours that is capable of harm and we lose the half of the other that is capable of good.

When we disconnect from either our own or others' full humanity, we set ourselves up for self-righteousness and lose the humility that keeps us human beings in check. Recognition and acceptance of this more complicated shared humanity sets the stage not only for reconciliation but for a quality of human connection that sends us farther along the path of human development—we become bigger in the process.

Forgiveness and Honoring Dignity: Two Ways to Restore Humanity

Restoring humanity in a relationship fraught with loss, pain, and conflict is difficult no matter how we approach it. There is no easy way. What is easy, and seems to come naturally, is our instinctive desire to lash back at the one who perpetrated the loss and pain. In the South African story, the mother who lost her daughter in the Heidelberg Tavern massacre said of the man responsible for ordering the massacre: "If I had met him then, I could have killed him with my bare hands." It is our first and primal reaction, hardwired deep within. Most of us have probably experienced the same impulse but in less extreme circumstances. The need for revenge is our default reaction to loss and threat.

In all the cases described in this chapter, each victim and perpetrator went through a process where they ultimately were able to control that dangerous and deadly impulse to annihilate the other. In some cases, such as with Ginn, with the help of her Christian faith, she embarked on the path of forgiveness. She was able to forgive Letlapa for killing her daughter, with astounding consequences. She said, "Letlapa has told me that in forgiving him I have restored his humanity." The forgiveness process enabled Ginn and Letlapa not just to reconcile but to develop a deep human connection that they never would have achieved if they weren't brought together by the tragedy.

Because of its power and the number of astonishing cases of reconciliation it has given rise to, not to mention the Christian imperative, forgiveness has become the clarion call for the healing of conflict relationships. But it is not the only way to bring about the restoration of humanity and reconciliation.

The chapter described several cases where reconciliation occurred, but forgiveness was neither asked for nor given. The story of Joanna Berry and Pat Magee details the nuances of another process that enabled them to restore the humanity to their relationship: a process I call *honoring dignity*.

Throughout my career as an international conflict resolution specialist at Harvard's Weatherhead Center for International Affairs, I have convened dialogues between warring parties all over the world. What I found common to all these conflicts was a cry from all sides to be treated with dignity. It was a cry that oftentimes was nameless, yet its effects could be felt in every discussion I facilitated. I also recognized that the flip side of a dignity violation is the key to honoring someone's dignity. I concluded that if indignity tears us apart, then dignity puts us back together again. Eventually, I put a name to the many ways that we can honor each other's dignity. I have called them the *Ten Essential Elements of Dignity*.[11] We extend dignity to others when we:

1. Honor their identity, so that others feel free to express their authentic selves without fear of being judged negatively, and they feel seen and valued for who they are without prejudice of race, gender, class, religion, or sexual orientation.

2. Recognize and acknowledge their perspective, that is, what is true for them. They feel they are paid attention to, are seen, and are being taken seriously for what they know and what they have experienced.

3. Include them so that they feel a sense of "belonging" at all levels (family, organization, community, nation), not to be marginalized and excluded from decision making that affects their lives.

4. Create safety for them, reducing a feeling of threat, both physically and psychologically.

5. Treat them fairly and with equality in an evenhanded way according to agreed-upon laws and rules.

6. Ensure freedom from domination (autonomy) so that they are able to act on their own behalf and are in control of their lives.

7. Seek understanding so that they feel they have been given the chance to explain themselves and their perspective— they feel understood.

8. Give them the benefit of the doubt so that they feel that they have been trusted with good intentions.

9. Respond to their expressed concerns—they feel listened to and heard—not treated as invisible.

10. Take responsibility for the harm that we have caused if we have violated their dignity.

By naming the behaviors, one can more easily "hold up the mirror" to see the sometimes subtle ways in which we consciously or unconsciously violate each other's dignity.

One of the greatest insights I achieved was becoming aware of a pattern of when I was most likely to violate the dignity of another: When I was hurt or threatened by someone's actions, I felt justified in treating them badly. That would take the form of aggression toward them ("fight response") or withdrawing from them ("flee response"). Both are hardwired, default reactions to being threatened.

The key to understanding dignity is not only knowing the *Essential Elements* (and I am sure there are more that I have yet to identify) but knowing the conditions under which we are likely to violate the dignity of others. These are the most difficult conditions, like what Ginn from South Africa felt initially—that she could kill with her bare hands the man who murdered her daughter. But the threat does not have to be that big to create an impulse to annihilate the person who delivered the threat. Many of us are naturally gifted at psychologically annihilating one another. A subtle remark that is hurtful and shaming can trigger our fight-or-flight reaction in seconds. Or no remark at all also can trigger our default reaction. My husband gets very upset with me if I ignore him or don't respond to something that concerns him. Humans have a need to be seen and to *be responded to* (*Essential Element 9*).

Each of the ten ways in which we violate the dignity of others makes us either want to fight (seek revenge) or withdraw (build silent resentment). Either way, the relationship breaks down, and we are at the ready for conflict.

A close examination of the nonforgiveness cases in the chapter shows that what was common to them all was that they extended dignity to one another. They did not seek revenge or harm but sought a deeper understanding of each other's perspective. Both the victims and the perpetrators *wanted* to hear each other's stories. Re-reading the stories, one can see that most of the essential elements of dignity were honored. It was clearly the case with Joanna Berry and Pat Magee. I especially appreciated Joanna's point about the inappropriateness of the forgiveness paradigm in their situation. Rather, Joanna felt that by carefully listening to Pat's story, she began to understand that she might have done the same thing were she in his shoes. She went on to point out that, for her, forgiveness felt condescending, locking them into an "us and them" scenario where the victim was "right" and the perpetrator "wrong."

By honoring Pat's dignity, Joanna not only acknowledged and recognized Pat's experience, she went a step farther and *identified* with him. She said, "Given any situation where I feel my rights have been taken away, I also could make decisions to be violent." For her, honoring Pat's dignity did not take away anything from her. In fact, she gained a deeper understanding, expanding her own meaning making. She remarked that forgiveness was irrelevant. She said, "Sometimes when I have met with Pat, I've had such a clear understanding of his life that there's nothing to forgive."

It's important to point out that Pat was not a passive recipient of Joanna's extension of dignity. He honored hers as well. Pat's willingness to sit through Joanna's painful story of loss and ultimately identify with her was equally moving.

Part of the magic of extending dignity is that it quickly becomes an interactive process. Unlike forgiveness, where the victim has all the power to shift the dynamics in the relationship, honoring dignity engages both victim and perpetrator. It is a reciprocal process that changes the victim and the perpetrator, sharing and equalizing the power between them. They both end up seeing the world differently; they both extend themselves to one another, creating a deeper space for compassion and learning and understanding.

The Berry–Magee story illustrates some key points about honoring dignity, but in all of the nonforgiveness cases, dignity was honored. They are all remarkable stories. In the process of honoring each other's dignity, humanity was restored, leaving everyone both "wiser and more mature." Martin Luther King would certainly have been proud of them.

The Need to Grieve

The final point I would like to make about reconciliation and the restoration of humanity to relationships crippled by tragic loss is the need for grieving. As Joanna Berry pointed out, if she were forced to forgive, she would be robbed of her understandable emotional reaction to the loss of her father. The need to express her emotions is a critical step in the process of her healing, not to mention in healing the relationship.

People who have suffered painful and traumatic experiences must be allowed to grieve and pass through the emotional maelstrom. Jumping into any process—whether it is forgiveness or honoring dignity—without time to experience and grieve the loss, can be retraumatizing. Imploring people to forgive before they are ready denies them the human need to be angry and outraged and to feel that what happened to them was wrong and unfair. In fact, it would be a violation of their dignity not to let them express these feelings. Martha Minow, in her book *Between Vengeance and Forgiveness,* points out that people need to be able to express anger after their dignity has been violated, helping them maintain a sense of self-esteem after the violation.

Whether they act on that anger is another matter. Part of maintaining our dignity is restraining ourselves from the understandable desire to lash back at those who have hurt us. However, expressing our outrage and lashing back are two separate things. It is important to express raw and uncensored feelings without shame and judgment. It is even better to be able to do it with caring people bearing witness, acknowledging that what happened to them was wrong and that what they are feeling is understandable and normal.

Many years ago, Elisabeth Kübler-Ross helped us understand the grieving process in her book *On Death and Dying.*[12] She originally wrote the book about people who were coming to terms with their own death but later expanded the relevance of her "grief-cycle" to include any kind of traumatic loss. She describes in detail the grief process, starting with shock and anger and ultimately ending in acceptance. She warns us that if we try to bypass these stages of grieving, true healing is jeopardized.

We need further discussion about how the grieving process works. My experience tells me that it needs to be done with the help of a trusted other—family, friends, and/or with professional assistance. As Archbishop Tutu explained to me after we cofacilitated *Facing the Truth,* a three-part television series produced by the BBC in 2006 where victims and perpetrators of the conflict in Northern Ireland were brought together for dialogue: "We (humans) seem to need a public ritual when we've been roughed up." I took this to mean that we need a ritual with witnesses (could be as extensive as a Truth and Reconciliation Commission or as intimate as a one on one with a loved one) to hear our story of loss and to receive acknowledgment that what we went through was wrong and unfair.

While acknowledging the need for individual grieving, I am reluctant to say that there is a neat and tidy way of going about it. We may all pass through Elisabeth Kübler-Ross' grief cycle, but every case has its own unique pace and circumstances. Grieving is a complex process, no less than what it takes to forgive or honor dignity. When we embark on the path of healing and reconciliation, we are making a profoundly emotional choice. There is no bypassing the pain and suffering. That said, my experience has shown that when we do make the difficult choice to go forward through the process of healing and reconciliation with "the other," we come out the other side feeling more whole, more insightful, and more open to our own growth and development. In fact, we ultimately realize that there is no "other." The wisdom and maturity that is gained by the process enables us to see ourselves in every human being we encounter. And when that happens, we know—from the inside out—the true meaning of shared humanity and being equal in dignity. As Archbishop Tutu reminds us: "We can only be human together."

Perspective
God's Dream for Humanity
Archbishop Desmond Tutu

> Desmond Tutu, recipient of the Nobel Peace Prize in 1984, retired as archbishop of Cape Town, South Africa, in 1996. He is a lecturer throughout the world and was a visiting professor at Emory University in Atlanta. He is the author of *No Future without Forgiveness* (1999).

God does have a sense of humor. Who in their right minds could ever have imagined South Africa to be an example of anything but the most awfulness, of how *not* to order a nation's relations and its governance? We South Africans were the unlikeliest lot, and that is precisely why God has chosen us. We cannot really claim much credit ourselves for what we have achieved. We were destined for perdition and were plucked out of total annihilation. We were a hopeless case if there was one. God intends that others might look at us and take courage. God wants to point to us as a possible beacon of hope, a possible paradigm, and to say, "Look at South Africa. They had a nightmare called 'apartheid.' It has ended. Northern Ireland (or wherever), your nightmare will end too. They had a problem regarded as intractable. They are resolving it. No problem anywhere can ever again be considered to be intractable. There is hope for you too."

Our experiment is going to succeed because God wants us to succeed, not for our glory and aggrandizement but for the sake of God's world. God wants to show us that there is life after conflict and repression—that because of forgiveness, there is a future.

In the act of forgiveness, we are declaring our faith in the future of a relationship and in the capacity of the wrongdoers to make a new beginning on a course that will be different from the one that caused us the wrong. We are saying, "here is a chance to make a new beginning." It is an act of faith that the wrongdoer can change. According to Jesus, we should be ready to do this not just once, not just seven times, but seventy times seven, without limit—provided, it seems Jesus says, your brother or sister who has wronged you is ready to come and confess the wrongs they have committed yet again.

That is difficult, but because we are not infallible, because we will hurt especially the ones we love by some wrong, we will always need a process of forgiveness and reconciliation to deal with those unfortunate yet all-too-human breaches in relationships. They are an inescapable characteristic of the human condition.

Once the wrongdoer has confessed, and the victim has forgiven, it does not mean that that is the end of the process. Most frequently, the wrong has affected the victim in tangible, material ways. Apartheid provided the whites with enormous benefits and privileges, leaving its victims deprived and exploited. If someone steals my pen and asks me to forgive him, unless he returns my pen, the sincerity of his contrition and confession will be considered nil. Confession, forgiveness, and reparation, wherever feasible, form part of a continuum.

In South Africa, the whole process of reconciliation has been placed in very considerable jeopardy by the enormous disparities between the rich, mainly the whites, and the poor, mainly the blacks. The huge gap between the haves and the have-nots, which was created and maintained largely by racism and apartheid, poses the greatest threat to reconciliation and stability in our country. The rich provided the class from which the perpetrators and the beneficiaries of apartheid came, and the poor produced the bulk of the victims. That is why I have exhorted whites to support transformation taking place in the lot of blacks.

For unless houses replace the hovels and shacks in which most blacks live, unless blacks gain access to clean water, electricity, affordable healthcare, decent education, good jobs, and a safe environment—things which the vast majority of whites have taken for granted for so long—we can just as well kiss reconciliation goodbye.

Reconciliation is liable to be a long, drawn-out process with ups and downs, not something accomplished overnight and certainly not by a commission, however effective. The Truth and Reconciliation Commission has only been able to make a contribution. Reconciliation is going to have to be the concern of every South African. It has to be a national project to which all earnestly strive to make their particular contribution—by learning the language and culture of others; by being willing to make amends; by refusing to deal in stereotypes by making racial or other jokes that ridicule a particular group; by contributing to a culture of respect for human rights and seeking to enhance tolerance, with zero tolerance for intolerance; by working for a more inclusive society where most, if not all, can feel they belong, that they are insiders and not aliens and strangers on the outside relegated to the edges of society.

To work for reconciliation is to want to realize God's dream for humanity—when we will know that we are indeed members of one family bound together in a delicate network of interdependence.

If we are going to move on and build a new kind of world community, there must be a way in which we can deal with a sordid past. The most effective way would be for the perpetrators or their descendants to acknowledge the awfulness of what happened and the descendants of the victims to respond by granting forgiveness, providing something can be done, even symbolically, to compensate for the anguish experienced, whose consequences are still being lived through today. We saw in the Truth and Reconciliation Commission how the act of telling one's story has a cathartic, healing effect.

True forgiveness deals with the past, all of the past, to make the future possible. We cannot go on nursing grudges even vicariously for those who cannot speak for themselves any longer. We have to accept that what we do, we do for generations past, present, and yet to come. That is what makes a community a community or people a people—for better or worse.

I hope that those who are at this moment enemies around the world might consider using more temperate language when describing those with whom they disagree. Today's "terrorist" could very well be tomorrow's president. This has happened in South Africa. Most of those who were vilified as terrorists are today our cabinet ministers and others sitting in the government benches of our national assembly. If those we disagree with today are possibly going to be our colleagues tomorrow, we might begin by trying to describe them in language that won't be an embarrassment when that time of change does come.

It is crucial too that we keep remembering that negotiations, peace talks, forgiveness, and reconciliation happen most frequently not between friends, not between those who like one another. They happen precisely because people are at loggerheads and detest one another as only enemies can. But enemies are potential allies, friends, and collaborators. This is not just utopian idealism. The first democratically elected government of South Africa was a government of national unity made up of members of political parties that were engaged in a life-or-death struggle. The man who headed it had been incarcerated for twenty-seven years as a dangerous terrorist. If it could happen there, surely it can happen in other places. Perhaps God chose such an unlikely place deliberately to show the world that it can be done anywhere.

3

MOVING BEYOND VICTIMHOOD

*When I talk of forgiveness, I mean the belief that you can come
out the other side a better person. A better person than the one
being consumed by anger and hatred. Remaining in that state
locks you in a state of victimhood, making you almost dependent
upon the perpetrator. If you can find it in yourself to forgive, you
are no longer chained to the perpetrator. You can move on and
even help the perpetrator to become a better person too.*

~~Archbishop Desmond Tutu

*The transformational power of forgiveness moves us from being
helpless victims of our circumstances to becoming powerful
co-creators of our reality. We learn how to see people with fresh
eyes, seeing them anew every day. In becoming more loving,
compassionate, and understanding human beings, we gain the
ability to have a deeper relationship with ourselves and with the
significant people in our lives.*

~~Dr. Eileen R. Borris-Dunchunstang,
author of *Finding Forgiveness*

Are some crimes unforgivable? Must victims of such crimes
remain victims? This chapter profiles men and women who
have overcome burdens that might have destroyed them, giving
them a new lease on life.

In 1997 Camilla Carr and her boyfriend Jon James went to
Chechnya to set up a rehabilitation center for war-traumatized

children. Three months later, they were taken hostage by Chechnyan rebels. Their ordeal lasted fourteen months during which Camilla was repeatedly raped by one of her jailers. After they were released, she basked in the euphoria of freedom and the love of her family. Then two months later, she collapsed and couldn't stop crying.

It took three years, Camilla says, until she found the space and silence to let go and surrender to weakness and vulnerability, and her nervous system could finally heal: "Rape is a terrible violation of a human being. I will never forgive the act, yet I can forgive the man who raped me; I can feel compassion for him because I understand the desperate and ignorant place he was coming from."

Many of Camilla's Chechnyan friends cannot understand how she and Jon can forgive. They feel tarnished by the guilt of their community. "I tell them that I believe forgiveness begins with understanding, but you have to work through layers to obtain it. First you have to deal with anger, then with tears, and only once you reach the tears are you on the road to finding peace of mind."[1]

I met Camilla and Jon in connection with the Forgiveness Project, an organization working to promote conflict resolution and restorative justice as alternatives to cycles of conflict, violence, and crime. At its heart is a touring exhibition, "The F-word: Images of Forgiveness," put together by photographer Brian Moody and writer Marina Cantacuzino. Camilla's story is one of the dozens displayed. By collecting and sharing people's stories and delivering outreach programs, the Forgiveness Project[2] encourages and empowers people to explore the nature of forgiveness and alternatives to revenge.

For some, bitter experiences from the past are crippling later in life; but others find these can lead them to a greater understanding of what is needed in the world. Mohamed Sahnoun, an Algerian diplomat who has been deputy secretary-general of both the OAU[3] and the League of Arab States and was special advisor on developments in the Horn of Africa to the UN secretary-general, is one such a man.[4]

As a youth, Sahnoun supported the struggle for his country's independence on a nonviolent basis. In 1954, when the first insurrection started, he was forced to hide as French authorities made no distinction between those who were violent and those who were not. Hidden by relatives in the south, he was later captured and over a period of two months tortured severely, nearly rendered deaf through beatings and underwater submersion. He saw death, he says, as the only way out of his hell.

Thanks to the intervention of French friends, a doctor was allowed to visit him, and the beatings were stopped. A few days later, an instruction from the French government forced the intelligence service to stop the torture, and he was sent to an ordinary prison. At his trial, along with thirteen friends, he was defended by a famous French barrister who was himself assassinated a few days later. After a few years in prison, his release date came due. Usually French paratroopers who employed torture waited outside the prison when prisoners were released. This time, some Christian French friends persuaded the head of the prison not to publish the release date in the usual way.

They escorted him from prison to the next boat and thence to France, where he was hidden in a monastery and then with a family in Brittany and with worker-priests in a Parisian suburb. He waited out the remaining period until Algeria's independence in Switzerland. Those years of struggle yielded wonderful friendships about which he speaks with great emotion. He expresses gratitude for what individual French have done for him and has refused to accuse the French of being his enemy.

In 2007 Sahnoun wrote an autobiographical novel, *Wounded Memory—Algeria 1957*. A reviewer in *Le Monde* calls the book "an extraordinary witness to human suffering and solidarity."[5] What the reader takes away from the book "is not barbarism but remarkable gestures of brotherhood." A reviewer in *La Croix* writes, "Tragedies have hardened this professional negotiator without embittering the man or making him cynical."[6]

From the very beginning of his diplomatic career, Sahnoun has been convinced that evil and good are shared by all. He brings his past experiences to his work of reconciliation. He writes in the book, "I try to bring help to victims as others did in times past for me."

Buried Alive

When quite young, Kenya-born Agnes Hofmeyr decided to devote her life to creating better race relations on the African continent. She died aged 89 in 2006 in South Africa and would surely have been pleased that at her funeral she was described as "a proud African." But her commitment was sorely tested in the 1950s. Her father,

Gray Leakey, was so loved by the Kikuyu that he was given the name *Morrangaru,* meaning "tall and straight." But things were not going well for the Mau Mau, a violent movement against the British colonial rule, and a prophetess said that the gods were angry and had to be placated by the human sacrifice of a good man. So Gray was taken and buried alive on the slopes of Mount Kenya.

Agnes was in the United States and in a turmoil, filled with hatred toward black people and wanted revenge. But through the turmoil, one thought came clearly: "Have no bitterness or hatred but fight harder than ever to bring a change to black and white alike." She was able only a short time later to return to Kenya and speak at a concentration camp where a thousand Mau Mau fighters were interned. "I want to apologize to you," she told them, "for the attitudes and arrogance of my people toward you that caused the bitterness and hatred that spawned Mau Mau, which in turn brought about the death of my father."

Later, at a reconciliation conference, she met face to face one of the men who had chosen her father for death and was able to say to him, "Thank God we have both learned the secret of forgiveness, or we could never sit here."

Over the years, Agnes used her experience widely, saying that she had drawn closer to people up and down Africa through her sorrow than she could ever have done without it. She believed that "in the darkest hour of the most inexplicable tragedy, if men and women will open their hearts to pain and open their minds to God's still, small voice, he will in unimagined ways bring some good out of it and weave it into the tapestry of a great master plan."

She answers the question "How can you forgive?" in her autobiography *Beyond Violence:* "For me the key to forgiveness is to see how terribly wrong I myself am. As I wrestled with my problem through stormy nights of tears, more and more my thoughts focused on what we whites had done in Kenya and what the Mau Mau had told us of the treatment by whites that had driven them into revolt. We whites were very conscious of the good things we had done. The blacks were very conscious of the bad things we had done. We people are more conscious of where we have been hurt than where we have hurt others. I had to identify with the wrong things we whites had done and realize that I stood in need of forgiveness and I did ask the Kikuyu for forgiveness. So perhaps a key to the question 'How can I forgive?' is to look at another question: 'How much do I need forgiveness?' "

Pennsylvania: Before the Blood Had Dried

The terrible tragedy that in October 2006[7] befell the peace-loving Amish community in Nickel Mines, Pennsylvania, the callous and pre-meditated murder of five young girls, shook the nation. The response of that community was, to some, almost beyond belief. From the first moment, it seemed that they were disposed to forgive.

How was this possible? A *Charlotte Observer* headline summed it up: "Amish forgiveness the result of a lifetime of nonviolence."[8] L. Gregory Jones, the dean of Duke Divinity School and author of *Embodying Forgiveness: A Theological Analysis,* describes how the grandfather of one of the slain Amish girls, less than forty-eight hours after the killings, urged a group of young boys to forgive the killer. "We must not think evil of this man," he writes. "Such words may sound bizarre to many of us. What we miss is how this grand-father's life has been formed by nonviolence, by patterns of prayer and worship, and by peaceful resolution of differences with others. Our task is to hope even against hope for communities and practices of forgiveness and repentance that can cultivate a future not bound by the destructiveness of the past."

Similarly, the *Philadelphia Inquirer* had the headline: "For-giveness is woven into the life of Amish."[9] It carried an article by Donald Kraybill, coauthor of *Amish Grace.*[10] He believes that the Amish are better equipped to process grief than are many other Americans. They see even tragic events under the canopy of divine providence, having a higher sense of meaning hidden from human sight at first glance. Their historic habits of mutual aid arise from their understanding that Christian teaching compels them to care for one another in time of disaster. "The Amish don't argue with God," he writes. "They have an enormous capacity to absorb adver-sity—a willingness to yield to divine providence in the face of hos-tility. Such religious resolve enables them to move forward without the endless paralysis that asks why, letting the analysis rest in the hands of God."

The Amish do not ask if forgiveness works, he writes, they simply seek to practice it as the "Jesus way" of responding to adver-saries, even enemies. "Forgiveness is woven into the fabric of Amish faith. And that is why words of forgiveness were sent to the killer's family before the blood had dried on the schoolhouse floor. Such courage to forgive has jolted the watching world as much as the killing itself."

Marie Roberts, widow of the gunman who killed the Amish girls, in a letter of thanks to the Amish, wrote, "Our family wants each of you to know that we are overwhelmed by the forgiveness, grace, and mercy that you've extended to us. Your love for our family has helped to provide the healing we so desperately need. The prayers, flowers, cards, and gifts you've given us have touched our hearts in a way no words can describe.

"Please know that our hearts have been broken by all that has happened. We are filled with sorrow for all our Amish neighbors whom we have loved and continue to love. We know that there are many hard days ahead for all the families who lost loved ones, and so we will continue to put our hope and trust in the God of all comfort, as we all seek to rebuild our lives."[11]

Poland: Revisiting Auschwitz

More than sixty years ago, at the age of ten, Eva Mozes was a human guinea pig in Auschwitz. She and her sister Miriam were Romanian-born "Mengele twins," young Jews operated on by the infamous Nazi doctor, Josef Mengele. That she survived at all is extraordinary. That she has forgiven Dr. Mengele is even more remarkable.

Arriving at Auschwitz in an early morning in May 1944, the two young girls were among the fifteen hundred sets of Jewish twins who were at Mengele's mercy as he sent whole families to their deaths. Within minutes of stepping onto the cement station platform and being identified as twins, their mother was dragged away, and their father and two older sisters were gone, never to be seen again. Their grandparents, uncles, aunts, and cousins were also killed, a total of 117 family members. A few hours later, the struggling Eva was held down by women SS and prisoners while a red-hot pen-shaped iron was dipped in ink and, dot by dot, the number A-7063 was branded on her skin, still visible today.

Three times a week over the next five months, she and her sister were subjected to gruesome experiments and injections with germs and chemicals. "It took every ounce of my energy to survive one day," she remembers, "to live through one more experiment. We did not cry because we knew there was no help. We had learned that within the first few days." She became ill after one injection and heard the doctors say, "Too bad, she's so young. She has only two weeks to live." Had she died, she knew that Mengele would have killed her sister with an injection to the heart and done comparative autopsies.

On a snowy day, 27 January 1945, four days before her eleventh birthday, the Russians liberated Auschwitz. "We were free, we were alive, we had survived, we had triumphed over the unbelievable." The first Soviet film footage to reach the world showed Eva and Miriam, two little girls holding hands leading other survivors out of the camp.

When the war ended, Eva lived in displaced-persons camps before going home to Romania and then, in 1950 she obtained a visa for Israel and went to an agricultural school. There were many such schools in Israel where orphans—traumatized by World War II, anti-Semitism, and prejudice—found acceptance and peace and learned to be proud of who they were. "I learned to like being Jewish," she says. At eighteen, she was drafted into the Israeli army for two years' service and stayed six more years as a career soldier, reaching the rank of sergeant-major. In 1960 she married an American tourist, Michael Kor, who was also a concentration-camp survivor, and came to live in the United States, becoming, as she puts it, "a proud American" in 1965.

Over the decades, she has had a passion to help other twins, to bring home the truth of what happened, and to battle for a more peaceful way of settling conflict. She is often in the news, appearing, for instance, on the *Oprah Winfrey Show* or when she was made Israel's "Newswoman of the Year." She was twice president of the Federation of Jewish Women and has written for children and grownups about her life. In 1978 she started looking for other twins. Between 1984 and 1987, with Miriam's help, she mailed out twelve thousand letters in a search for fellow survivors and located 122 of them. And since 1997 she has given twenty-five hundred lectures to schools, universities, synagogues, and civic groups.

With Miriam, she was cofounder in 1984 of CANDLES, which is an acronym for "Children of Auschwitz-Nazi's Deadly Lab Experiments Survivors," an organization dedicated "to heal the pain, to teach the truth, to prevent prejudice." In 1995 in Terre Haute, her home city in Indiana, she set up the CANDLES Holocaust Museum and Education Center. In 2003 it was firebombed. She told the press that she had forgiven the Nazis but now she had to forgive those who destroyed her museum. With gifts from all round the country, it was rebuilt and reopened in 2005. She says "I didn't give up in Auschwitz and I'm not giving up here."

In June 2001, she spoke in Berlin at the Kaiser Wilhelm Institute, which had been in charge of the wartime experiments. She told her audience, "We are meeting here as former adversaries. I hope we can part as friends. My people, the Jewish people, are hard working, intelligent, and caring. My people are good people. We did not deserve the treatment we received. No one deserves such treatment. Your people, the German people, are hard working, intelligent, and caring. Your people are good people, but you should never have permitted a Hitler to rise to power. There is a lot of pain that we, the Jewish people, and you, the German people, carry around. It does not help anyone to carry the burden of the past. We must learn to heal ourselves from the tragedies of the Holocaust and help our people to heal their aching souls. I realize that many of my fellow survivors will not share, support, or understand my way of healing. But this is the way I healed myself—and I dare hope it might work for other people."

Eva Mozes Kor originated and directed the observance of the fortieth anniversary of the liberation of Auschwitz, returning to the camp and holding a mock trial of Mengele. In 1992 she and her sister Miriam were interviewed for a German TV documentary "Children of Fire." A German doctor from Auschwitz, Hans Münch, was also interviewed.

In July, Kor received a phone call from Dr. John Michalczyk of Boston College, asking her to do a lecture at a conference on Nazi medicine. Michalczyk added, "It would be nice if you could bring a Nazi doctor with you." She replied, "Dr. Michalczyk, where am I going to find a Nazi doctor? The last time I looked, they were not advertising in the *Yellow Pages*." "Think about it," he said.

Through the help of a German-speaking friend, Tonny Van Rentergham, she arranged to meet Dr. Münch. When they did so, she asked him if he knew anything about the operation of the gas chambers. "This is the nightmare I live with," he replied. He had signed the death certificates. At her request, he agreed to sign a document testifying to what had actually gone on. She was delighted that she would have a document that would help her combat revisionists who claimed there were no such gas chambers. He also agreed to accompany her to Auschwitz to observe the fiftieth anniversary of its liberation. Wanting to thank him, and realizing that no one could take from her the power to do so, she decided to write him a letter of forgiveness.

So in January 1995 she and her children, and he and his children and grandchildren stood together by the ruins of the gas chambers. Dr. Münch's document was read, and he signed it. Kor read her Declaration of Amnesty and signed it. "I felt like a burden of pain was lifted from my shoulders. I was no longer a victim of Auschwitz. I was no longer a victim of my tragic past. I was finally free. So I say to everybody: 'Forgive your worst enemy. It will heal your soul and set you free.'" She also says, "The day I forgave the Nazis, I forgave my parents because they did not save me from a destiny in Auschwitz and I also forgave myself for hating my parents."

She knows that her forgiveness of the Nazis and Dr. Mengele is not welcomed by many fellow Jews and emphasizes that she speaks only for herself: "I forgive not because anybody asked me or imposed it on me but because I realized by taking back my power, by forgiving somebody, I actually give myself the gift of freedom." She recommends forgiveness as "a skill for a good life like reading, writing, and arithmetic," and says, "It took me fifty years to be free inside."

In May 2006 a film about her experiences, *Forgiving Dr. Mengele,* was released. A reviewer wrote of the film in the *New York Times:* "Ms. Kor, a stout little sparkplug of a women with energy to burn, charges around Terre Haute in a red-white-and-blue pantsuit, selling houses, giving speeches, and cheerfully reminding her interviewer that 'there's more to life than Auschwitz.'" The review concludes, "Whether or not you agree with her decision to forgive her torturers, it's impossible not to be moved by her fierce capacity for life."[12]

Kor firmly believes that forgiveness is an essential issue that needs to be discussed, explored, and taught, and that she has a contribution to make in that effort. But she made one request to me if I wrote about her, that I should not put a religious frame round her story "because I am <u>not</u>," she underlined, "religious. My forgiveness has nothing to do with God or religion; it has to do with our ability to heal ourselves by forgiving. I believe that people do not have to believe in God to forgive."

Germany: Norwegian Confronts Nazi Jailer

It has been said that forgiveness belongs to the brave. It is certainly not a soft option: it takes courage. A Norwegian friend, Leif Hovelsen, has that quality. As a young man, he joined the underground resistance in Norway when the country was overrun by the Germans in World War II. The only trace of that experience you notice when you meet him today is his deafness, a result of Nazi beatings.

Leif comes from a hard school. His father was a pioneer of the dangerous sport of ski jumping. In a biography of his father, Leif describes how his father took him to a national jumping tournament when he was only eleven years old. A week before the event, his father took him to the top of the jump, the steep slope down which the competitors must ski before launching themselves into the air. Leif's father told him he wanted him to start the tournament with a jump. Leif looked at the hundred-meter drop and was scared. "No, I won't," he said. "Are you a frightened sissy?" asked his father.

During the week, Leif went back and climbed to the top of the jump again, paralyzed with fear. It started to get dark, and he knew he couldn't tell his father that he had been there and hadn't dared to jump. Finally, he plucked up courage and tried. He fell on landing but wasn't hurt as badly as he expected. He tried it again with the same result. On the day of the tournament, he realized that what had been wrong with his practice jumps was that he hadn't dared to go full speed. "When the red pennant waved and the trumpet call sounded," he says, "I knew I had no other choice than to go flat out—and so I did." He jumped 125 feet and landed on his feet.

To Leif, it was a great achievement, putting him onto the next stage of jumping. His father said something Leif has never forgotten: "You might be scared, my son, but you're not a coward."

Leif learned another lesson from his father. He was cheated out of some money by a local thug. His father made him go back and recover the lost money. "I still recall how painful and humanly difficult the experience was and how puzzled I was that it should be so hard to go straight up and challenge that man, even though truth was on my side."

Leif believes his father wanted him to learn a basic lesson for life. "Whenever a man condones what is wrong," he says, "whenever he gives in when a fight is needed, he gradually, often without noticing it, becomes an accomplice in that wrong. Whenever a man keeps silent when his conscience urges him to speak out, it corrupts and corrodes his will and human dignity. On these very issues and choices hang the freedom and personality of man."

These early lessons helped lay foundations in Leif's life. As a young man in resistance to the Nazis who occupied his country, he was betrayed by one of his friends and incarcerated in the Nazis' infamous Grini prison. He was condemned to death and was only saved by the ending of the war.

Shortly after the liberation, Leif found himself with roles reversed: as one of the guards taking it out on his former captors, including the Nazi camp commandant, Alfred Zeidel. He did so with enthusiasm, humiliating them with the same punishment drills they had inflicted on him. A Nazi guard, Wilhelm Heilman, begged Leif for some water. Leif took a bucketful and threw it in his face. His Norwegian comrades laughed. But Leif had an uncomfortable feeling as he went home that he had done something wrong. His conscience told him "There is no excuse. What you did was rotten."

"I knew inside it was true and I despised myself," he says. "I wanted to fight for justice, but this was lust for revenge. It hurts to see the naked truth about oneself. In my own nature, as a Christian and a Norwegian patriot, I had the same evil demons in me for which I was accusing National Socialism and the Germans."

As he was walking in the hills one day, he thought about the Gestapo agent, Otto Suhr, who had tortured him and suddenly, clearly, and unexpectedly, he thought, "Tell him you forgive him." The thought had never crossed Leif's mind before, but it was, he says, an inner imperative. "If people hear about it," he thought at the time, "they will think I'm a nut." His mother encouraged the idea. "Say that I am praying for him," she said.

So when it came Hovelsen's time to do guard duty, he summoned Suhr, and they stood face to face. "He knew me," recalls Leif, "and his glance was uneasy. I looked him in the eye and said words that had come to me and added what my mother had said. He shook all over but did not say anything, and I put him back in his cell. When I answered the Nazis with the same treatment meted out to me, their spirit had conquered me. When I forgave, I had conquered National Socialism."

Leif did not press charges against the guard. Others did, and the guard was condemned to death. The minister who attended him told Leif afterward that the man had asked for Communion. "That shook me," says Leif. "I knew in the moment he repented, he was as welcome as I would have been. I have no right to judge and condemn people. It is in God's hands."

Forgiving freed Hovelsen from the past, and he went to Germany soon after the end of the war, stretching out the hand of friendship to his former enemies. His work paved the way for the first visit to Norway after the war of a German cabinet minister[13] and later for the first German head of state[14] to come to the country since 1905. Hovelsen's parents were visited in their home by the German ambassador to Norway,[15] who thanked them for permitting their only son to come to his country and work tirelessly for the moral reconstruction of Germany. His parents were deeply touched. The last Germans in their home had been the Gestapo members who had arrested Leif.

Hovelsen went on to support the dissidents in the Soviet Union, and when Russia became free of Communism, he worked to help shore up the country's moral and spiritual infrastructure. In 2006 his memoirs, in Russian, were published in Moscow. He wrote to one Russian: "Anyone can be given the gift of being a free man, free of hate, revenge, and bitterness. What happened to me was a divine intervention. At the moment when I acted on the compelling thought that had come to me, I neither understood nor grasped what I did; nor did I fully realize how deep my fear and hate against the Gestapo and the Germans were. But by obeying it, I became a free person. And because of that, I was used in an amazing way to build reconciliation between our two countries."

This story has a postscript, one which underlines the point that forgiveness is not only something that may happen at one moment in time but means embarking on a journey and being ready to see new truths. Fifty-two years after his wartime experiences, Hovelsen suddenly realized that he had never thought of apologizing to the prison camp guard he had thrown water at so callously. In 1997 Leif wondered for the first time what had happened to Heilman. "God's spirit touches you in the middle of the night," he says. "Suddenly you see another side you had overlooked or were not ready to see." He had never reflected on the effect his action had had on the German. Deep down he had considered what the German had done was worse than what he himself had done. "So many accuse others for the evil they do," he says. "but refuse to see that we ourselves might be part of it. Whatever I did of evil I am responsible for a need to restore if possible."

He decided to go to Germany to seek out Heilman. After an extensive search, he discovered that his captor had died five years earlier and learned that while Heilman was in Norway, his father, mother, and four sisters had been killed in a British bombing raid on Germany. Finally, he located Heilman's surviving daughter. He told her about the camp, about the punishment drill, and the bucketful of water, and that he had realized how wrong he had been. "I wanted to tell your father how sorry I have been and to ask for his forgiveness." "I forgive you," she said, "and I know that my father would have too." A few weeks later, Leif went together with the daughter and her husband to Heilman's grave. He placed three roses there. He says, "Standing there, I knew God had healed the wounds of the past, the evil that I had inflicted on an enemy and on myself."

Leif wrote me in 1993, "The ways of God are inscrutable. When he struck me like a bolt from the blue, prompting me to forgive the Gestapo man who had tortured me, it could not have been more illogical, more unpopular, and more crazy to the human mind, especially in those days of May 1945. Many friends could not understand me; some even looked upon me as a traitor. I did not even grasp it myself. However, I could not resist the call that God stirred inside me. Today the perspective of forty-five years' time has proven that God's way was the providential way, throwing me into his orbit, and making me free from the grip of hate and bitterness that was enslaving me.

"It was also the salvation for the Gestapo man who was executed because of his crimes but who found peace with his maker and victory over death. It also has become a door-opening experience to many people—Germans, Russians, Poles—in their struggle to find inner freedom and deliverance from the evil of hate."

India: Beyond Revenge in Gujarat

The Indian state of Gujarat, birthplace of Mahatma Gandhi, was long known for tolerance, moderation, and nonviolence. Civil rights leader Martin Luther King Jr. said, "I came to India as a visitor but I go to Gujarat as a pilgrim." In recent years, however, it has been seen by many as a laboratory of hate against Muslims, who make up 13 percent of the billion population of India, 82 percent of whom are Hindu. This is the story of one man, Juzar Bandukwala, who at great personal toll stands up for his wounded community without a trace of bitterness.

On 22 February 2002, a trainload of Hindu activists was returning to Gujarat from a campaign at the disputed religious site at Ayodhya. At the railway station in a small town called Godhra, a compartment was set alight, resulting in the horrific burning alive of fifty-eight people, many of them women and children. The idea was swiftly and influentially spread that the arson was organized by Muslims, and this was used to exploit hatred against the Muslim population. The result was that Gujarat became the scene of mass violence on a scale and brutality rarely seen in modern India. More than two thousand men, women, and children were killed, and more than two hundred thousand people were rendered destitute, their homes and livelihoods destroyed. It later transpired that the initial fire was possibly an accident.

In 2006 Prashant Jha of Jawahrlal Nehru University wrote in *Countercurrents:* "Today Gujarat is a society sharply polarized; and prejudices about the 'other' are deeply entrenched and a state that happily engineers everyday hatred. In its wake lies a community that lives in fear. The violence is invisible. It operates systematically, as well as subtly, at the establishment and social level."[16]

Harsh Mander, a senior civil servant who resigned in protest at the state government's inability to prevent the murder of Muslims, lays out the issues: "The carnage that convulsed the state of Gujarat has left in its wake a profound human tragedy that does not heal or abate. The agony of Gujarat, its blood-drenched humanity soaked in ideologies of hatred and divide, has hurtled the people of our vast country into a defining crossroads. The manner in which they respond today will determine the kind of country and world that we leave behind for our children. At stake is the affirmation of justice, our pluralist heritage, indeed our very survival as a people who care, and a polity that is genuinely democratic and humane."

Dr. Bandukwala consistently has worked to shore up that pluralist heritage. He is president of the Gujarat People's Union for Civil Liberties. The Gujarati Muslim grew up in a business family known for trading in guns and ammunition. The name even means "one who deals in guns." But having no interest in the family business, and fascinated by Albert Einstein and the atom bomb, he dreamed of finding a scientific solution that would make atomic bombs redundant. In 1967 he went to the United States where, in 1972 he gained a doctorate in physics, specializing in the behavior of objects that travel faster than light. While there, he met a nun who told him that he could do more for his people if he returned home rather than staying in the United States.

"That conversation changed my entire life," he says. "I destroyed my green card." He realized that his research was too cut off from everyday problems facing the world and returned to India, in late 1972, joining the physics department at the University of Baroda, where he still teaches. "I plunged into the one issue that has focused my life for the past thirty-five years: how to uplift the Muslims of India."

After his return, he got involved in social reforms among the state's Muslims. Priority for him was—and is—modern education, which must accompany religious education. "This required I be as honest as possible with both Muslims and Hindus. But the extreme elements on both sides found me very irritating." He faced stiff opposition from conservative Muslims for having liberal views on women's rights; girls' education; on the need to widen Muslims' view of the world, making it more in tune with modernity and science and able to reach out to non-Muslims. He called for reform of traditional *madrasa* education and questioned the sharp sectarian differences that many Muslim leaders had a vested interest in maintaining.

In the late 1980s, in the wake of the controversy over *Satanic Verses*, a book that repelled him, he said that the *fatwa* to kill Salman Rushdie was un-Islamic. "The notion that a writer pay with his life was equally repulsive to me." Even from an Islamic angle, he found the Prophet's treatment of his enemies as most humane, even by modern standards. The right way to oppose the book was to offer a counterperspective, he said. For saying this, he had a *fatwa* imposed on him as an "enemy of Islam." He was even accused of turning girls into prostitutes because he had been arguing for modern education for Muslim girls.

Unexpected backing came from a Bombay organized-crime boss who liked his arguments about modernization and organized a public meeting in his support. It silenced the mullahs and inspired him to carry on with his efforts to promote social reforms among Muslims. "Since then, there has been no question of my acceptability within the Muslim community," Bandukwala told me. "It is ironic that my final acceptance was due to the intervention of a Bombay [organized-crime] figure. It was not due to my own qualifications, whatever they may be, of head and heart."

On the night before the Gohdra train massacre, he spoke in Baroda, the educational capital of Gujarat, of Savarkar[17] as no Muslim ever did. He thought it would cement Hindu–Muslim relations there. He ended with the words: "Friends, there are only two paths before the country: the path of Mahatma Gandhi, which is inclusive, in which every Indian child will feel that this country belongs to him. The other alternative is the path of Savarkar, in which many Indians feel that the country does not belong to them."

Within twelve hours of his speech, the Gohdra train burning took place, which he was quoted widely as condemning. But he became the first victim. Attempts to enter his house were frustrated by Hindu neighbors, a point that he urged the press to highlight. But then began what he calls "the longest day of my life." With the concurrence of police who were supposed to protect him, his house was burned down while he escaped first to a friend's house, where he had to hide in the bathroom, and then by plane to Bombay, having first appealed on national TV for sanity and compassion. "All over, I could see fires burning and roadblocks to prevent any Muslim escape. By God's grace, I was a respected figure in the city but on the drive to the airport, I felt like a hare being hunted by the hound. I shuddered at the thought of what must have happened to my fellow Muslims."

The following week, he flew to New York to be with his son. A childhood friend in an important position in the U.S. government suggested that he seek political asylum. He refused, saying that Gujarat was his *karmabhoomi*:[18] "I can never abandon it while it burns."

He returned after three months when a police inquiry was held about the burning of his house. He refused to name the policemen who had joined hands with the mob and said "I pardon them."

To him, the remarkable feature of Gujarat in 2002 was that Muslims survived and emerged from the pogrom "stronger, wiser, and economically stable." Education and business became the "in thing" in Muslim homes. Religious obscurantism was out. The immediate priority was to bind the physical, economic, and psychological wounds of a ravaged community. There was little government support, but "in a remarkable show of solidarity, millions of people, cutting across religious lines, all over India and even from abroad, poured out their hearts and opened their purses to put these victims back on their feet."

Bandukwala does not want Muslims to answer hate with hate. "It is a tribute to the Muslims of India that we have not responded with the weapon of terrorism, despite the provocation for the same. Osama bin Laden is not the answer to the problems facing Muslims in Gujarat and India. His approach can be suicidal for us. His methods violate the basic precepts of Islam, wherein killing of innocents is an unpardonable sin."

The situation is still tense, he says. At first, the feeling was one of revenge. Now it is not. "Some of us are strong believers in nonviolence. We have been repeatedly urging them to leave justice to God: Revenge will mean only more trouble for the whole community." It would have been good, he told the *Times of India,* if the Hindu leadership had felt remorse and sorrow. "The standard comment remains, 'Muslims deserved it.' If they just said the simple word 'sorry,' we'd come forward and forgive, and the process of reconciliation would begin." The Germans have apologized for the killing of Jews and the Japanese for killing Chinese, but "too few Gujarat Hindus have had the courage to speak against the killing of Muslims."[19]

In his frequent letters to the papers and in speeches, he returns to the dual mission of helping Hindus face what has happened and to changing his own people. "We must engage in deep introspection and critique our own selves; find out and rectify our own faults." He has also been working with Hindus of different kinds and acknowledges when they take positive steps. He sees the development of a modern middle class as one way to solve the Hindu–Muslim problem.

In 2002 he e-mailed me: "Peace and reconciliation are possible with the magic word 'Sorry.' The next few decades will be crucial for India and, by virtue of [India's] size, for the world. If India can contain this passion for revenge and turn it into reconciliation and brotherhood, the world would have gained a great deal."

In an article at the height of the worst violence against his people, the respected newspaper *The Hindu* described him as a physician-turned-peace activist, who suffered like the rest of his community, but had no words of bitterness. The article about him was headlined "A sane voice in an insane clime."[20]

Rwanda: Tutsi Works for Reconciliation

The prisoner in the central jail in the capital, Kigali, was an emaciated shadow of his former self, brought low from his position as an all-powerful mayor. Looking at him, Joseph Sebarenzi couldn't summon up any hatred. "When I saw him, miserable and malnourished, I felt compassion," he told me. "Instead of thinking evil, that he should die, I decided to give him some money."

"Don't you remember what he did," said the surprised USAID worker whom he was accompanying. Joseph remembered well. Here was a Hutu who helped direct the killing of Tutsis like himself in a mass slaughter where more than eight hundred thousand men, women, and children died, including both his parents and siblings. Joseph remembered; he couldn't forget, but "slowly, slowly," as he puts it, his hatred had been ebbing. Particularly as he worked with an NGO in rural areas and saw Hutus suffering and as scared of Tutsis as he had been of them.

Joseph Sebarenzi is a Rwandan survivor from those terrible times brought to the conscience of the world and later dramatized through the film *Hotel Rwanda.* As a child, he glimpsed the tribal violence that would later engulf his country; but as a young person, he "kind of accepted injustice" and didn't know what he could do about it. His parents sent him away for schooling in Congo, where he also got a bachelor's degree in sociology.

Later, after the killings, he was consumed by negative thoughts and questions of why people who had been friends, had shared everything, had killed his father and mother. He was angry: angry at church, angry at God, angry at Hutus, although it didn't always show, just as the horror through which he has lived doesn't always come through as he speaks. "In Rwandan culture, people don't always externalize their feelings. They may, out of fear of further victimization, say it's OK when it's not OK," he says. At first, he wanted revenge. But he made his way back to his Christian roots and "negative thoughts diminished." By 1996 he was ready to accept the truths his father had taught him, to work for justice and for reconciliation. He remembered the Scripture teachings that one should overcome evil with good, that one should forgive not just seven times but seventy times seven. "I also felt that, for the sake of future generations, the best way to prevent further violence and protect those who were to come was to engage in reconciliation."

After a period in exile, he felt it was safe to return to Rwanda and help in its reconstruction. He was soon on the council of the Liberal Party. Elected to be a member of Parliament, he worked to build strong institutions, provide accountable government, and advance reconciliation and was subsequently elected Speaker of Parliament. As a Human Rights Watch report stated, "It was apparently this commitment to good government that won Sebarenzi approval among ordinary people, Hutu as well as Tutsi." Instead of using his position to wreak revenge, he pushed for peace and reconciliation. "Revenge," he says, "is like adding guilt to victimhood. It solves nothing. At some point, we have to ignore the past and envision the future."

His efforts to establish some autonomy for Parliament and his outspokenness in holding government ministers accountable for alleged corruption led to pressure on him to resign and, when threatened with assassination, he sought asylum in the United States. He completed a master's degree at the School for International Training and now teaches conflict resolution there and works with its program CONTACT, an acronym for "Conflict Transformation across Cultures." He is respected by both ethnic groups and keeps close friendships with many in the Hutu community but feels that it is still not safe for him to return home—not because of Hutus but because the current regime does not tolerate dissenting views.

In his lectures and public speaking, Joseph draws on his personal experiences and his thesis work, which was on reconciliation and the need for a Truth and Reconciliation Commission for his country. He also is writing a book about his experiences. He is heard frequently on the BBC and the Voice of America on their Kinyarwanda programs broadcast to Rwanda. He champions a broad process of restorative justice and calls on Rwandans to embrace reconciliation and forgiveness. He told an NPR station, "I am a victim of genocide. But we cannot judge one million people—no jail is large enough. Retributive justice could lead to another cycle of killing."

Building on the work of the Truth and Reconciliation Commission in South Africa, he believes that Tutsis and Hutus should be given the opportunity to speak about and listen to the respective sufferings of their people and that they should discuss and put in place mechanisms to prevent future violence. Confronting the past gives voice to victims on both sides. This should not be interpreted as equating the abuses suffered by each side. "Each abuse stands alone. The only thing abuses have in common is that they are all wrong."

He is not surprised when he hears some Hutus denying the genocide of Tutsi in Rwanda or when he hears some Tutsis denying the crimes committed against the Hutu. "People naturally hate talking about their offenses to others, but they enjoy talking about the offenses done to them." In South Africa, the victims, across racial lines, were given a safe space to tell their stories, and the perpetrators equally were given the opportunity to disclose their awful acts and to apologize.

To establish a shared truth, there were requirements for both the victims and the perpetrators. For the perpetrator, it required acknowledging the wrong done, apologizing, resolving not to repeat the wrong, and, finally, making reparation—to the extent possible. On the other hand, the victim was required to forgive and to commit not to take revenge. "Without these steps on each side, reconciliation is unlikely and even impossible."

Through his teaching experience with CONTACT and research in conflict transformation, he came to believe in the crucial necessity for human beings to recognize that all humanity must support each other rather than destroy each other. "Those who think they can overcome violence with violence are mistaken. As long as we don't understand that violence begets violence we will have a hard time to overcome the legacies of conflict, war, and genocide."

Joseph feels grateful for his capacity to process his terrible trauma at the personal and communal level. "However, tragically, one of the consequences of trauma is that affected individuals and communities are predisposed to revenge. Even if they don't have opportunities to take revenge, if the conflict continues to fester and if it is not transformed, they tend to pass on the memory of persecution and the desire for revenge to future generations, who may grow all too eager to avenge what happened to their families, tribe, or ethnic group." He believes that victims have choices to make: between revenge and reconciliation, between death and life.

He speaks of constructive relationship building, forging a nonviolent partnership in which you are no longer enemies seeking to defeat each other. "You are embarked on the path toward reconciliation, which is the ultimate goal of dialogue. The farther and longer you travel down that road, the harder it becomes to return to old ways, to destructive patterns of behavior."

If you set out to harm the one that harms you, he believes, you are failing to seek the higher ground by stopping the forces of destruction. "Responding to violence with violence is unethical, expensive, and ineffective," he says.

He came to realize through his own experience that dwelling in the past was harmful. He discovered that his own best interests lay in reconciliation—not in revenge or in any other type of violence. As he tells his students, looking back he can see three reasons why he chose the path of reconciliation. First, the creation of peace for future generations. "There is absolutely nothing I can do to bring back my loved ones. But there is something I can do to build the foundations for peace for those who survived, for my children and grandchildren, for all generations of Rwandans. Engaging in revenge perpetuates the cycle of violence; reconciliation breaks the cycle."

Second, such an approach was faithful to his own spiritual integrity. "The Bible instructs us 'not to take revenge, not to be overcome by evil, but to overcome evil with good.' One of the great messages from Jesus to his followers was 'you have heard it said, "eye for eye and tooth for tooth." But I tell you do not resist evil by evil.' I believe that if we truly respect our spiritual teachers and if we uphold the best in our religious traditions, we need to embrace reconciliation and reject revenge."

Third, reconciliation contributed to physical and emotional well-being as anger and resentment were the great enemies of such well-being. "I have learned that forgiveness is just as important to my health as eating the right foods. Engaging in resentment not only damages your health, but also cripples you to the point of becoming a perpetrator. You become the very sort of person you profess to despise. Revenge is like adding salt to the wound and guilt to victimhood."

On the tenth anniversary of the 1994 genocide, a Kigali memorial center was opened. The site was chosen because of the mass burial of 250,000 victims. On its wall are the words of a survivor, Yolande Mukagazana: "There will be no humanity without forgiveness. There will be no forgiveness without justice. But justice will be impossible without humanity."

England: Liverpool Mother Stirs a Nation

In July 2005, a young black man in Liverpool, Anthony Walker, was brutally murdered with an ice axe to his skull after being chased by white racist thugs.

Anthony was a bright eighteen-year-old student whose ambition was to be a lawyer and a judge. He loved performing, looked after his five siblings when his parents separated, and was a devout Christian who had declined an invitation to take part in trials for the England basketball team because they fell on a Sunday. Thousands took part in an antiracism vigil and also in a candle-lit walk to the park where he was attacked.

In December 2007, his killers came to trial, were found guilty, and jailed for life. They were boys from Anthony's school who had shared the same playground. Minutes after the verdict, Anthony's mother, Gee, a special-needs teacher, faced the press. "It's been real hard going," she said, "but I feel justice has been done. Do I forgive them? At the point of death, Jesus said, 'I forgive them because they do not know what they do.' I have got to forgive them. I still forgive them. It will be difficult, but we have no choice but to live on for Anthony. Each of us will take a piece of him and will carry on his life." The London *Times* headlined her statement across a page: "I forgive them, says mother."[21]

After the murder, a number of people urged Anthony's father, Steve, to take revenge, even saying that they were ready to unleash the kind of violence that blighted the area in the eighties and offering to provide him with a gun so that he could hunt down his son's killers. But he made it clear that he wanted his son's death to be a catalyst for racial harmony, not further bloodshed.

The murder, reported BBC News Liverpool, "united a community in anger at the ferocity and senseless nature of this racist attack."[22] The family's generous response stirred the whole country and was even commented in the archbishop of Canterbury's Christmas message that year.

Determined that Anthony's death not be just another murder statistic, Gee and other members of the family set up the Anthony Walker Foundation "to play a small part in teaching the next generation of children to be more tolerant of each other regardless of the color of their skin." She and the family have been active in many areas of the life of Liverpool and Britain. The foundation has hosted a National Union of Teachers lecture on promoting racial harmony, and Gee has gone into schools to talk to young people about respecting and valuing people's differences. In September 2006, she opened a peace garden at a local school. "Peace is not just about one day," she said. "It's something lived every day. Don't let other mothers cry like me, teach your children tolerance and peace." She said afterward, "If I can change just one of their minds to think positively and be respectful, that will be enough because it will reach a whole family." Daughter Dominique has been running workshops and hosting concerts with the same aim.

In the summer of 2006, Gee helped organize the Anthony Walker Festival of Sport, Music, Art, and Education at a Liverpool sports academy, which was a huge success.

In October 2006, an Anthony Walker bursary was launched to promote racial harmony, particularly among young people, through funding school workshops focusing on sports, music, and education.

In December 2006, Gee Walker and Dominique, in recognition of their work to promote racial harmony, met the queen at Buckingham Palace. Gee is quoted in the *Liverpool Echo* as saying of Anthony, "I am sure he is looking down at us and laughing at the fact that we are off to Buckingham Palace. It's a bit much to put into words. It's nice to be recognized."[23]

In January 2007, the charity was given £15,000 by the Football Association. The money had been collected at the season's curtain-raising game between Liverpool and Chelsea. It will fund a twenty-minute DVD drama to be shown at secondary schools across Merseyside to educate pupils about racism and racist violence. Dominique says, "It is important to get this message across to children, and sport or modern technology like DVDs is the best way to do it."

Gee has received numerous local and national awards, some of which also have been instituted in Anthony Walker's name. One is the first ever Profile in Courage award from the National Black Crown Prosecution Association for the family's "calm dignity in the face of tragedy."

In January 2007 Gee was given an honorary degree by Liverpool Hope University for her work in promoting racial harmony. The citation, which spelled out her many achievements, said that "In the aftermath of his murder, his mother spoke movingly of her grief and pain at his loss and of how she could not begin to understand what could have motivated these two young men to carry out a completely unprovoked and brutal attack on her son. The quiet dignity with which this remarkable woman spoke to journalists and TV reporters made a lasting impression on all who heard her." It concluded: "As one of our alumni at Liverpool Hope University, you are an inspiration to all who would make a positive contribution to racial harmony and social cohesion in this country."

Trevor Phillips, head of the Commission for Equalities and Human Rights, spoke in Liverpool cathedral that week[24] about the dignified way in which the Walker family had handled their grief, the example of forgiveness and reconciliation that they had set, and the energy they had committed to their antiracism campaign.

"Gee," he said, "you stand out in an age of part-time parenting when our children face full-time peril; an age of shallow, instant notoriety when our people need role models of stature; an age of crass anything-goes commercialism when our country cries out for a renewal of its deeper values. At a time when we needed to be reminded what morality and courage in the face of evil looks like, Gee Walker and her family showed us the consolation of faith, the promise of hope, and the tender face of charity. We have much to thank you for, and though few of us could show the fortitude and forbearance you have shown, you and the young people we celebrate tonight show us all what being human can be at its best. You have shown that the behavior of individuals can make a difference.

The Walker family is a great inspiration to us all, that against great adversity it is possible to create harmony.

"It is not all plain sailing. 1980 will come again. There will, sadly, be more Anthony Walkers. We cannot always forestall the same thing happening to others but we can learn the lessons. Every time we fail, we recover faster. Anthony's life ended too early. It is our responsibility to make those whose lives go on better, richer, more equal, and more harmonious. We can do this but we have to want to, to have the courage to take action into our own hands and make the community better. That is the debt that we owe Anthony."

A New Sense of Empowerment
Dr. Margaret E. Smith

Dr. Smith is scholar-in-residence at American University and teaches in the division of International Peace and Conflict Resolution in American University's School of International Service. She is the author of *Reckoning with the Past: Teaching History in Northern Ireland*, published by Lexington Books in 2005.

Something dehumanizing has occurred that cannot be erased, and the residue of this occurrence clouds the breathing space of victim and perpetrator alike. We are all aware of the burden carried by perpetrators—the pretense that past behavior has no relevance to the present, guilt, self-justification, the need to hide the event or to split oneself off from it psychologically, the necessity to sidestep or turn a blind eye to the obvious consequences suffered by the victim.

We also know that victims need to hear an acknowledgment of the ills they have suffered. They deserve to see a legal regime that holds wrongdoers accountable and, in many cases, they deserve reparations. Political systems and social institutions should be altered to make it harder for such events to happen again. And groups need to find ways of remembering so that societal wounds are not forgotten.

But beyond all of this, victims still carry a burden because they live with the dilemma of how to think about, and behave toward, those who harmed them. This dilemma is even greater for groups than it is for individuals. While individuals who are in conflict can decide never to see the other party again, social groups and countries must deal with each other for a variety of reasons.[25] In either case, the experience of harm is more than substantive injury: it signifies that perpetrators have seized a position of power over victims by committing acts that define subsequent realities.

The word *victim* must therefore be understood in two senses. In a value-neutral sense, the victim is the person to whom harm was done. In a normative sense, the victim is the one who has been subjected to an assertion of power from the outside. This latter aspect of victimhood creates an acute dilemma for the victim.

How can a person break out of the overbearing sense that someone else's behavior has had lasting repercussions upon his or her life? For some, moving on as if nothing had happened is the best way to signal that the perpetrator's power is not lasting. But for others, the difficulty with this stance is that something *did* happen. Moreover, even if the victim gains some satisfaction from the fact that he has not lost stride, he may suffer from the ongoing insult that the perpetrator has not recognized the degree to which he offended the moral universe.

Another option open to the victim is to retaliate. The impulse for revenge is understandable and strong and is linked to our instinct for self-protection. It is problematic because it sets up a victim–perpetrator cycle, so familiar in civil wars, that can continue for generations. While the original victim may gain some satisfaction from this, he is put in the unhappy position of becoming just like the perpetrator.

Deciding to forgive, says Miroslav Volf, professor of theology at Yale Divinity School, is a way for a victim to protect himself or herself from a vengeful outlook that could lead, in Wolf's words, to "mimicking or dehumanizing the oppressors."[26] But does the gesture of forgiveness on its own generate sufficient empowerment for the otherwise disempowered victim? Forgiving might nonetheless seem too much to resemble resignation or a willingness to sweep matters under the rug. It still might suggest to the outside world that the victim lacks self-respect.

This leads us to a third available option for the victim: to discover a newly empowered sense of self. One way victims have done this is in undertaking a task or project that models a different kind of future. It is in the endeavor to build a different future that we most easily can understand the willingness to forgive. When those harmed reach out to create some transformative venture, they are taking power into their hands in a way that acknowledges the past but also makes it possible to move on.

Perhaps a matter for further study is the kind of transformative practices that people who have been harmed choose subsequently to engage in. One example would be endeavors undertaken with the perpetrator. In this case, the perpetrator would have to have recognized and acknowledged the harmful act and, presumably, asked for forgiveness. Without such a gesture, any common endeavor of the victim and perpetrator would surely seem less than authentic.

On the other hand, what is the victim to do if that apology is not forthcoming? Many of those placed in this dilemma have found themselves taking positive action of their own regardless of whether the one who did them insult has sought atonement. In many cases, this takes the form of helping others who have suffered in a similar way to the victim.

So, why forgive? Because the stance of forgiveness is attractive to a victim when it is part of some form of empowerment—not empowerment over the perpetrator, which would place the victim in danger of becoming like the perpetrator, but empowerment characterized as a new sense of identity and self, demonstrating that the victim is able to act upon the world.

The idea that forgiveness involves a shift in the sense of self underlines the fact that forgiveness is rarely something conferred or expressed in one particular moment. It grows over time as the person who suffered harm turns the kaleidoscope of his life to a new position. This way of thinking about forgiveness also sheds light on the role of reparations. Reparations are important, in a material sense, to restore what was destroyed. But they are also a gesture of recognition of how difficult it will be for some victims to turn that inner kaleidoscope without material help. Reparations or compensation for some people will be a prerequisite for forgiveness in the way I have defined forgiveness. This might not be so for everyone, but it will be increasingly so the more totally a person's life has been blown apart by the injurious act.

Forgiveness is not a matter of condoning or ignoring wrong. Forgiveness is not a matter of ignoring legal redress. It is a recognition that the harmful act can be transformed to something else if the victim finds a new sense of empowerment to repair the world.

Perspective
The Righteous Chariot
Rajmohan Gandhi

Rajmohan Gandhi, author and former member of the Indian Parliament, teaches at the University of Illinois at Urbana–Champaign. Among his books are the biography of his grandfather *Gandhi* and *Ghaffar Khan,* his 2004 biography of the nonviolent Pashtun leader.

Let me, a Hindu living next to many Muslims, among others, try to address two questions here. One, is forgiveness an "issue" for Hindus? Two, is forgiveness more of an issue for Muslims than for adherents of other faiths?

I know of Hindus who thank God for what they see as the innate and, through history, uninterrupted peacefulness of the Hindus. I know, too, of Hindus who derive from the sacred text of the Gita (which opens with a battlefield scene) the doctrine of holy war—*dharmayudh* in Sanskrit or Hindi, which can be translated fairly as *jihad* in Arabic. And I know of Hindus harboring both beliefs who therefore hold that Hindus seldom, if ever, need to be forgiven. They do not kill or harm non-Hindus; if at times they appear to do so, they are only, and reluctantly, discharging a religious duty.

Yet, Hindu lore is replete with gore and includes, for example, the story of the hero of legendary times, Parasurama, who filled several lakes with blood to avenge a humiliation. And our world's modern-day violence has sadly included ample contributions from those calling themselves Hindus in Sri Lanka and Nepal and in several states of India, including Gujarat and Assam. It has also included (not always in headlines) the oppression of weak, supposedly "lower" caste or "untouchable" Hindus at the hands of stronger, supposedly better-born Hindus.

So forgiveness is indeed an issue that Hindus should frontally face. We have harmed fellow Hindus as well as non-Hindus. Often such harming was avoidable. Hence, we need to be forgiven. Often, we have been harmed too. So we need also the difficult ability to forgive. Luckily Hindu tradition upholds forgiveness.

I am hardly alone among Hindus in acknowledging this. Many Hindus are well aware that noble Hindu teachings against violence have not prevented Hindus from lapsing into cruelty and that noble Hindu teachings in favor of forgiveness have not always melted hate and anger from wounded Hindu hearts.

When my grandfather, the Mahatma, declared that the battle-field scene in the Gita was allegorical and that the real *dharmayudh* was against the baseness inside our hearts, he was following a rich Hindu tradition in favor of such an interpretation.

The Ramayana epic (which, though ancient, continues to stir and inspire millions of Hindus) tells of the fight of Rama, the divine prince, with Ravana, the demon-king. "Ravana is in a chariot, and you are on your feet. How will you fight?" Rama is asked. In a famous reply, Rama describes "the real meaning of a chariot":

> Listen, friend, the chariot that leads to victory is of another kind. Valor and fortitude are its wheels; truthfulness and virtuous conduct are its banner; strength, discretion, self-restraint, and benevolence are its four horses, harnessed with the cords of forgiveness, compassion and equanimity. . . . Whoever has this righteous chariot, has no enemy to conquer anywhere. (From the "Lanka" chapter of the Ramayana, Tulsidas version)

Through the ages, a majority of ordinary Hindus have accepted this deeper meaning of holy war and of a holy chariot and thereby prepared themselves to live in peace with people who may be difficult or different.

These ordinary Hindus, who, let me repeat, comprise the majority, are being targeted by a minority of militant Hindus who (a) demand acceptance of Hinduism as a call to righteous war and (b) portray today's Hindu millions, residing largely in South Asia, as weak, vulnerable, and under siege by Muslim and Christian forces and needing to fight a war against the presumed attackers.

Like extremists from other backgrounds, Hindu extremists play on fear—today, in particular, the fear of terrorism—and on the past, which is often specially constructed in order to excite revenge. But the spirit of Hinduism calls for constructing the present and the future and calls for the primacy of confidence rather than the sway of fear. This means a willingness, when necessary, to seek or grant forgiveness.

Do Muslims find it harder than, say, Hindus or Christians or Buddhists or Jews to forgive? The very question gives off a smell of falseness, for it suggests a challenge to the similarity in all of God's human creation. But let us examine it in the light of the fact that, save one, each of the 114 chapters of the Quran starts with the words: "In the Name of the Almighty, the Merciful, and the Compassionate," which also happen to be the words Muslims most often use when in joy or sorrow or danger or suspense. Can forgiveness be a strange notion to those asking several times a day for mercy and compassion?

It is indeed true that in recent years many terrorist acts have been committed by people bearing Muslim names and often in "the name" of Islam. (Many but hardly all. Some have been committed also by persons holding Christian, Jewish, Hindu, Buddhist, or Sikh names. And it was not many decades ago that terrorism was openly avowed by some Hindu and Jewish groups.)

That the world's Muslims have to find ways of isolating the extremists who have sought to hijack Islam is only too true. And a great many of them are trying to do just that, with creativity and courage both. We make their task harder if we go along with the segregating and illogical notion that there is a class of humanity, distinct from every other class or category, namely the world's Muslims, who are uniquely predisposed in favor of violence and terrorism.

Can forgiveness be reconciled with a sense of a flawed religion, race, or community? Are there some, wearing suitable badges, who are entitled to forgiveness, while others, lacking those badges or sporting a different badge, are not? Without universality, "forgiveness" is commerce.

4

taking responsibility

An old Cherokee grandfather is talking to his grandson who has come to him with anger at a friend who has done him an injustice. The grandfather tells him a story: "I too, at times, have felt a great hate for those who have taken so much, with no sorrow for what they have done. But hate wears you down and does not hurt your enemy. It is like taking poison yourself and then wishing your enemy would die. I have struggled with these feelings many times. It is as if there are two wolves inside me. One is good and does no harm. He lives in harmony with all around him and does not take offense when no offense is intended. He will only fight when it is right to do so and in the right way. But the other wolf, ah! He is full of anger. The littlest thing will set him into a fit of temper. He fights everyone all the time, for no reason. He cannot think because his anger and hate are so great. It is helpless anger, for his anger will change nothing. Sometimes it is hard to live with these two wolves inside me, for both of them try to dominate my spirit."
The boy looks intently into his grandfather's eyes and asks,
"Which one wins, grandfather?"
The grandfather smiles and quietly says, "The one I feed."

~~The Wolves Within, a Cherokee legend

Around the world, men and women of differing backgrounds are stepping forward in their communities to take the lead in overcoming division.

The Solomon Islands deal with the legacy of a five-year civil war and tit-for-tat killings. One man who put his life at risk to bring peace was Matthew Waletofea, an accountant and school director active in the South Seas Evangelical Church. Waletofea, who has been an advisor to two prime ministers, set up the Civil Society Network, which mediated between warring factions.

When thirty thousand of his Malaitan people were evicted, the Malaitans mounted a coup and overthrew the government. When beheadings and delimbings became accepted as a normal part of resolving differences, Waletofea spoke out against the militias on both sides and was hated by both. Throughout the conflict, despite being punched and kicked and gun-butted, with his office vandalized and his house ransacked, and being accused of taking sides, he held fast to his belief that forgiveness was a vital part of building peace.

Waletofea told an international conference in 2005 that he had said to his wife and six children that he, and even one of them, could be killed but that he wanted them to know that he had forgiven the perpetrators for any wrongdoing. He told them that if he were to be killed, he hoped that they too in time would have the grace to forgive.

At one point, his brother was mistaken for him and nearly killed. "I remember praying that night. I thought I was doing God's work—speaking out when nobody wanted to speak. And I told God that I would rather he took me and not the militia. Afterward, I had a strange sense of being liberated." The worst moment was when his wife was away in Australia, and three men burst into his house. Four of his children were at home. "One of them pulled out an assault rifle, put it to my chest, and pulled the trigger. It didn't fire. He took out the magazine, put back one bullet, then pulled the trigger again, but it didn't fire. We're very superstitious in the Solomon Islands— so I said to him, 'You can try one more time, but you can guarantee it will fire out the other end!' He pulled back his rifle and left."

Since peace was established in 2003, Waletofea has continued his work, including pioneering with others in the setting up of a national branch of the anticorruption group, Transparency International, and is working to establish human rights and truth and reconciliation commissions. To address the critical problem of ethical leadership head-on, he founded the Solomon Islands Democratic Party.

A major division is the Israel–Palestine conflict whose effects spill over into every nation where Jews and Arabs live. In Britain, the two communities live side by side, and both are minorities and significant contributors to society. They share a common experience of having to address hostilities that derive from mistaken stereotypes of their religions and cultures and also have more in common with each other than with other religions. Yet, particularly since 9/11, the country has witnessed a significant and alarming growth in anti-Semitism and Islamophobia.

This was the challenge faced by Dr. Richard Stone, a leader in the Jewish community who served on many prestigious councils and on the panel of two government inquiries into racism. "I fill gaps, I go for the gaps," he told me.

A former medical doctor, Stone chaired the Commission on British Muslims and Islamophobia from 2000 to 2004 and, as chair of both the Jewish Council for Racial Equality and the Islamophobia Commission, he found himself in a unique position bridging Muslim and Jewish communities. For many of the British Muslims, 80 percent of whose families come from the Indian subcontinent, he was the first Jew they had met.

In the early 1980s, a British Muslim husband-and-wife team set up a charitable foundation, Calamus, to promote dialogue between the three Abrahamic faiths. The Jewish community responded with the Maimonides Foundation, and for ten years the two groups sustained—with dinners and an annual lecture—dialogue between Muslim and Jewish leaders. Stone, who had been a founding member of Maimonides, recognized the need for a more "grassroots" contact that didn't just involve a few leaders, as well as a forum for more informal contact to be pursued throughout the country.

"In 2003 I decided to seek interested British Jews to meet friends and colleagues from many Muslim communities around Britain. I had the privilege of being introduced by my Muslim commissioners. It took two years of quiet, steady growth to develop a group strong enough to go public with two events in 2004." They recognized that "an attack on one community is an attack on all communities."

The result is Alif–Aleph UK, which aims to work jointly for the mutual benefit of the two communities in Britain. *Alif* and *Aleph* are the first letters of the Arabic and Hebrew alphabets, the languages of the Quran and the Torah, the holy books of Muslims and Jews. Their meetings are chaired jointly by a Jew and a Muslim, "a good practice" model for all communities in the United Kingdom who find themselves divided, usually by conflicts from abroad spilling over to create division in the United Kingdom.

In a 2007 pamphlet, *Faith and Foreign Policy*, for the Foreign Policy Centre, Stone wrote about the five or more wars since the founding of Israel in 1948 and "the grumbling conflict" between Jews and Palestinians for one hundred years, even before the Balfour Declaration of 1917, which gave British government support for a national home for the Jewish people: "With no resolution, neither side is the victor, and the narratives of each have become polished and polarized, with each side pointing the finger at the alleged faults of the other. These are then used as ammunition in a war of words that always blames the other side for failure to make peace. Both sides see themselves as the victims of the other's murderous domination."

He points out that, privately, Jews and Muslims express distress at the plight of "ordinary people" on both sides, but publicly it is hard for Anglo-Jewry to do other than leap to the defense of Israel where the five million Jews are 80 percent of the population but less than 50 percent of the population of the Israeli and Palestinian territories added together. And the Muslim leadership in the United Kingdom is naturally drawn to supporting the Palestinians, about 90 percent of whom are Muslims.

One Muslim with whom Stone has conducted some fifty meetings is Imam Abduljalil Sajid, who is attempting to mirror positive national relations in his community. He has developed a good relationship with the five rabbis in his local Jewish community in Brighton, and at one synagogue he was the first non-Jewish speaker to give the annual memorial lecture. He was the first Muslim to invite a famous Jewish national religious leader, Rabbi Jonathan Magnoet, to address the congregation of his Brighton mosque. He finds that relations are strengthened when both parties work on shared tasks and create coalitions—even representing the interests of others: for instance, cooperating on food issues, such as animal slaughter and reverence for the animal, with the chair of the Bengali traders association and the chair of the Jewish traders association campaigning together on local "bread-and-butter" issues.

Imam Sajid holds many national offices, including the chair of the United Kingdom's Muslim Council for Religious and Racial Harmony. He tells me that the Muslim Council of Britain and the Board of Deputies of British Jews meet regularly to discuss issues of mutual concern. He speaks of the importance of creating safe spaces in which dialogue can take place and mentions the need for "informality, independent facilitators, staying small, equal representation, sensitivity, comfortable topics, and agreed-upon ground rules."

He feels that there is no political or religious reason for Muslims and Jews to do other than rebuild together a "Golden Age" as they did in thirteenth-century Andalusia and in eighteenth-century Salonika. And even if not "golden," it was better for their communities than their "negative experiences in Christian Europe." In 2006 he visited Norway, Indonesia, Australia, Fiji, New Zealand, and the United States to promote a peaceful Islam. The *Jakarta Post* headlined his words: "Extremism 'alien' to Islam."[1]

Fiji: God Has No Favorite Race

I entered the conference hall early. The chairs had been laid out neatly. But a trim disciplined-looking man had taken it upon himself to line them up even more exactly. His actions reminded me of a sergeant-major preparing his soldiers for a review, and as I talked to him, I learned that he had indeed held that rank in the British army, where he served twenty-three years and was decorated by Queen Elizabeth. He was also a traditional chief from his country, Fiji.

Ratu Meli Vesikula, after his years in the British army had returned to his Pacific island country to work in provincial administration, thinking that the needed economic, political, and social changes would be accomplished by the normal parliamentary process. However, in 1987 a coup was proclaimed "in the name of the indigenous people." Out of touch with events in the capital, he readily accepted this justification and was soon enlisted as a leader of the Taukei nationalist movement, whose slogan was "Fiji for the Fijians." The Indians they were attacking made up at that point 48 percent of the country's population.

"I advocated violence, instigated violence, talked of sending Indians away from Fiji," he says. "I was in the thick of things." As a spokesman for the movement, Vesikula got a Fijian crowd to dig a hole in the middle of Suva and start a fire over it, threatening to put Indians into this *lovo* (a Fijian oven in the ground). He became a cabinet minister in the interim government. When later removed from the post, he led a breakaway and even more extremist faction.

It took Vesikula five months to realize that the coup had not been mounted to benefit the indigenous people but rather to restore a certain group to power. This realization came through the help of a Fijian pastor and a forty-day period of prayer and fasting, seeking divine guidance, which resulted in a "personal revolution": "The change that took place within me involved the awakening of my spirit. I had come to realize that the 'us and them' attitude I held was divisive and damaging. Once played upon by the use of race, it awakened prejudice within me and generated fear, hatred, and greed. My group and I had become a powerfully divisive and damaging force in the land."

Honoring his new freedom from hatred, he went to see Dr. Timoci Bavadra, the deposed prime minister, and apologized for what he had said and done against him. His apology resulted in his being persecuted, arrested, jailed, sued, and labeled a betrayer of his own people.

Vesikula had begun to look at his country differently. "I saw a Fiji that included everyone, a multiethnic nation free of prejudice, hate, and division and encompassed in love. For the first time, I found in the effort to bring our people together a purpose for my life."

He realized, he says, that God had no favorite race. "We are all his children, standing equal in his sight. I began listening to God, and new ideas were put into my heart."

In 1989 he attended an "Initiatives of Change" conference in Sydney. This led to him putting relationships right in his own life and to the thought that came to him "as sharp as an arrow" that he must apologize publicly to the Indian leaders and leaders of other races for the way he had treated them. He made his first public apology at a conference at the University of the South Pacific in Suva in September 1990: "I want to turn to my brothers and sisters from the Indian community. I would like to apologize for all the hasty words and actions I carried out three years ago. I ask you to forgive me for all those unkind words and unkind deeds I did."

Indians responded and took his hand. Y. P. Reddy, a respected leader of the south Indian community, said, "There is a great change.

He is sincere. He and I and all of us can work together for the betterment of Fiji." Which is what they have since done.

The English-language and Hindi press published widely Vesikula's apology and his commitment to reconciliation. "The Indians were victimized and made scapegoats," he said. New awareness about what had been happening in Fiji gripped him so tightly, he said, that he wanted to take on single-handedly those who had led the coup. But instead, he learned to forgive.

It came as a shock to the country and to Vesikula when a coup took place in 2000. He along with others from both the Fijian and Indian communities were at the heart of efforts to get hostages released and to bring people together. In 2001, at the first session of Parliament after the general election following the ending of the coup, he repeated an apology made in the upper house on national television. That year, he joined the Citizens' Constitutional Forum's (CCF) steering committee, an NGO formed to protect Fiji's 1997 Constitution and to fight for good governance and against racial discrimination and corruption.

The training and development of young people became a priority for Vesikula. In his efforts to address poverty and find employment for young people, he has helped to send twenty-five hundred young men from all ethnic groups to join the British armed forces. Hundreds of Fijians are also in the Australian and U.S. armies, and more than a thousand men are working as security guards in Iraq and Kuwait, with nurses and caregivers also finding work overseas. His office also has been working to apply for development funds to help the running of small projects, especially in rural areas.

In March 2005, he moved back to his village about thirty miles outside of Suva, to give much needed help to improve his people's standard of living. In two years, they raised over $80,000, one-third for educational needs, one-third as a contribution to government for a new water system, and about $24,000 for the work of the church. In an e-mail to me in 2007 he wrote: "We have also embarked on a small-scale bee-keeping enterprise for honey processing as well as pig-raising. We have sixteen hives so far and nearly one hundred pigs to sell, with a lot of piglets coming through. We volunteered to host courses for the above projects attended by people in the district. We also observe a conservation program on some of our reefs and lagoons, which is paying off when we go in to harvest sea-produce to eat or sell. These initiatives have improved household incomes all around the village. We are looking at a small fishing project next."

December 2006 saw another coup in Fiji. "This last coup is different from the three earlier ones with the Fijian military ousting a bad Fijian government; that is, it's Fijian versus Fijian but the worry is, if there was a counter struggle, the nonindigenous would still end up as scapegoats. This is why our work with CCF is so important."

Working with the CCF, he initiated a conference at the University of South Pacific in 2006, "New Hope from Fiji: Making this Vision Possible." The invitation asked, "Why have we allowed narrow sectarian thinking to stunt our national growth? Is it time to embrace a new spirit, to rid ourselves of prejudice, selfishness, hatred, fear—the blocks that divide us from each other?" And continued: "Could we heal past wrongs through honesty and forgiveness, transforming our historical differences into a deeper care? Could we, through a new honesty and selflessness, tackle the causes of poverty? And begin to care for our environment as the national treasure it is, sustained and maintained for our children and grandchildren?"

The conference was a joint effort of the Ministry of National Reconciliation, Initiatives of Change, and the New Zealand Agency for International Development and was opened by the country's vice president, Ratu Joni Madraiwiwi. It drew representatives from around the Pacific including twenty-two from the Solomon Islands. The vice president underlined the conference's timeliness in the light of the political tensions: "Whatever happens, this is our home," Madraiwiwi said, "We will need each other and the strength that comes from our interconnectedness. I am the richer and humbler for the experience of reaching out to others."

Israel: Asking Questions

Her first words to me were, "My work is not work. It's my life—twenty-four hours a day." She was several hours late for our phone interview, underlining the fragile environment in which this "non-work" takes place. Merri Minuskin is director-general of the Center of Education for Reconciliation and Cooperation (CERC). She spends several days a week in Jordan, where the border had just been closed, which was why she couldn't get back to talk to me at the appointed hour. In Jordan, she is often welcomed as "the ambassador of peace." She builds on a life that has known prejudice and frustration, which perhaps gives her a sensitivity to the feelings of others and an infectious persistence.

.   Merri's family came originally from a part of Belarus (White Russia) that is now in Poland and emigrated to the United States, where she was born in 1954. Her grandparents survived the Holocaust, but their brothers and sisters all died in the gas chambers. As a child, she was introduced early on to injustice. She lived first in a largely Jewish community in Brooklyn, then, to improve their lot, the family moved in 1959 when she was five to the Bronx. There, she was beaten up and called "a dirty Jew." They moved two years later to Queens, where she encountered the prejudice against people of color, even in her own family. She wanted to deal with the injustice and prejudice she encountered and was elected representative of black students in her large high school. At seventeen, when Merri moved alone to Israel, she felt she was going home. "It was what I wanted all my life." She went to live on Kibbutz Afik the night before the outbreak of the Yom Kippur war. Merri was surrounded by bombings and death.

One day, in a valley near the Kibbutz, she came across a diary of a Syrian who had been evicted. It told of this woman's commitment to building peace and it opened Merri's eyes to what had gone on before. She feels it was a marking event in her life and propelled her into peacemaking. "I needed to begin asking questions."

Another marking event in her life was in 2000 when she attended a conference in Caux, Switzerland, and felt she was meeting for the first time people who shared her values and commitment. "They didn't just talk about them, they lived them. It changed my life completely." It confirmed for her that she was on the right path. "It is at Caux and through the people there that I get the courage to continue." She has found allies in her desire to build trust across divides. Discovering Palestinians present there, she took the opportunity to apologize "for the sorrow and loss of dignity" her people in Israel had inflicted upon them and for the "choice to be ignorant" that her people make every day. "Every morning I make a choice to be different," she says.

One follow-on from this was the decision in 2003 to set up the CERC, which works in Palestine, Jordan, and Israel at three levels: government, civil society, and grassroots. It has a thoroughly diverse group of directors with peacemaking experience. They aim to bring people together, both the different ethnic groups within Israel and also Palestinians and Jordanians. In these efforts, Merri is building on her work over the years as a teacher at the Arab teachers' training college in Beit Berl and as head of the Middle East division at the international institute where she ran training programs for people from different countries and organized "people-to-people" meetings between Israelis and people of other countries and faiths. In May 2007 she accepted the further responsibility of becoming director of the Israel-Jordan Chamber of Commerce.

In her efforts to reach government, she has had senior Middle Eastern officials together in her home. She has brought Jordanians and Palestinians into the Israeli Foreign Ministry. She has received funding from the foreign ministries of Israel, Germany, Sweden, Poland, and Canada. In 2007 she developed a reconciliation program for the Knesset, Israel's legislature, involving people from the far right and left—Arabs, Jews, Muslims, and Druse.

Her grassroots work means that she is sometimes in Jordan three times a week, which she says can be "an island of peace." She works in refugee camps, with the poorest people, on women's health issues, giving them the ability to work as volunteers teaching other women. "The most important thing is the trust relationship between them and me." She brings women together in interreligious dialogue, sometimes bringing them to Israel where they, of course, also want to see their old homes. She has brought teams of young boys to play soccer matches in Israel. "Parents had to know me first to trust me." She also has brought mayors together from the border areas.

At times it is frustrating: Merri still lives in Israel and loves her country, but her "eyes are open." People are being killed, and houses destroyed, and she feels that her government is doing nothing to promote peace and a lot to make it more difficult. However, she is sustained by the thought of the people waiting for her when she comes into Palestine. "There is so much happiness, new relationships being built, changes on the ground." Those she works with don't want to continue with violence. "They don't want to kill Israelis, not any more." Families who have been approached by Hamas or Al Qaeda for cooperation tell her they have turned down these requests. "What greater gift can I have than that? It tells me something has been effective. This is what sustains me. Even those who have lost family and friends or spent years in Israeli jails are working for peace. God is watching and bringing our hands together. I cannot stop believing."

She has had brushes with death. Once she was set upon by illegal Palestinian workers when she was returning an Arab Palestinian couple to their home and was unloading toys and blankets for children. "Go, go, go," they shouted, slamming the car's trunk. She escaped, with bullets chasing after her. She felt at first betrayed and stayed home, sitting for twenty-four hours in darkness. She could have been captured or killed or both. "I realized I had no anger. It was not their fault; the war had turned them into this."

On another occasion, she was showing solidarity with some Palestinians when their houses were being destroyed. Her son happened to be in the Israeli Defense Force unit sent in to remove them and recognized her. He was afraid she would be hurt. His commanding officer said he didn't need to participate. "The soldiers were incredibly kind to us," she remembers.

Merri's goal is to help people reach out to those that have hurt them most.

Reconciliation is an important ingredient in her work to promote cooperation and understanding within Israel and between Israel and neighboring countries. Sometimes it means opening wounds in order to heal them, going deep and being honest. "I have sat in groups where people have screamed, yelled, released so much hate. But they come back because it is in the human spirit to forgive. To live in peace, you must live peace. We must stretch out our hands to 'the other.'"

Many people, she says, think she is crazy to do what she does. "But once people meet 'the other,' they may not love them, but they can respect them," she says. "Our work saves lives and changes people's attitudes." She says that each side needs to admit that the other side has real truth. "I hope we can find the connecting points of the two truths and build a new truth. We cannot afford any more to work only in our own community and to make peace only with ourselves."

An evaluation of the center's work on Israeli–Jordanian cross-border cooperation was undertaken in 2005 by the Economic Cooperation Foundation for the Friedrich Ebert Stiftung, a German foundation promoting understanding and peace between peoples. Its report on three years' work says: "Cultural barriers have been dismantled; former enemies across the river have met each other on a regular and completely voluntary [basis]; and the seeds of practical civic cooperation have started to appear." If the initiative succeeds "it might prove that Israel and its Arab neighbors can generate and sustain joint ventures for the benefit of all peoples in the Middle East." It is described as "a rare successful example of cooperation between different social groups that are usually at odds with each other. Kibbutz members from the Beit Shean Valley Regional Council and the Beit Shean city residents share responsibility for creating a new model for an Arab–Israeli 'people-to-people' cooperation."

It concludes that the center's cross-border cooperation initiative in northern Jordan was "the most elaborate and sustained venture so far, designed for reshaping the nature of the peace accords between both countries and converting it from the governmental level to the civic level."

Merri Minuskin says, "Peace lives in every person. Bring two people together, and soon their families will come and soon their neighborhoods and then their nations. Peace is not difficult to create as long as we reach out and help those first two people and continue to embrace those who follow. Just trust."

Sierra Leone: No Thirst for Revenge

Revenge was John Bangura's deepest desire.

His Sierra Leone village had been burned down. There had been a massacre, with nine family members killed, and to this day he does not know what happened to his sister or to his closest friends. "I was fuelled with a lot of hate," he says. "I was willing to do whatever I could to seek revenge, not so much on the rebels, for I could have been one of them. I was angry at the leaders who laid the foundations of the war and had the money and the means to get out of the country. In my thirst for revenge, my intention was to join other Sierra Leoneans in the diaspora with a similar state of mind to work out a master plan for this mission."

Sadly, Bangura's traumatic experiences have been shared by thousands in Sierra Leone—a West African country made up of 60 percent Muslims, 30 percent Christians, and 10 percent people of indigenous beliefs—as they suffered a ten-year civil war.

In 1991 the Sierra Leone Revolutionary United Front (RUF) launched a bush war against what they felt was the corrupt and inefficient government in Freetown. The following year, there was a military coup. Bangura, a businessman who felt that any kind of military government would be a disaster, joined in opposing the new regime. It was then that his village was destroyed and family members killed. He managed to get his wife and children to safety and escaped to Europe. He did not return home for nine years.

He had the necessary visas and expected to be able to join relatives in the United States. But, as he discovered, appeals for political asylum have to be made in the first foreign country reached, in this case Denmark. For twenty-three months, under immigration control, he was well looked after, staying in a Red Cross refugee camp as his case was investigated. A local clergyman, Torben Juul Christensen, befriended him.

Despite Christensen's friendship, dark thoughts welled up against those he believed were traitors to their country. Some had escaped abroad; others had remained and joined the military government. "I contacted a friend who introduced me to a member of 'Hell's Angels' in Denmark. One day I was invited to his home. I was impressed by what I heard and thought I could use some of their expertise to track down certain people and eliminate them." He began to plan a secret operation, modeled on techniques used in another West African country, using kidnapping and murder.

As he grappled with this tension between the "good" and "bad" influences, he studied and gained management skills, attending the National Transport School and learning Danish, which speeded the immigration process. Granted political asylum in 1994, he became a bus driver. He was joined by his wife, Aminata, and two young daughters whom he had not seen for five years.

The following year, encouraged by Christensen, he attended an Initiatives of Change (IofC) conference in Caux, Switzerland. He thought he had left the past behind, but there, as he met others who had suffered, it came rushing back. In quiet moments in the morning, he felt a voice telling him that he was driven by hatred and needed to search his conscience. "I was able to revisit what was deep down and arrived at the thought that the resources I was planning to use to take revenge would be better spent to bring healing to my nation, to help my country."

Bangura also felt that when he returned from Caux, he should apologize to his wife, Aminata, for not treating her right in the past years. "What I had been doing was not in harmony with family life," he says and recalls how he knelt down before her and admitted to doing things he shouldn't have been doing in the years they had been apart. A year later, a further change came as he attended a conference in Tanzania. He remembers vividly the scene as he sat under a tree with storm clouds darkening around him and heard a voice saying, "John, your country is on fire; your people are dying. I'm asking you to go back home to take the message of peace and reconciliation. I will bless that mission, your people, your family."

The first steps would have to be taken from Denmark, as it was still too dangerous to return. The challenge was to find trustworthy people in Sierra Leone whom he could build on. Aminata and he decided to begin with her uncle. Bangura phoned him in Sierra Leone and asked three questions: "Are you ready to work for your country without being paid? Are you ready to pack your bags and go on a journey of healing, sometimes even risking your life? Would you be able to do so without pointing fingers or blaming anyone?" The uncle answered "yes" to all three. Somehow, an awareness of Bangura's sense of vision and calling had gotten through. "I want you to get together ten people of credit, men and women, and hold your first meeting," he told his uncle. "I will call you again in a week."

The uncle duly gathered the people, and Bangura called, asking the group to consider two points. First, what had gone wrong in Sierra Leone. "Do not point fingers. Do not argue among yourselves." If they ran into difficulties, they should pause and observe a quiet time: "God will speak to one of you." Second, "Find allies you think you can work with." He said he would send $100 so they could fax reports after each meeting.

Out of what might seem an inauspicious beginning was born, in 2001, an NGO: "Hope-Sierra Leone" (H-SL). "We got together a group of people," says Bangura, "who put country before selves."

Within the country, the United Nations had deployed seventeen thousand peacekeepers to disarm seventy thousand former combatants, nearly seven thousand of them children who had been conscripted into the fighting forces. Most were restored to their families. And by 2001 it was safe for Bangura to return to the country, which now faced the task of reconstruction and rehabilitation. He spent six weeks there, meeting people on all sides. H-SL teamed up with other civil society groups who built a foundation of trust among rebels, clearing the way for UN peacekeepers to return to the north, where some had been taken prisoner. He risked his life going to the area where the rebels who had killed his family lived and was reconciled with them. "One way to convince the rebel groups," he says, "was my own personal change." It was the first of fourteen visits to Sierra Leone over the next six years.

"My strategy has always been top-down and bottom-up, running parallel," says Bangura. For instance, he realized that the war had "stolen" young people from their communities. In order to "kick-start" development, it was vital to help the ex-combatants to get back to work. He started village programs with themes like "honest conversations" and "healing through forgiveness and reconciliation." He approached the paramount chief of the region, who provided one thousand acres of land for "integrated farming" projects and engaged more than five hundred young people in this work. Get them work and education, Bangura believes, and they won't go for guns. He helped young people be welcomed back into areas where they may have killed the locals. One villager said, "Some killed my children. But now we are here. I'll not get my children back, but I would like to forgive them because they do not know what they were doing."

H-SL soon had a high profile in the country, and Bangura found himself appearing on television. He met leaders of the Revolutionary United Front (RUF); former officers from the Armed Forces Revolutionary Council (AFRC) that had briefly taken power in 1997; and the pro-government Civil Defense Force (CDF). All said they would work for peace—and did so. Taking courage from his own victory over revenge, he invited former junta leader Johnny Paul Koroma (AFRC) and Koroma's bitter enemy, the deputy minister of defense (former head of the CDF), to the IofC conference in Caux. There, they were challenged by Rajmohan Gandhi, a grandson of the Mahatma, to find a nonviolent way to resolve their differences. The two men agreed to sign the peace process. The formal ending of the war came on 18 January 2002.

Following the war's end, Bangura made two trips to Sierra Leone, running workshops based around questions such as "What are some God-given resources in you that, if given the opportunity, you would like to make the most use of? If you had the opportunity, would you like to be a light in your community or family?" At the end of one workshop in the key town of Makeni in Northern province, a peace-and-reconciliation tree was planted: "These guys stood there with shovels and hoes in their hands saying 'Today is the best peace agreement we are signing. Nobody has paid us for it. We are signing the peace with our blood and our sweat. And from today, we will never take up weapons against our own people.'"

As UN peacekeepers began withdrawing, Bangura saw that Sierra Leone's police and military forces needed to be prepared as "custodians of peace and [to] become part of healing the country." He invited the deputy inspector-general of the Sierra Leone police to Caux in 2003 and returned the following year with the joint forces commander of the armed forces. At Caux, they began to heal the deep distrust toward those they felt had hurt them. The policeman said, "I also experienced some terrible things. I'm still their boss. I thought it was my time to take revenge and punish them. But being here at Caux, I see that is not right. I am going back home to forgive them."

These senior officers requested training for their people and so, with the backing of the government, Moral Foundations for Democracy (MFD), a course for reconciliation and change, was set up. They enlisted members of an international NGO with experience in facilitated training, particularly in eastern Europe. In 2005 two six-day pilot courses were held, followed by training that qualified twenty-three Sierra Leoneans to deliver the course over the next five years. Australian journalist Mike Brown wrote, "Scanning the testimonies of participants gives an impression of battle-hardened men and women gaining new confidence in personal integrity and professional disciplines: abandoning schemes of personal revenge, facing family violence and alcohol abuse, ending the 'envelope' system of collecting bribes and distributing them to their officers; senior policemen together assessing their mistakes in silence and sharing their vision as a regular part of operations."[2]

In 2002, in the run-up to UN-supervised elections, H-SL was accredited as one of sixteen monitoring organizations to provide voter education, observe the elections, and supervise the counting. In November 2006, Bangura was publicly thanked by Minister of Internal Affairs Pascal Egbenda for "a remarkable initiative." Speaking at the official launching of its "mutual farming for peace and reconciliation project" at the Makeni Town Hall, Egbenda said that Hope-Sierra Leone had "helped to reshape the minds of people living in these communities through its various projects." In his speech, reported in the newspaper *Awoko*,[3] he said that government had done a lot in achieving food security, but this should not be left to government alone; it needed the concerted effort of all to achieve it.

A month earlier, the UN Peacebuilding Commission recommended war-ravaged Sierra Leone for support from a newly established fund to assist countries emerging from conflicts in rebuilding efforts and to prevent them from falling back into bloodshed. John Bangura and Hope-Sierra Leone are among those working to avoid such a relapse. Bangura says that whether talking with ex-combatants, cabinet ministers, or farm workers, his most effective "weapon" has always been the sharing of his own experience. "I then invite them to join me in the vision I have for my country."

In August 2007, a team from H-SL was among official observers at the country's presidential and parliamentary elections and afterward developed a campaign to stem a wave of violence that threatened to engulf the country when the presidential results were inconclusive.

Bangura could have settled down in his new country, leaving the horrible memories behind him, but decided instead to give his best to Sierra Leone. He still earns his living driving a bus in Denmark, where he is chairman of the Denmark–Sierra Leone Friendship Association. Looking back at the disaster that Foday Sankoh—former leader of the RUF, another hate-driven exile thirsting for revenge—inflicted on Sierra Leone, he says that one could easily conclude: "Hate that is not healed, and revenge that is not spiritually transformed into love and care as it happened in my situation, could be disastrous for a whole nation and people."

A testimony to his work, a nomination for the prestigious Tannenbaum Peacemakers in Action Award states: "His reputation for integrity and selfless concern for the well-being of fellow citizens has won the respect of leaders from many sections both in rural communities and among the national leadership. John has no doubt that he owes everything to the God who saved him from bitterness and revenge. It is his faith that sustains his efforts and enables him to keep going, no matter the cost."

India: Praying for Compassion for the Aggressor

When I talk of forgiveness I am talking about a wider transaction than just a person or a nation forgiving what has been done to them. It is about what each of us can do, through an apology or simply reaching out to the other, to help free a person or nation of hatred. It is about creating community.

Sushobha Barve embodies this in a wonderful way. Her initiatives in building community have grown in most inauspicious circumstances. This high-caste Hindu, who runs the Delhi-based Centre for Dialogue and Reconciliation, has become known through South Asia for her work to help people of different religions and castes come together.

The prestigious *Hindu* newspaper writes, "Sushobha Barve is a woman of uncommon courage. She addresses the intractable problem of building goodwill among communities in extraordinary circumstances. She has gone about this task in situations of bloody conflict such as the 1984 anti-Sikh riots, the 1989 Bhagalpur riots, the 1992–1993 Bombay blasts, and the 2002 Gujarat riots."[4]

Her mission began dramatically. In 1984 she was traveling by train when the news broke of Indian Prime Minister Indira Gandhi's murder by Sikhs. In her compartment, were two Sikh businessmen. Fellow passengers discounted the Sikhs' fear of vengeance. But as the hours ticked by, the train began stopping, and there was a rumor that a Sikh had been pulled off the train and shaved—an affront to his faith. Sushobha was concerned about protecting the Sikhs. She moved from the window to the door, and the men hid in the top bunk.

In one town, a gang of young people entered the compartment, but Sushobha managed to talk them out of causing trouble. At the next stop, however, the train was surrounded by villagers armed with sticks. Three times their compartment was searched. The fourth time, the intruders discovered the two men in the bunk. Sushobha tried in vain to shield them and was seized. The men were pulled out, severely beaten, and then thrown back into the compartment, and everything was looted. At the next stop, the men were thrown off, stoned, and set on fire. Sushobha and her traveling companion were the only ones who had tried to prevent the violence.

Sushobha says that she never dreamed that her generation would witness killings comparable to those that took place after the partition of India and Pakistan in 1947. "It was gruesome," she wrote to a friend, "but even when the villagers held me by the neck, I felt comforted by God's love and protection." "But," she asked, "what was God's purpose in allowing us to go through this? How are we going to repent and cleanse our sins? Is it possible to heal the wounds between Hindus and Sikhs?"

Sushobha had been brought up in an orthodox and broad-minded Hindu family. Her parents and grandparents encouraged her to ask questions about religious beliefs and traditions and inculcated a strong sense of right and wrong. "This did not prevent us from doing wrong," she says, "but we knew when we had strayed from our path, and our conscience would weigh heavily." She had never been taught to hate any religious, racial, linguistic, or caste groups, but only rarely had people of different backgrounds intruded on the family's life. There had been little interaction with other religious communities.

An incident in college, however, prepared her to be a bridge builder between different religious communities. It was there that she had her first encounter with a Muslim—Abida, a fellow student with whom she shared a table. One day, Abida spoke to Sushobha of her relations who had come from Pakistan. This was only two years after India and Pakistan had been at war, and Sushobha found herself thinking that she could not trust Abida. Several months later, Sushobha had the uncomfortable thought that she should apologize to Abida for the invisible wall that she had allowed to grow between them. Her reaction to Abida brought into focus the unspoken prejudices and distrust that she felt are deeply embedded in the Hindu psyche. "How could I have allowed myself to be swayed emotionally and begin to distrust someone who had done no wrong to me?" she thought. After Sushobha's apology, Abida was in tears. She had sensed that something had come between them, but she had not known what it was.

"This encounter opened the windows of my heart and set me off on a road to build friendships with Muslims right across the length and breadth of India," says Sushobha. "Since that day, distrust and prejudice toward Muslims have never brushed my mind or entered my heart. Somewhere along the line, I realized that if true understanding was to come between people and communities, I must also try to understand history from their viewpoint."

Sushobha describes the train experience as a watershed. "It not only shook me physically and emotionally, but it made me realize that any one of us could become victims of violence in today's India." A month later, she still felt anger and guilt about those hours on the train. "I was tortured at night by the thought of not being able to save the lives of the two innocent men." She decided to accept responsibility for what Hindus had done. "It was a painful process," she recalls, "but once accepted, I was shown the steps I should take." She felt that she should write letters to Sikhs—some known by her, some not, apologizing unconditionally. Khushwant Singh, a well-known writer and Sikh spokesman, replied in a handwritten note: "I was in tears as I read your letter. As long as we have people like you around, we will survive as a nation."

It was one thing to write letters but another to visit Sikhs in person. Sushobha went to see a Sikh couple whose farmhouse had been attacked. Again she made an unconditional apology for the deep wounds and humiliation. Husband and wife were in tears. Usha, the wife, held her hand. "To hear what you have just said," she told Sushobha, "makes me feel that all we have gone through during the last two months was worth it and is healed."

Later, Sushobha discovered that, amazingly, the two men in the train had survived, badly burned, and were free of bitterness at a time when they had every reason to be bitter. "Even the most inhuman suffering had not killed the fine human qualities of courage, compassion, vision of the future, and gratitude to all who had helped them."

From 1984 onward, after those traumatic hours in the train, Sushobha's life and work took on a new urgency. She set out to build bridges of trust within India, and between India and her neighbors, and to go where people were in need, sometimes taking teams of people with her. In December 1992, for instance, when the Babri Mosque at Ayodhya was destroyed and ten days of violence in her city, Mumbai, left six hundred people dead and its millions of inhabitants in shock, she moved into Dharavi, the worst affected area, and lived there in dangerous circumstances for a week. On her initiative, the state governor and the chief minister set up the Citizen's Non-political Peace Committee, on which she was asked to serve. While the rest of the city burned in January, there was peace in Dharavi as hundreds of Bombay citizens turned out to help.

"One day," she says, "I had the thought that I must pray for compassion also for the aggressor. For me, it meant praying for my own people with whose actions I had totally disagreed. It is important for those of us in crisis situations to keep our hearts open to listen to all sides. Unless we listen, we will never know how to help and we will never be used. When we listen, we are actually helping people toward finding solutions."

With her Center for Dialogue and Reconciliation, she is active in Kashmir. In January 2007, writer Arundhati Ray described her work on Changemakers.net: "Sushobha Barve throws herself into some of India's most vicious conflict zones like the northernmost state of Jammu and Kashmir—an alpine idyll transformed into bloody killing fields by a territorial dispute between India and Pakistan and the Hindu–Muslim divide—in order to encourage traumatized populations to overcome their distrust and begin the process of healing and reconciliation.

"Gently but adroitly, she persuades the warring sides to engage in conversation, drawing strength from her uncompromising belief in the healing power of dialogue. By facilitating person-to-person dialogues on both sides of the India–Pakistan border, Barve builds civilian bonds that span the border and exert pressure on leaders of both countries to reach an accord."

Barve's book *Healing Streams*[5] is dedicated to "the victims and survivors of violence in South Asia." She has seen in some ordinary men and women of India the magnanimity to forgive and a spirit of accommodation. They have shown both the courage and the humility to accept wrongs and acknowledge the pain caused to others. "We have numerous examples of men and women," she writes, "who have shown the courage to break the chain of hate and revenge. They inspire us at a time leaders have failed to inspire. We need urgently to increase their numbers."

British-Japanese Relations: A Tale of Two Flags

In May 1998 a news photo went around the world of former British prisoners of war of the Japanese turning their backs on the emperor of Japan and Queen Elizabeth when they rode through London together. This discourteous act, testament to persisting bitterness and a legacy of World War II, was probably all that many people heard about the Japanese state visit. According to the *Guardian,* the act "left an indelible image of shock and humiliation on the faces of Japanese VIPs passing them in royal procession."[6] But there's another story to be told.

Two British veterans of World War II, each with a different agenda, waved Japanese flags that day, one as a sign of support, the other as a sign of protest. The former was Richard Channer, wounded at the battle of Imphal and awarded the Military Cross, a decoration for gallantry. Years earlier, he had traveled with another veteran to Kohima to lay wreaths at the British and Indian cemeteries and also beside a tree marking where a Japanese sniper had fought. Their laying a wreath for the thousands of Japanese soldiers who were killed there was described in the *Daily Telegraph* as "one of the more remarkable gestures of reconciliation."[7]

On London's ceremonial mall that day in May 1998, Channer made himself a megaphone out of cardboard and shouted his welcome to the Japanese emperor. As the royal party passed, he waved his flag in an arc, and he and two other ex-servicemen yelled *"Banzai!"*

Channer was waving the flag on behalf of a fellow veteran, Les Dennison, not well enough to attend. Dennison had been one of thousands of British and Australian prisoners of war and Asian laborers to drive a rail link through the mountainous barrier between Thailand and Burma. Thousands died. During his three and a half years of incarceration, Dennison watched fourteen of his fellow prisoners decapitated. His weight dropped from one hundred sixty pounds to seventy-four pounds.

In an article in his local paper, the Coventry *Evening Telegraph,*[8] under the headline "Time to call a truce on lasting bitterness," Dennison wrote:

Reading the letters and articles demanding compensation and apologies from the Japanese government, I am saddened by the negative display of bitterness and hatred after fifty years.

I write as an eighty-three-year-old ex-serviceman who served in the Far East, was defeated and taken prisoner in Singapore, helped clear up the dead and debris with a handcart in Singapore, had a spell in Changi prison, then back up-country to Thailand, then marched two hundred miles through swamp and jungle to Soukuria, the death camp. After completing one stint of fifteen kilometers of railroad and one of the bridges over the River Kwai, four hundred survivors out of sixteen hundred moved on into Burma.

Yes, I still have nightmares and even imagine the sweet stench of the dead waiting to be burnt on a pyre, rain permitting. But with the passing of fifty-five years, there has been growth, maturity, caring for wife, family, and friends.

In 1962 I reluctantly attended an international conference. Reluctantly, because I learned there was a Japanese delegation attending. One of the Japanese who spoke before the eight hundred delegates, General Sugita, who attended the surrender of Singapore, bowing low, said, "I knew what happened during the campaign. I can never expect you to forget what happened." Then, bowing once more, he said, "I am sorry. Please forgive me and my nation."

It was then that the healing of bitterness and hatred began. Since then, I have experienced the care and friendship of many Japanese who have shown sincere remorse and apologies. I find the many unforgettable memories can be lived with in the deep healing peace that is nurtured out of one's basic change of attitude.

In a BBC interview broadcast from Hiroshima on the fiftieth anniversary of the dropping of the atomic bomb, Dennison was asked to describe his wartime experiences. The last question to him: "If you could speak Japanese fluently and were to stand up in front of the Japanese nation on this day, what would you say to them?"

His reply: "I would bow low in humility and I would just beg their forgiveness for my callousness at the time when I heard of the bombs being dropped on the cities of Japan and I would humbly ask their forgiveness for the years of my bitterness, resentment, and hatred against the people of Japan. That is what I would simply do."

The waver of the second flag on the mall that May day was Jack Caplan, and he set his on fire as a protest just before the royal couples passed. Like Dennison, he had been captured at Singapore and worked on the Thai–Burmese railway. The picture of him brandishing the burning flag made him an instant celebrity around the world. His action reflected his obsessive preoccupation with Japanese wartime brutality and hatred of anything Japanese.

A remarkable Japanese woman, Keiko Holmes, now living in England, saw the picture of Caplan burning the Japanese flag. She felt strongly that he needed to go to Japan to be "set free." The founder of Agape: Working for Reconciliation, Keiko has, since 1992, taken nearly four hundred British ex-servicemen and their families to Japan, something for which she was awarded the Order of the British Empire by the queen in 1998.

A few weeks after Keiko saw Caplan's picture and thought of what a visit to Japan might mean for him, she had an unexpected call from him, and they met soon afterward. She invited him to join one of the parties of ex-servicemen. He was not ready for it then, but four years later he accepted.

Caplan was fearful that a fanatic would try to kill him but was overwhelmed by his reception in Japan and the desire of Japanese to learn what he had gone through and to apologize to him. "These people were sincere, compassionate, and humane. They queued for hours to meet me and have photos taken with me, and women actually cried tears, asking for my forgiveness." After the visit to Japan, the difference in him was, according to his wife Claudia, "like black and white." She said, "He changed completely. He was bowled over by the Japanese." An article sent out by the Japanese news agency Kyodo reported that in the years before his death in 2004, he struck up many strong relationships with Japanese people who became regular visitors to his home. He also forged a deep relationship with the Japanese ambassador to Britain at the time, who voiced admiration for Caplan's ability to let go of anti-Japanese feelings.

An article in the *Jewish Telegraph* reported: "The Glaswegian whose picture was flashed around the world when he burned the Nippon flag during Emperor Akihito's visit to London in May 1998 is now one of the Japanese people's best friends."[9] Caplan told reporter Rhonda Cowen: "My whole perception of the Japanese has been turned around. I have realized that our enemy is not each other but war."

Jack Caplan died at the age of 88. His widow says he never regretted waving the burning flag because he thought he achieved something important. Her husband's actions, she feels, may have influenced the British government's subsequent decision to make a special payment to former POWs held by the Japanese. He also maintained his conviction that the Japanese government should make a full apology and offer compensation. But after his visit to Japan, he no longer blamed the Japanese people. She was sorry that his ability to quell his simmering anger came so late in a life haunted by memories of prison camps.

Keiko feels it important that Japanese learn their history, understand, and apologize. In 2004, speaking of her motives for organizing the trips to Japan, she said, "I'm doing it for both countries because people need to be set free. Deep inside, both British and Japanese former soldiers want to be freed; inside they are crying out to be freed of the war."[10]

Liberation through Responsibility
Dr. Mohammed Abu-Nimer

Dr. Nimer is associate professor at American University's School of International Service in International Peace and Conflict Resolution in Washington, D.C., and director of the Peacebuilding and Development Institute. He is cofounder and coeditor of the new *Journal of Peacebuilding and Development.* Recent books include *Reconciliation, Coexistence, and Justice in Interethnic Conflicts; Peacebuilding and Nonviolence in Islamic Context: Theory and Practice; Contemporary Islam: Dynamic, Not Static.*

The reconciliation process is a complex journey. If we imagine it as a road with many stations, taking responsibility for our own actions would be one of the first stops that people in any conflict have to make before traveling forward in the path of transformation.

By taking responsibility for their actions, parties to a conflict open the way to justice and peace while at the same time addressing their past, present, and future relationships. Indeed, taking responsibility may be the greatest challenge in the reconciliation process, as many believe "no justice without peace and no peace without justice."

For justice to be done, there is a necessary precondition of acknowledgment and recognition of past wrongdoings or some form of responsibility that has to be taken by actors in the conflict. The notion of justice must be modified from its initial absolute terms to a version in which both parties can begin to negotiate their possible future relationships. In the cases shared in the foregoing chapter, many of the actors started with a strong desire to avenge injustice. When British soldiers Les Dennison and Jack Caplan, John Bangura from Sierra Leone, and Ratu Meli Vesikula from Fiji, found themselves in safe spaces, they moved from the need for revenge to a change of heart and a readiness to take responsibility; a new sense of restorative justice emerged.

As stories in this chapter illustrate, when perpetrators take responsibility for the wrongs done by themselves or their communities, victims are able to move beyond their injuries and pain, to transcend the desire for revenge, to rise above the ongoing cycles of violence and assert their right to a different kind of life.

The reconciliation process requires liberating ourselves from the trap of the past and the web of conflict that force us to relive our fears and hatred of the "other." This often fuels the victim's quest for revenge as he or she thinks that it is the only path to restore the lost harmony and balance in their lives. As exemplified by this chapter's cases, taking responsibility for past actions (through verbal confession, active peace work, compensation, and so forth) can transform an individual who inevitably will affect others around him or her.

These five moving stories are a source of hope and inspiration, illustrating the power of an individual's actions. When a person, especially from the dominant majority, expresses sincere intentions and systematically takes actions that reflect his or her capacity for self-critique, inevitably someone from the other community ("the enemy side") will reciprocate. These pairs of "good doers" become shining lights in the midst of darkness. The Japanese soldiers reciprocated the gestures of the British soldiers who acknowledged the wrongs of their countries by speaking on behalf of each other's sin in their own respective country, while Imam Abduljalil Sajid reciprocated the courage of Richard Stone, chairman of Britain's Islamophobia Commission, by bringing Jewish rabbis to his mosque.

Some disparage the impact of "individual actions." However, even if these pairs of activists could not point to great success in

moving the public opinion, their efforts at reconciliation neverthe-
less remain crucial for keeping alive the hope of many who long
for peaceful coexistence yet do not publicly take action themselves.
Also, these stories show that when the actors involve in their efforts
key decision makers and leaders—for example, Bangura inviting
an ex-commander from the civil war to Caux and Ratu Meli in Fiji
reaching out to the powerful business community—successful outcomes are more likely.

Similarly, the impact of responsible actions is greater when
actions have tangible outcomes. For example, initiating development projects and improving people's lives in a conflict context like
Fiji has far more outreach than only denouncing violence and issu-
ing statements to the press. Bringing employment, vocational rehabilitation, and joint projects to rival ex-combatants in Sierra Leone
was taken seriously by the local communities, and Merri Minuskin's
Israeli–Jordanian border cooperation project motivated Arab participants in need of economic development.

"A web of trust" is woven by people who take responsibility for
wrongs done by their own community. They create a much needed
and rare space where trust enables revenge, hatred, and fear to be
replaced by coexistence, cooperation, interdependency, and forgiveness. In the Sierra Leone story, Bangura's conscious decision
to forgive and not seek revenge for the killing of nine of his family
members opened such a space for many others in his homeland.
Similarly, the Hindu peace activist Sushobha Barve, who traveled
the country during sectarian riots and put herself in the midst of
violence, appealing to local leaders to stop their followers, created
safe space for dialogues that allowed people to break out of their
cycle of hatred and revenge.

Another condition that increases the likelihood of an act of
responsibility being successful is when the individual is affiliated
with the dominant group. In a conflict context, members of the
privileged communities are often perceived as careless and even
beneficiaries of conflict. Thus, when a person like Sushobha Barve, a
high-caste Hindu who has access to power, apologizes to Sikh leaders and victims, she is immediately credible and gains legitimacy in
the eyes of the minority groups. Also, when a Jewish Israeli accepts
individual responsibility for the consequences of the occupation
system, Palestinians are able to reciprocate, too.

Risk-taking and vulnerability are always associated with taking responsibility. Activists can lose their lives, and family members can become isolated from their communities, and even be accused of treason. This risk was evident when Sushobha Barve was held by the neck by the Hindu mob who searched her train compartment for Sikhs and when Merri Minuskin was escaping gunshots while transporting aid to Palestinian refugees. These risk-takers are the peacemakers who stand in the middle of the fight and preach a different message. Such peacemakers are rare because of the physical and psychological danger associated with these actions.

Risk-takers are usually motivated and sustained by their personal experiences of transformation, which are their most powerful weapons to counter hatred and the desire for revenge. Because all people, regardless of their nationality or history, long to be liberated from their deepest feelings of hate, revenge, and animosity, the efforts of risk-takers toward reconciliation often spread fast. Keiko, the Japanese woman who arranged for the British soldier to visit Japan, captured this assumption: "Deep inside, both British and Japanese former soldiers want to be freed; inside they are crying out to be freed of the war."

This is the internal force buried within each human and often touched by unilateral and unconditional acts of forgiveness and justice. It is the same force that allowed the British soldier to be liberated after living forty years with his hatred of Japanese people. Similarly, Bangura from Sierra Leone says his most effective weapon is sharing his own experience of how his life was transformed.

Taking responsibility for one's own actions allows people in conflict to imagine a different future for their relationships. A vision can emerge only if the cycle of violence is broken through the combination of actions and statements denouncing violence and revenge. These concrete actions become the foundation for building a shared vision among the fighting parties. For example, Bangura was transformed by his own experience of suffering as an immigrant in Europe and as a survivor of a brutal civil war. Working with ex-combatants who have taken responsibility for their actions and admitted their role in massacres and killings in rural areas allowed him to reach out to thousands of people in his country and inspire many leaders to engage in reconciliation and the forgiveness process.

Developing a new vision for the future is an essential dimension step in the reconciliation process that can be taken only if ownership of past actions is accepted. For example, Israelis and Palestinians locked into a cycle of revenge and accusations of "who did what and when" waste their energy and are unable to imagine a different future.

Taking responsibility for one's own group or nation is extremely difficult, but when it is done in an unconditional way, it opens wide realms of possibilities, and one never knows how it will affect people on the other side. Japanese General Sugita, who attended the surrender of Singapore and was addressing an international conference in 1962, could hardly have expected his words to reach Dennison (the World War II veteran): Bowing low, he said, "I knew what happened during the campaign. I can never expect you to forget what happened." Then, bowing once more, he said, "I am sorry. Please forgive me and my nation." Such courageous steps "set free" people like Dennison, who are trapped in revenge and hatred. That is the hidden power of the stories in this book. May these stories travel around the globe and contribute to the reduction of human suffering.

Perspective
The Great Forgiver
Benazir Bhutto

Benazir Bhutto was prime minister of Pakistan (1988–1990 and 1993–1996) and led the Pakistan Peoples Party (PPP). She was assassinated on 27 December 2007 a few months after writing this essay.

"If any show patience and forgive, that truly would be an exercise of courageous will and resolution in the conduct of affairs."

~~Al Qur'an: Sura 42: 43 Counsel

My greatest challenge in learning to forgive was following the murder of my father, the former president and prime minister of Pakistan, Zulfikar Ali Bhutto. After being removed as prime minister in 1977, he was put on trial for conspiracy to murder a political opponent but was himself judicially murdered with the blessing of a military dictator, General Zia-ul Haq. I was in my twenties, a graduate of Harvard and Oxford universities; because I had not only championed for my father's freedom but had also taken up leadership of the political party he founded, the Pakistan Peoples Party, together with my mother, I was myself subjected to long periods in jail in solitary confinement and also detained in my own home. In all, I spent nearly six years of my life as a political prisoner from 1978 to 1984. In such circumstances, the challenge not to feel hatred and a desire for revenge was tremendous.

When I reemerged into the world, living first in exile in London for two years, I felt that the world had gone topsy-turvy. Because of my own imprisonment, I had not been able to grieve properly for the loss of my father. But as time passed, I realized, with the help and advice of my family and friends, one of whom was the late Dr. Charis Waddy, that healing from the pain I felt came from forgiveness, from letting go of past hurts, however agonizing the experiences may have been. Even today—nearly thirty years after these events—I remain grateful to Dr. Waddy for the wisdom and kindness she gave to me in my hour of need. As I have now learned, and as she wrote in her inspirational book, *The Muslim Mind*, "In bridging the gap between man and man, forgiveness plays an essential part. Magnanimity is a sign of strength."

More challenges to forgive came with the murder of my two younger brothers, both young men in their prime; Shahnawaz was murdered in France; Mir Murtaza was killed during a gun battle on the streets of Karachi. But through this adversity, I have learned to have a strong purpose in my own life, a purpose built on a deep understanding of right and wrong. I have realized that however much one has to suffer at a personal level, there are others who have had, if not similar experiences, then equally grievous ones from which they too have had to recover. Throughout history, our literature is littered with treatises on the need to forgive. After World War I, there was a need for forgiveness after the tragic loss of so many lives in a terrible and unprecedented war of attrition. And invariably it is those who have suffered most who have demonstrated an extraordinary capacity for forgiveness. Before his death at the hand of an assassin, Martin Luther King Jr. told his supporters in the United States of America that the person who was devoid of the power to forgive was also devoid of the power to love. In the present day, the need to forgive both at a personal and political level is as great as it ever was. Today, our focus of attention is on the wars in Afghanistan and Iraq, where there will be more widows, more fathers and mothers grieving for the loss of their loved ones; they too will be seeking the strength to learn to forgive.

My own personal suffering and the need to learn forgiveness has also engendered in me a profound sense of duty toward my fellow human beings; my leadership of my father's political party, the PPP, has been inspired by witnessing the sacrifices others have made for a political goal—in order to see a democratic, vibrant society develop in the country of my birth, Pakistan. This support has been a lifeline, and I feel humbled by their commitment.

Above all, I have been helped by my faith in God as a Muslim. My parents always taught me that a good Muslim is one who forgives. And I know that we share in common this important teaching with the Christian faith. As Mother Teresa is also renowned for saying, if we really want to love, we must learn to forgive. From childhood, I have studied the Quran and taken comfort from the verses that relate to forgiveness. Among those which have given me strength, I should like to share the following: "Be foremost in seeking forgiveness" (Sura 57: 21 Iron); "Race toward forgiveness from your Lord; restrain anger and pardon men" (Sura 3: 133 & 134 Imran); "Requite evil with good, and he who is your enemy will become your dearest friend" (Sura 41: 34 Expounded). God, I truly believe, is full of forgiveness. He is the great Forgiver.

5

CREATING safe space

*We should consider these propositions: that forgiveness
without repentance is a hand extended that never completes
itself in a handshake; that repentance without forgiveness is
paralyzing—a cry for help which goes unanswered, leaving a
penitent imprisoned in the past; that, therefore, forgiveness and
repentance need each other if they are to usher in a partnership
that sets human feet together onto a road toward reconciliation.*[1]

~~Donald W. Shriver Jr., author of *An Ethic for Enemies*

*Tolerance and forgiveness are the key methods of minimizing
hatred. You cannot feel hatred or disrespect toward your guru,
so you cannot learn tolerance and forgiveness from him. You can
only learn these things from your enemy. When you meet him,
that is the golden opportunity to test how much you practice what
you believe.*

~~The Dalai Lama, at Mountain House, Caux in 1983

Dwarfed by high-rise buildings in the city, London's business
district, is a structure that would not look out of place in the
North African desert. It is called simply "the Tent." Erected in the
garden courtyard at the back of Saint Ethelburga's church, Bishopsgate, it is a unique sacred space where people of all faiths, or
none, can meet with others from different traditions and explore

141

differences in a spirit of friendship and respect. Made in Saudi Arabia and with art works donated from Morocco and Turkey, it has eight stained-glass windows that have been described as "a superb exercise in religious and cultural tact."[2] Actually, the windows are based on the seven main language roots and contain no religious symbols at all. The sixteen-sided structure is covered in woven goat's hair like a Bedouin tent.

In 1993, having survived the Great Fire of London and the Blitz, Saint Ethelburga's, one of two remaining medieval churches in the city, was largely destroyed by an IRA bomb. Using much of the original stonework, it was reopened in 2002 as a center for reconciliation and peace. The center's aim is to explore the complex relationship between faith and conflict—faith as a *source* of conflict and a *resource* to transform it. I have a particular interest in this church: my parents were married, and I was baptized, there; my father's office at 80 Bishopsgate was next door.

Since the rebuilding, Saint Ethelburga's has hosted hundreds of events toward achieving its aim. Even before 9/11, it was pursuing dialogue with Muslims. However, Saint Ethelburga's soon recognized a situation that faces many who enter in goodwilled fashion into dialogues with faiths other than their own. The fact that Saint Ethelburga's was a Christian church meant that Christians were always the hosts and non-Christians the guests, which could put limits on frank discussion.

The building of the Tent outside Saint Ethelburga's was a deliberate attempt to create a space where religious dialogue could exist between equals, a space that through its architecture recalls the desert from which many faiths have emerged. Its opening was attended by the Prince of Wales and leaders of nine faith traditions in Britain, who all brought to the occasion copies of their respective holy books. The prince unveiled a plaque to a former rector, John Medows Rodwell, who in 1861 published the first reliable version of the Quran in English.

The manifesto of the Tent at Saint Ethelburga's, "Sharing the Space," proclaims: "Christian and Muslim scriptures endorse neither coercion nor violence in pursuit of their invitational missions. However, the reality around the world is that tension between Christianity and Islam is expressed in the form of violence and other forms of conflict and repression. No conversation that ignores the reality of these issues will be fully grounded in truth."

I have a close connection with another "safe space"—Mountain House, Caux, a conference center for reconciliation and trust building in Switzerland. I was first introduced to the work of Caux as a teenager. I had been evacuated with my brother to the United States for safety during World War II[3] and, hoping a visit would help to reestablish family unity after the war, we went to Caux in 1947. It did, indeed, have that effect but, more than that, it launched the whole family on a commitment to a work for reconciliation and change then known as Moral Re-Armament and now as Initiatives of Change (IofC).

As my brother Gerald writes: "It helped develop a transparency in our relationships within the family and in our dealings with others. This was reinforced by hearing from others, who told of significant change and reconciliation, both personally and in wider conflict situations they had lived through. From them, we learned the discipline of a daily time of quiet in the early morning, 'listening to the inner voice' or 'seeking God's guidance.' They highlighted that if you want to put right what is wrong in the world, you have to be ready to start with change in your own life. A consequence was that my brother and I and our parents took on a commitment to what in those days we called 'remaking the world.'"

Mountain House continues its work to this day. In April 2007, for example, forty Burundians, including three former heads of state, politicians, religious leaders, members of the rebel Palipehu-tu-FNL movement, and people from civil society lived together in Caux and conducted an "honest conversation" to consolidate the fragile peace in their country. This was part of a long process that started five years earlier. In six days at Caux, they built on the experience gathered from sixty years of the center's operations. The first two days were devoted to "creating a spirit of dialogue" and were divided as such: first, "the fears," and second, "the wounds," both of which are obstacles to dialogue. In the atmosphere created, a frank and moving dialogue took place. The third day was about creating conditions for dialogue and particularly how to create a space for dialogue in Burundi. The fourth day was headed "Reinforcing personal responsibility and initiating a code of good conduct," and the fifth day was left to the Burundians to be alone together.

The work continues on the ground with the support of the Swiss Foreign Ministry. Ambassador Pierre Combernous, who had himself been involved in Burundi peace efforts, spoke at Caux of the "special relationship" between the Swiss government and Caux. "This relationship is in the context where the spirit of Switzerland's foreign policy is marked by ideas of solidarity, universality, and human values," he said.

In 1946, when the Caux conference opened, the first words of Frank Buchman to those assembled from many nations were "Where are the Germans?" Strenuous efforts were made to cut through difficulties and red tape to allow Germans to leave their country. In this chapter, I tell the story of what happened at that time through the experience of a French woman who came the same year that we did. It is a saga that led to Mountain House being twice nominated for the Nobel Peace Prize and to Dr. Buchman being decorated by France and Germany.

Then, at the end of this chapter, with the help of Dr. Barry Hart, we take a further look at the need for places where people can come without feeling threatened.

Switzerland: Irène Laure at Caux

In 1946 a group of Swiss, at great personal sacrifice, bought the run-down Caux Palace Hotel overlooking Lake Geneva as a place where warring nations of World War II could meet. It was the fulfillment of a thought that had come to a Swiss diplomat, Phillipe Mottu, three years earlier: If Switzerland was spared by the war, its task would be to make available a place where Europeans torn apart by hatred, suffering, and resentment could come together. Renamed Mountain House, this distinctively turreted building, which in 2002 celebrated its centenary, is set in restful grounds with a panoramic view of the peaks of the Dents du Midi and has been host to several hundred thousand people from all over the world. It is owned and operated by a Swiss foundation, Caux—Initiatives of Change.

The summer of 1947, the year I first went with my family, five thousand people from some fifty countries attended sessions at Caux. They included the Swiss president and the prime ministers of Denmark and Indonesia; Swedish UN emissary Count Bernadotte; a U.S. congressional committee; twenty-six Italian Parliament members; U Tin Tut, the first foreign minister of independent Burma;

and G. L. Nanda, a future Indian prime minister. Also in attendance was Irène Laure, representing Marseilles as a member of the French Constituent Assembly and a leader of three million socialist women in her country.

Madame Laure would have felt at home in the presence of dozens of Allied service personnel recently demobilized and would have been reassured by meeting former resistance figures like herself. She would have appreciated what historian Scott Appleby highlights as "the service of Caux in providing a neutral and secure place, where antagonists can meet at a physical and psychological distance from a conflict zone and in an atmosphere of civility and mutual respect, to discuss their differences and what they hold in common."[4] She was not, however, prepared to meet Germans, even those who had been anti-Nazi or had suffered because of Nazism. Germans at that time were not welcome at other international conferences. She might have been appalled had she known that the first group of Germans was welcomed to Caux by a French chorus singing in German. She was certainly not aware that the first words of Buchman on arriving for the opening of Caux the summer before had been "Where are the Germans?" Already that first summer, sixteen Germans had come, and one hundred and fifty came in 1947.

The Germans came to Caux as equals. The Hamburg *Freie Presse,* in a report from Caux, commented, "Here, for the first time, the question of the collective guilt of the past has been replaced by the more decisive question of collective responsibility for the future. Here in Caux, for the first time, Germany has been given a platform from which she can speak to the world as an equal."

Laure was an internationalist. Between the two world wars, she cared for German children in her home. But her experience in the resistance when Germany occupied her country, and the torturing of her own son, had left behind a passionate hatred. When Allied bombers flew overhead, Laure rejoiced at the destruction that would be wreaked on Germany. After the war, she witnessed the opening of a mass grave containing the mutilated bodies of some of her comrades. She longed for Germany's total destruction; she never thought that understanding was possible and never sought it. Invited to Caux, she hesitated at first because she knew at some point she would have to come to grips with the question of Germany's future. But she finally accepted, welcoming the chance of a break from the political wrangling in Paris and the opportunity of some good food for her children, malnourished from the privations of the war.

The presence of Germans was a shock. Every time a German spoke, she left the hall. Although she noted the Germans were saying things she had not heard them say before, that they were facing the mistakes of the past and their own nation's need for change, her gut reaction was still "I will never stay under the same roof as the Germans." She packed her bags to leave and then ran into Buchman. "Madame Laure, you're a socialist," he said to her and, echoing his remarks the year before, "How can you expect to rebuild Europe if you reject the German people?"

Her immediate response was that anyone who made such a suggestion had no idea what she had lived through. Her second response was that perhaps there might be hope of doing something differently. She retired to her room. "I was there two days and nights without sleeping or eating with this terrible battle going on inside of me. I had to face the fact that hatred, whatever the reasons for it, is always a factor that creates new wars."

Emerging, Madame Laure was ready to have a meal with a German woman. She hardly touched her food but poured out all she felt and all she had lived through. And then she said, "I'm telling you all this because I want to be free of this hate." There was a silence, and then the German woman, Clarita von Trott, shared with the Frenchwoman her own experiences from the war. Her husband, Adam, had been one of those at the heart of the 20 July 1944, plot to kill Hitler. It had failed, and he had been executed. She was left alone to bring up their two children. She told Laure, "We Germans did not resist enough, we did not resist early enough and on a scale that was big enough, and we brought on you and ourselves and the world endless agony and suffering. I want to say I'm sorry."

After the meal, the two women and their interpreters sat on the terrace overlooking Lake Geneva. Then Madame Laure, the Christian socialist, told her new German friend that she believed that if they prayed, God would help them. She prayed first, asking to be freed of hatred so that a new future could be built. And then Frau von Trott prayed, in French. Instinctively, Madame Laure laid her hand on the knee of the former enemy. "In that moment," she said later, "the bridge across the Rhine was built, and that bridge always held, never broke."[5]

Laure asked to be given the opportunity to speak at the conference. Many were aware of her background, but few knew what conclusion she had come to in her room or the effect that her conversation with Frau von Trott had on her attitude. "Everyone was fearful," she remembers. "They knew what I felt about the Germans. They didn't know I had accepted the challenge." It was a risk for the organizers. They did not believe that the best way to get across new ideas to Germans, who had lived all those years under Nazism, was to put them in the dock.

Laure spoke to the six hundred people in the hall, including the Germans. She told them honestly—and, as she says, disastrously—all that she had felt. Then she said, "I have so hated Germany that I wanted to see her erased from the map of Europe. But I have seen here that my hatred is wrong. I am sorry and I wish to ask the forgiveness of all the Germans present." Following her words, a German woman stepped up from the hall and took her hand. To Laure it was such a feeling of liberation that it was like a hundred-pound weight being lifted from her shoulders. "At that moment, I knew that I was going to give the rest of my life to take this message of forgiveness and reconciliation to the world."

Rosemarie Haver, whose mother was the German woman who took Laure's hand, said to Laure more than thirty years later, at Caux in 1984: "Your courage in bringing your hatred to God and asking us Germans for forgiveness was a deeply shattering experience. When I saw my mother go up to you, my whole world collapsed about me. I felt deeply ashamed at what Germans had done to you and your family. I slowly began to understand that these Germans who had also brought much suffering on my own family had acted in the name of Germany, which meant in my name also."

Peter Petersen, a young German who later became a senior member of the Federal German Parliament, was in the hall that day. As he told the story: "I arrived in Caux with very mixed feelings. I fully expected people to say, 'What are these criminals, these Germans doing here?' I was ready with counter accusations to whatever we were accused of. Instead, we were really made welcome. A French chorus sang, in German, a song expressing Germany's true destiny. Every door was open to us. We were completely disarmed. Three days after my arrival, I learned of the presence in Caux of Madame Laure. I also learned that she had wanted to leave when she saw us

Germans arriving. A violent discussion broke out amongst us. The question of guilt and who was to blame, the question that was so dividing Germany at that time, could no longer be avoided. We all recognized that this Frenchwoman had a right to hate us but we decided that if she expressed her hatred we would reply with stories of the French occupation in the Black Forest."[6]

When Laure spoke in the meeting, Petersen and his friends sat at the back, ill at ease and asking themselves if it would not be better if they left the hall. After her speech, Peter said, "I was dumbfounded. For several nights it was impossible for me to speak. All my past rose up in revolt against the courage of this woman. I suddenly realized that there were things for which we, as individuals and as a nation, could never make restitution. Yet we knew, my friends and I, that she had shown us the only way open if Germany was to play a part in the reconstruction of Europe. The basis of a new Europe would have to be forgiveness, as Madame Laure had shown us. One day, we told her how sorry we were and how ashamed we were for all the things she and her people had to suffer through our fault, and we promised her that we would now devote our lives to work that such things would never happen again anywhere."

Irène Laure could, with every justification, have blamed the Germans. She did not do so. In fact, many years later she said, "From the moment I decided to talk with them as friends instead of blaming them, the only thing I wanted to do was to apologize for my own hate." And, as in myriad other examples over the years, her generous attitude provoked soul-searching in those to whom her words were addressed, whether German or other nationalities.

In her three weeks at Caux, Laure was exposed to many other aspects of the center's approach. Along with the restful setting, there is the nature of the meetings and workshops, the chance for leisurely talks at mealtimes, and the use of theater and arts to present universal truths. A gracious sense of hospitality is expressed: Swiss families give of their best to furnish the place; volunteers take infinite care in the preparation of rooms, with fresh flowers there and in the public rooms; meals take into account the cultural sensitivities of different peoples.

In plenary sessions, formal presentations are kept to a minimum, and the emphasis is on participants sharing their experiences. Laure would have heard others tell personal stories of change, stories that intended to inspire and motivate change in others, without preaching or advising. She herself spoke six times. Just as with Laure and the Germans, when adversaries meet at Caux, the approach may open the way to a change in relationship. Rabbi Marc Gopin observes that hearing the public testimony of parties to a conflict is critical to the Caux conflict-resolution process: "Empathy is evoked by the painful story of the other party, and in this religious setting, both parties refer to God's role in their lives. This, in turn, generates a common bond between enemies that has often led, with subtle, careful guidance, to more honest discussion and relationship building."

Unhurried meals are an integral feature at Caux. They are a way of "putting people in the way of others"—bringing individuals who are grappling with life's tough dilemmas together with others who have met similar challenges—whether through careful planning or by the chance "decisive encounters" as French Catholic philosopher Gabriel Marcel in 1958 called these interactions at Caux.[7] In the case of Madame Laure and Frau von Trott, a mealtime at Caux brought enemies to a place of new understanding and possibility.

The encounters he observed at Caux convinced philosopher Marcel that he was seeing a new world conscience evolving. "What strikes me before all else is that you find there the global and the intimate linked together in a surprising way. For the first time in my experience, I sensed a true global awareness in the process of being formed. It is shaped through encounters."

Laure's own change of heart was a soul-shaking one for her. She began to believe it could happen to others, even to employers. She probably discovered early on that some of the persons serving her at meals were from the class that she hated. And getting to know employers—particularly French ones—with a new motive, helped her to move beyond her class-war attitudes. In fact, she had first thought Caux was "a capitalist trap." But by the end of her time at Caux, she was working with employers to plan an industrial conference in the north of France.

Some encounters will have been in the serving teams, which are a central feature of life at Mountain House. All guests are encouraged to take a share in the running of the house. Gopin notes: "The Caux center is organized by work teams, with the specific intention of creating relationships through shared work. This is a cost-effective equalizing of relationships and a powerful nondia-logic way of developing relationships." He refers to the bonding that occurred between him and some Arab students at Caux in 1991 when they found themselves together on a service team, depen-dent upon each other and cooperating to solve practical questions quite separate from the Middle East. Laure's husband, Victor, soon became a regular bread baker in the Caux kitchen.

Another feature of the Caux conferences is the use of theater to present ideas. One of the first acts after the purchase of the Caux Palace Hotel had been to turn the hotel ballroom into a theater. For, as Marcel observed, "Buchman and his associates have made a real discovery. They have realized that people nowadays are far more profoundly influenced by seeing something acted than you could expect them to be by hearing a sermon." Laure saw plays in the theater, sometimes presenting challenging experiences in daily life, sometimes historical or biographical stories. One was *The Good Road,* a musical with humorous sketches of contemporary life and a moving pageant of history that proclaimed dramatically the basic ideas of freedom and the necessary conditions of a sound society. She saw *The Forgotten Factor,* an industrial drama that contained the basic principle of the work of Caux—it is not *who* is right but *what* is right that matters—and she recognized in the unfolding clashes between employers and workers something of her own experience of Marseilles. Later she was to have that play staged in France.

Also shown that summer was *And Still They Fight,* a dramati-zation of the life of a Norwegian patriot, Freddie Ramm, who had helped his country before World War II be reconciled with Den-mark and who died during the war as he was being repatriated from a German concentration camp. With the horrors of the Holocaust shocking the world, Germans were very much on the defensive. After Reinhold Maier, minister president of the state of Wuert-temberg-Baden, saw *And Still They Fight,* he slipped away from the Caux theater and threw himself on his bed "completely shattered" with shame at what his country had done. "It was a presentation without hatred or complaint and therefore could hardly have been more powerful in its effect," he later wrote.

Laure returned home from Caux for an election campaign. In a speech before leaving, indicating how far she had come in her thinking, she said, "I ask you to understand the suffering and needs of the working people, as I shall ask myself in campaign speeches to remember that employers are not always wrong either." To the Germans, she promised that she would fight for reconciliation between France and Germany. "Here at Caux," she said, "my heart has been liberated from bitterness against Germany. I shall use my position in politics to see that France and other countries do not have any desire that Germany should starve. France, too, has been an occupied country just as Germany is today. We have all been wrong. Now we must build a bridge of caring across the Rhine."

Responding to Laure's words, Madleen Pechel of Berlin, who had been with her husband in a Nazi concentration camp, said, "I shall take Madame Laure's words to the women of Germany. Many times, tears of joy have come to me at Caux. I do not think from 1934 to 1947 I have ever laughed with such a full and open heart as in the last eighteen days, here among people who have every right to hate us Germans."

More than five thousand French and Germans took part in Caux sessions between 1946 and 1950. Harold Saunders, a former U.S. assistant secretary of state, said at Caux in 1992, "If the changes in the human arena involving the French and German people who came to Caux after 1945, if that human relation had not been changed, there would be no institutions of the European community today, or they would at least have taken longer in coming." The journey of discovery of comparatively few individuals had led on to a greater vision of cooperation and coexistence among many Europeans.

In *The Psychodynamics of International Relationships,* Joseph Montville singles out the change of Irène Laure at Caux as "perhaps the signature event in terms of psychological breakthroughs in the Franco–German conflict" and "one of the most dramatic examples of the power of a simple appeal for forgiveness."

Laure, reflecting on her visit to Germany after her weeks in Caux, said, "Can you think what it meant for me to go there? In my heart, I had willed the ruins of World War II. I am a mother and a grandmother. I am a socialist and all my life I have talked about fraternity, yet I had longed for a whole people to be destroyed. I had to ask forgiveness for my hatred from those people who were living in the ruins. I had to ask forgiveness from fifty thousand women whom I saw, gray with fatigue, clearing the rubble in Berlin. I do not forget the ruins in my own, or other countries, that the Germans caused. Not at all. But the thing I had to do was to face my own hatred and the part it played in dividing Europe and to ask forgiveness for it. Change in me brought forth change in many Germans. An idea strong enough to answer the hate I had is strong enough to change the course of history."

Transformative Spaces for Change
Dr. Barry Hart

> Dr. Hart is a professor of Trauma and Conflict Studies in the Center for Justice and Peacebuilding at Eastern Mennonite University. He has developed and led training programs in conflict transformation, restorative justice, trauma healing, and peacebuilding in East and West Africa, the Balkans, and Northern Ireland. He is the academic director of the Caux Scholars Program.

When complex and violent conflicts alienate people and break the human bond of interdependence, it is essential to create a process for healing and rebuilding relationships. An important part of this process includes providing safe and hospitable space for remembering the past and building toward a more just and peaceful future. Theories of change tell us that this process needs to be both dynamic and realistic, with goals that reflect real-world relational and structural circumstances. In addition, it must include the ways and means for people to do significant self- and group-reflection. As part of this process, skills and related tools of intervention such as deep listening, dialogue, negotiation, mediation, and storytelling help create transformative spaces for change to take place. Creating the most conducive space to address what is on the minds and hearts of individuals is an essential and critical step in the process of transforming the conflict in both the short and long term.

Creators of Space

A conflict transformation process that helps move individuals and groups of people toward a more equitable and stable future requires individuals who are willing to make changes in their own lives and who will risk challenging members of their own ethnic or religious groups to do the same. It is creators of change who provide the welcome and hospitality, as well as the facilitation and negotiation expertise, that help key individuals find ways to remember and change as well as over time (often very long periods of time) develop strategies for just peace conditions in their communities and societies.

This conflict-transformation process seems almost impossible to imagine when considering, for example, the Israeli–Palestinian conflict. This *intractable* conflict has persisted for nearly six decades and seems to have no end. But even in this case, there is hope due to the work of individuals and groups who challenge representatives of both sides of the conflict to find ways to stop the violence and begin or restart the peace process. Harvard professor Herbert Kelman, who began bringing together leading Israeli and Palestinians in small confidential workshops in the mid-1980s, has been part of this process, as has former Norwegian Minister of Foreign Affairs Johan Jorgen Holst, who hosted the Palestinian and Israeli negotiators in his family home as a critical step in the Oslo Accords negotiations.

Other individuals and groups such as Peace Now, Seeds of Peace, and Bat Shalom have worked to create the necessary space for Israelis and Palestinians to hear each other and do the important self-reflection required for change to take place. This personal change among many is usually the first step in a long process of transforming difficult conflicts. The "simple act" of personal change has an essential role in the requisite systems change necessary to build sustainable peace during and after complex conflicts.

Geopolitical and other variables that impact and hinder the work of the above-mentioned individuals and groups do not diminish the fact that acts of hospitality and trust-building interventions, as well as mediation, negotiation, and other skills, *contribute* to peacebuilding in the region. Behind peace agreements and subsequent strategic peacebuilding processes are individuals and organizations whose values, courage, and desire for peace are at work and will ultimately be a factor in the creation of stable and just relationships.

Conflict transformation did take place in this part of the world, resulting in the Camp David Accords of 1978. President Jimmy Carter hosted Menachem Begin and Anwar Sadat at Camp David, Maryland. There, a historical peace agreement over the disputed Sinai region was reached between Israel and Egypt. How this happened is of key importance. President Carter's "one text" negotiation approach was not working—Sadat and Begin refused to meet face to face, and Carter became frustrated with the men and the process. Not until Carter asked the parties to come together in a more informal manner did a breakthrough occur.

In this informal setting, President Carter created a new kind of *space* at Camp David, a more personal space where the parties could experience each other in less of a political sense and more on the level of their common humanity. This was further enhanced when Carter showed photos of his grandchildren to Begin and Sadat, which prompted them to take out photographs of their grandchildren. Through this simple, yet important exchange, these leaders decided they wanted a more peaceful future for their grandchildren and all children in Israel and Egypt. This opened the way for working out the important technical details of the resolution of Sinai conflict.

The space for change that President Carter created may have been unexpected, borne of frustration, but it offers a clear lesson for peacebuilding, showing that processes need to address both the tangible and intangible elements of a conflict. In this case, the intangible issues of identity–identity threat and human dignity— were involved along with the tangible issue of state sovereignty and security. The humiliation Egyptians experienced with the taking of the Sinai by Israel in the 1967 war needed to be dealt with, as did Israeli security issues related to the attack by Egypt at the start of that war.

Camp David's nonthreatening space was essential for this transformational experience to take place, and it helped create another kind of space, one about children and their future and the need to work together to assure this future. Carter was clear about the need for the first space, the physical beauty and quiet of Camp David, but it seems he may have "happened upon" the second space—the one that exposed the *need for the other*, a recognition of interdependency, which proved to be the tipping point of the negotiations.

Society of Friends

When the Society of Friends, commonly known as Quakers, deals with complex conflicts, their chief concern is "being in human solidarity with all parties." They engage all parties of the conflict in discussion to find a way out of the violence. Their *witness* to others is premised on "equality, justice, peace, simplicity, and truth," and they work to engage parties separately with a care and respect that promotes peace. They then act as a "bridge" between the parties, and since they are trusted by both sides, the information they share and encouragement to peace and justice they promote is respected and often positively acted upon.

Quakers carried out this peacebuilding role in the conflict between whites and blacks in Rhodesia in the late 1970s. Along with the Catholic Church and members of Moral Re-Armament (now Initiatives of Change), they played a significant role in creating spaces for individuals to make decisions that protected life and eventually helped transform the conflict. Central to their work as bridge builders was the art and practice of *listening*. According to Dr. Ron Kraybill, founding director of the Mennonite Conciliation Service:

> Listening was, for the Quakers, no mere prelude to serious talk. Listening was itself a genuine contribution to change—a means to support the dignity, credibility, and rationality of the individuals with whom they were interacting. And because the Quakers consulted widely each time they expanded their role, listening was also a manifestation of their political values. Rather than give advice, the Quakers *sought* advice about what they should do and at all times presented themselves as quiet servants of the needs of the parties. Theirs was the politics of transformative listening.[8]

The transformative listening of the Quakers and other groups working for change in the Rhodesia conflict created an environment that allowed individuals to hear their own deep thoughts or, for some, to reconnect with their moral or spiritual selves. Effective, empathic listening by another, according to Virginia lawyer and mediator Larry Hoover, "provides us the opportunity to clarify our thoughts and emotions, to feel cared for and empowered to take the next step, or to begin or continue the healing process."[9] In Rhodesia, the next step was honest conversation between whites and blacks and the creation of a nonviolent process that led to the development of the new state of Zimbabwe.

Woodrow Wilson Center for Scholars

In a context specifically designed to train leaders, the Woodrow Wilson Center for Scholars creates space for change for Burundian leaders. The center's Burundi Leadership Training Program (BLTP) began in late 2002 to build on the Arusha Accord of 2000. This accord began a fragile peace process between the Burundi government and rebel factions. Military commanders from all sides and a cross-section of other Burundian leaders—ninety-five in all—were invited to take part in this eighteen-month long capacity-building (training) initiative.

The initiative's object was "to build a cohesive, sustainable network of leaders who could work together across all ethnic and political divides in order to advance Burundi's reconstruction."[10] These important workshops featured training in interest-based negotiation, communication, conflict analysis, and strategic planning, but may have been just as critical in providing a space for these leaders to *breathe* and reconnect with themselves and, through the safe and creative environment of the training venue, to reconnect with the humanity of their *enemy.*

Several stories from the workshops are telling in terms of the change process that began to take place among these leaders. One general spoke about the importance of the setting for him, since for the first time in three months he was able to *think* and not just react to his surroundings. In one sense, he was clearly defining what happens in times of war and high-energy leadership in which one is mainly functioning in the instinctual or emotional part of the brain and not in the frontal cortex, or thinking, part of the brain. This general, through the workshop *and* its environment of safety and a place of learning, was able to find the space he needed to think about both the important information he was receiving and the power and importance of not having just to react to the world around him.

A second example of the change process came in a conversation with Wilson Center's Steve McDonald[11] when he was asked how issues of trauma and trauma healing were dealt with in the group. Since trauma was not a subject of the training, Steve inferred that some healing may have happened when the wives of the leaders (mostly men) were invited for social weekends. McDonald implied that these women helped not only bridge the gap between faction leaders but, through their presence, brought a certain sense of calm to the gathering. Perhaps, too, they represented a stable past and, as mothers, a hope in the future since children represent and need a stable future, as we noted in the Camp David example.

Initiatives of Change

As Henderson describes in this chapter, Initiatives of Change (IofC), at its center (Mountain House) in Caux, Switzerland, has played a significant role in the reconciliation of Europe after World War II and continues to provide the physical, emotional, and dialogical space to help individuals and groups coming from regions in crisis to hear the stories of others, to listen to their inner voice for direction, and to tell their own stories of anger, pain, or forgiveness.

In Caux, there has been "a tradition to carefully prepare for the meeting of groups alienated from each other."[12] In one example that occurred years ago in Caux, uninterrupted listening helped begin a process of change between a group of Palestinians and Maronites from Lebanon. Each group was given unlimited time to speak their minds independently—no one stopped them as they expressed their perspectives of what had happened in their conflict and how they felt about it. They were *listened* to and cared for by their IofC hosts. Through this deep listening process and, in this case, a friendly discussion between a Palestinian and Maronite women about the dress one of them was wearing, their husbands started to talk to each other, which led to a deep discussion between members of both sides.

There is intentionality in the planning of these meetings in Caux, as Henderson has described. It begins before parties arrive—relationships have been built over time, friendships have been established with individuals and groups by members of the IofC network. So, when the conflicting parties arrive in Caux, there is already trust in these friends and now hosts. This is the foundation for more listening, which includes listening to other participants at Caux whose stories of transformation often become further encouragement to individuals just beginning to explore their own attitudes toward those they consider "other."

Another tool for change used in Caux is bringing parties together at the dinner table. Sitting together to eat good food, the parties in conflict begin to engage each other in new and profound ways. Food is an equalizer of sorts, and the table is a "space" both familiar and safe. Additionally, there is an IofC tradition of service to others. Guests participate in the running of Mountain House and therefore are part of work shifts in which they find themselves serving food or tea with members of the other group. Maybe more importantly, as part of the rotation process of service, they eventually serve each other. These activities, tied to deep internal and external listening, create various spaces for choices to be made in order that change of attitude and direction might take place.

In conclusion, intentionally created spaces help create other spaces for change in and among individuals and groups. New narratives emerge in contexts where people are encouraged to think and feel rather than just react or maintain their hatred and stereotypes of "the other." Listening, talking, and learning to speak with greater care happens in the spaces created by people who deeply respect and want the best for their guests and those they represent. Ongoing listening and talking also can lead to a commitment to sustained dialogue, which in turn builds more trust and space for new ideas and transformative action.

Shifting both mind and heart comes more through experience than learning, and both are necessary for personal and subsequent institutional shifts to take place. Whether the Quaker challenge of *human solidarity* leading to truth and justice or the Wilson Center's training approach to *build sustainable networks for leaders,* or Initiatives of Change's *starting with oneself* through deep internal listening, it is critical to know that creating space within people and around people and their issues is an essential step in the transformation of complex conflicts.

Perspective
What a Woman Can Do
Betty Bigombe

Betty Bigombe was a Ugandan cabinet minister and is currently a distinguished scholar at the Woodrow Wilson International Center for Scholars in Washington, D.C.

Conflicts and violence have plagued Uganda since 1966.[13] Idi Amin's military coup in 1971 was followed by successive governments being overthrown, with Yoweri Museveni's National Resistance Movement (NRM) coming to power in 1986. When Museveni defeated General Tito Okello Lutwa, the northern war became initially a popular revolt by Okello's ousted army troops and their numerous civilian supporters who formed the Uganda People's Democratic Army (UPDA). On the other side was Alice Auma Lakwena who claimed to be a prophet and formed the Holy Spirit Movement. These two rebel groups enjoyed popular support in the north from the Acholi population that was both angry and alarmed at the new Museveni regime. Fear of national marginalization by the government they perceived to be dominated by western Ugandans was at the center of the rebellion. Alice Auma Lakwena's Holy Spirit Movement was defeated in 1987 and she fled to Kenya, while the NRM government negotiated and signed a peace agreement with UPDA. While these rebellions ended, Josep Kony started that same year what later became known as the Lord's Resistance Army (LRA) and the northern conflict entered an entirely new chapter. Joseph Kony's worldview is steeped in apocalyptic spiritualism and he uses brutality and fear to both maintain control within LRA and sustain the conflict.

In 1988, as an Acholi member of President Yoweri Museveni's cabinet, I was appointed Minister of State for Pacification of north and northeastern Uganda resident in Gulu. It was hard leaving my children, but at least I knew that, unlike the children in north and northeastern Uganda, they had food, shelter, school, and their father. Reactions to my appointment were mixed: most were skeptical whether a woman could manage such a task; others thought Museveni wanted to kill me. "Why appoint someone without military experience to such a task," they asked. Others even believed I was a girlfriend he wanted in a place he could access alone. The rebels felt insulted that the president had sent a "girl," as they put it. I had to show them what a woman could do, coping with everything from poisonous snakes to assassination attempts, going through ambushes, and escaping land mines, in order to reach people in internally displaced camps (IDPs). Two thoughts prevailed at my lowest moments: if God does not call your number, you will not die; and if you have been given a mission, you will be able to accomplish it. Each time I went to the camps, it gave the people hope. On these visits, I did not simply stay for a few hours and leave, nor did I lecture people and praise the government. Rather, these visits entailed pitching camp in IDPs to listen to people vent their anger. The visits enabled me to identify rebel collaborators so that I could later make direct contact with the rebel leader.

In 1992 I established contact with Kony and met with him four times between 1993 and 1994. I went to the jungle to meet him although I knew the chances of being killed or held hostage were high. I talked to him daily through radio communication. We got very close to reaching a peace agreement; a date and venue for signing had been agreed upon. But two weeks before signing, President Museveni cancelled peace talks and opted for a military solution. This devastated me, as I had invested heavily in the peace process.

In 1997 I joined the World Bank in Washington, D.C. While preparing to go to Burundi on a World Bank mission, I saw a CNN "breaking news" flash indicating that the LRA had massacred about three hundred people in IDPs in Lira district. They had set huts alight, shooting anyone who ran out. The reporter said that I was the only person who had met this bizarre leader and gotten the rebels and government close to peace—and my picture came up on the screen. I remember whispering, "Oh, my God, I can't believe it's still happening. This can't go on."

Should I go back, I asked myself, could I afford to lose my World Bank job, could I leave my college-age daughter behind? Maybe, I thought, I can give it another try. I did so. As a rationale for accepting talks. I told the president, "You're a father, you have beautiful children; if they were abducted how would you feel; look at the economic cost, the way it is affecting the country, allow dialogue." I persuaded the LRA to accept a negotiated settlement. I said to them, "you have been fighting for twenty years, you have a terrible image, you have a chance to talk, to get to the table." I spent eighteen grueling months as chief negotiator between the LRA and the Ugandan government. My only weapon was the trust I had established. As a peace activist, I encourage parties to seek dialogue as the first option.

I spent hours every day talking on cell phones, coaxing, encouraging, and scolding the UPDA officers and the rebels—and listening, which is a part of making peace. You can't address problems without hearing what people think and feel. Even the devil wants to be listened to. Sometimes, one of my most powerful tools is not talking at all. Silence works wonders.

I am confident that peace will eventually be reached through the Juba talks that began two years ago. True, a peace deal will not be arrived at easily. When people have been killing one another, they do not overnight start seeing one another in a different light. People who have been fighting for twenty years are very suspicious.

They think, "We've been enemies for so many years, can I start trusting so-and-so?" I have learned as a mediator that it is important not to jump straight into talks but to spend time in confidence building, where the parties can interact with different people and among themselves to move toward understanding. When people are given a chance, they can reform. Even the spoilers, those who benefit from war, can become promoters of peace. It does not matter who you are as long as you are human, we all deserve peace.

Amnesty encouraged LRA members to risk coming out to integrate into their communities. They find it as difficult to integrate as those communities do in forgiving them for their crimes. Forgiveness is very personal. Traditional justice alone—accountability, truth, and compensation—might not always reach the heart and soul of people who have borne the brunt of the situation. Traditional justice is not an alternative to international and national justice. People want peace and justice sequenced. "Let's first have peace," they say, "then justice will follow."

I have a lot of hope. I see promising commitment from both sides that the process should continue. Back in the United States again, I remain immersed in my quest for a settlement, thinking about the situation when I go to bed and on my computer after waking.

We easily could be discouraged by the continued failure of the international community to do more to end the misery in the camps and the years of warfare. But we owe it to the tens of thousands of children to keep pressing to bring the nightmare of LRA atrocities and suffering to an end. Armed conflict has had disastrous effects on children in Africa. How do you deal with children who are one day victims of the perpetrators of violence and the next day perpetrators themselves? In the case of northern Uganda, children have become protagonists of war when they are forcibly recruited to be combatants and are instilled with hate, the skills of warfare, and devotion to armed factions.

Young people in conflict areas are often displaced, lose educational opportunities, suffer the destruction of family structures, and struggle with physical and psychological trauma. My concern always has been that if these youths are not supported to recapture their childhood and make them productive members of the community, they will be poverty strapped for the rest of their lives. They will also be a source of insecurity. That is why finding strategies to alleviate the suffering of children and rehabilitate them and their communities is imperative.

Asked what I would regard as success, I say it is when the war ends, people are resettled in their homes and are able to live in dignity, children go to school, all have access to basic services. It is a daunting task but doable. I have a long way to go. I'll try to remain young so I can achieve that.

6

acknowledging the past

*Apology is more than an acknowledgment of an offense together
with an expression of remorse. It is an ongoing commitment by
the offending party to change his or her behavior. It is a particular
way of resolving conflicts other than by arguing over who is bigger
and better. It is a powerful and constructive form of conflict
resolution embedded, in modified form, in religion and the
judicial system. It is a method of social healing that has grown in
importance as our way of living together on our planet undergoes
radical change. It is a social act in which the person, group, or
nation apologizing has historically been viewed as weak, but
more than ever is now being regarded as strong. It is a behavior
that requires of both parties attitudes of honesty, generosity,
humility, commitment and courage.*

~~Dr. Aaron Lazare, author of *On Apology*

*I own I am shocked by the purchase of slaves
And fear those who buy them and sell them are knaves;
What I hear of their hardships, their tortures and groans
Is almost enough to draw pity from stones.
I pity them greatly, but I must be mum
For how could we do without sugar and rum.*

~~William Cowper 1788

In March 2007 a solemn bicentenary commemoration of legislation that ended Britain's slave trade was held in Westminster

Abbey and was attended by Queen Elizabeth and Prince Philip and by then-Prime Minister Blair and other dignitaries. This legislation, as the film *Amazing Grace,* released the same month, dramatized, was inspired by a great abolitionist movement across the country, led in Parliament by William Wilberforce.

The Abbey proceedings were suddenly interrupted, however, by an African, Toyin Agbetu, who strode out in front of the altar and shouted out that the queen should apologize, and Africans present should walk out. "This is an insult to us," he said, "You should be ashamed."

After being hustled out, thirty-nine-year-old Agbetu, founder of the African pressure group *Ligali,* explained, "The queen has to say sorry. There was no mention of the African freedom fighters. This is just a memorial of William Wilberforce."

Dr. John Sentamu, archbishop of York, Britain's first black archbishop and formerly a judge persecuted in Uganda by General Idi Amin, said he was grateful that the protestor had been allowed to speak and added, "I hope the depth of anger he expressed is matched by that he should have toward those African chiefs who grew fat through the capture and sale of their kith and kin for trinkets."

As this protest at the Abbey, criticisms of the film, and the archbishop's words make clear, attempts to honor heroes from the past or even to own up to terrible injustices are both essential and fraught with difficulty.

In the United States in 2007, significant steps were taken to confront slavery, which has been called the country's "original sin," as the nation marked the four hundred years since the founding of the first European settlement in Jamestown, Virginia. It was there, in 1619, that one finds the first recorded instance of slavery in the New World, when a Dutch ship landed at this colonial outpost and unloaded twenty Africans in chains who were to be sold as indentured servants. By the early eighteenth century, slavery had become crucial to an economy built on the cultivation of tobacco and cotton.

E. Stanley Jones, missionary and theologian, wrote in 1925: "*The Mayflower* that carried the Pilgrim Fathers to religious liberty in America went on her next trip for a load of slaves. The good ship *Jesus* was in the slave trade for our fathers. Is it to be wondered at that race and color prejudice still exists in the West in spite of Christianity? It came with it." Whether these words from Jones are accurate or not it seems that the first slave ship to the Americas bore that very name and is a trenchant reminder of an evil whose ramifications are still with us today. One doesn't have to tread far into the minefield of race relations to know that acknowledgment and healing for the past are still appropriate and often resisted. Many families are discovering surprises about their past.

I found in my family papers two pages from the Radnor plantation journal of February 1831. The pages detail the activities of the slaves on this Jamaican coffee plantation. How they came to be removed from the journal and why we have them is a mystery. Perhaps some opponent of slavery had taken them to use in the campaign against slavery, which two years later was outlawed in British colonies. There may be a more shameful explanation. I may never know. But it serves to remind me that none of us knows the extent to which our families or our people were tainted by or benefitted from the exploitation of the labor of others, even with Native Americans keeping slaves or, as Archbishop Sentamu pointed out, Africans selling slaves.

I was at a dinner party recently, and the subject of apology for the slave trade came up. Around the table were Christian men and women who quickly wrote off, even made fun of, the idea that apologies of any kind were needed for something that happened so long ago. The central weakness of their arguments was that they were all white and had, one assumes, never put themselves in the shoes of black people whose ancestors had suffered or whose position in society was still a reflection and legacy of that past injustice.

The subject must certainly be approached with care and with an awareness that political capital is easily made of it. Apologies are better made because one's conscience demands it rather than because it is demanded by someone else. Sometimes circumstances make an apology appropriate and even unexpected for the one who apologizes. Veteran American journalist Charles Overby had such an experience on a trip to West Africa in 1999. He met—and was challenged by—America's past. As chairman and chief executive officer of the Freedom Forum, he had gone with a delegation to learn more about the news media, particularly in Mali and Senegal. But in the process, he says, "We learned more about ourselves."

As they prepared to open a two-day conference in Senegal, he could not shake off the image of West Africans being shipped to the United States as slaves. He had not expected to feel as he did and decided to apologize to the West Africans for the American role in slavery. "It was presumptuous of me to do so," he says, "but I couldn't help it.

"Seeing some of the buildings where the slaves were kept before their departure, I felt a lump in my throat. How could I—the head of an American organization that promotes freedom around the world—stand in front of West African journalists, students, and government leaders and carry on as if the only thing between us was the Atlantic Ocean?"

Overby said to the audience, "In traveling to Senegal, I am acutely aware of the historical link between the United States and West Africa. The slave ships that transported your ancestors from here to my country represent a sad and tragic time in my country's history. I cannot change the past. But I can apologize for it. To each of you, I deeply apologize for the outrageous and barbaric actions of my countrymen and my personal ancestors in the eighteenth and nineteenth centuries."

He recalled the words of an old African American Baptist preacher, often quoted by Martin Luther King Jr., "We ain't what we want to be. We ain't what we're going to be. But thank God we ain't what we were." And went on, "It is in that spirit—repentance for the past and hope for the future—that I open this conference and dialogue."

And what a dialogue it was, says Overby.

He reported this experience in the forum's monthly *News*. "West Africa is where slavery began," he wrote. "The events of previous centuries affected us dramatically. I could speak as only one American, as one Southerner. I apologized profusely."

He was immediately met with some ugly responses, ranging from "No apology could ever suffice" to "You have no right to apologize" from conservative friends who felt we were not required to apologize or repent for the sins of our fathers, just our own. But overall, he told me, the response was balanced, with some people expressing curiosity and others support. "My biggest concern," he told me, "was not to come off as something I wasn't—I wasn't an official spokesman for my country. I wasn't attempting to portray myself or my organization as a paragon of virtue. I wasn't trying to whitewash the past with what could be interpreted as an empty rhetorical gesture. I spoke from the heart with what I was feeling at the time—a small, insignificant person confronting a piece of history and trying to deal with it on a personal level. I think most people understood that."

Overby was not deterred by the possibility of criticism. When he was executive editor of the *Clarion-Ledger* in Jackson, Mississippi, in the early 1980s, he decided that the paper should apologize as an institution for its past support for segregation—even though it had changed hands since those days and was now owned by Gannett newspapers. In his editorial, he apologized for the paper's active complicity in attempting to keep African Americans from learning and working and playing equally alongside white people. It had done that through the news and editorial columns, through what the newspaper covered and what it didn't, through the active support of politicians and leaders who vowed the South would never change. He began his editorial "We were wrong, wrong, wrong." That, too, triggered some ugly calls, he says. He challenged public officials running for office to renounce their previous racial attitudes. Some did, most didn't. "But it was an interesting exercise," he comments.

This chapter is about acknowledging the past. Most of us realize that some kind of apology, preferably sincere, keeps normal human interaction going. But when is it appropriate to apologize on larger issues? Is there a statute of limitations on exhuming the past? When and where do reparations come into the equation? Who is deserving of an apology? Are there any precepts we can follow?

Whether you hold a "black armband view" of history or a "three cheers view" of history (as Australians have characterized the debate over whether their country's past was a disgraceful story of imperialism and exploitation or largely a success story), the concluding perspectives of Joseph Montville, which are the fruit of years of pioneering work in the healing of history, give us pause for thought.

Healing in the Slave Triangle

Imposing and identical fifteen-foot-high stone figures in a close embrace, symbols of "reconciliation," stand today on three continents—in Liverpool, England; in Benin, West Africa; and in Richmond, Virginia.

Five thousand people attended the unveiling in Richmond on 30 March 2007 at the site of the city's former slave market where three hundred thousand kidnapped Africans and their descendants were torn from their families and "sold down the river" to Southern plantations. Water from a cascading fountain flows over a map of the slave triangle, where an inscription describes the suffering of the millions of Africans transported from their homeland and concludes with the words: "Their forced labor laid the economic foundations of this nation." A delegation from Liverpool, including a representative of the city council, was present as well as four West African ambassadors. The ambassador of Benin, Segbe Cyrille Oguin, called it a "blessed completion" of a triangle of new relationships between three places that had profited hugely from the traffic in human flesh.

Seven years earlier, in February 1999, President Mathieu Kerekou of the Republic of Benin had visited a black church in Maryland, knelt before the congregation, and asked them to forgive the sins of his ancestors in helping to perpetuate and sustain slavery in his country. Bishop David Perrin said that the president's message was so genuine that even the children were moved to tears. On the president's invitation, Perrin and his wife and three others visited the West African nation and were commissioned by him to invite a hundred leaders in the African diaspora to come for a reconciliation and leadership conference. At the same time, he invited European leaders to come and publicly repent for their sins. He wanted to bring all parties together to prepare for the millennium with a reconciliation conference that would involve repentance and forgiveness.

Kerekou was conscious that there was still a divide in Benin between families who were descendants of those whose family members were captured and sold into slavery and those who captured them and was also aware of the resentment still felt by some in the diaspora.

The conference took place in December 1999. A number came from Richmond. From Liverpool came Lord Alton, who brought with him the official apology of the Liverpool City Council. Earlier in the month, as a final act before the millennium, the council had passed unanimously a motion recognizing the "trade in human misery" through which it had become rich. The city had joined the trade in 1699 when the *Liverpool Merchant* set out carrying 220 slaves from West Africa to Barbados. Part owner of the ship was Sir Thomas Johnson, known as the founder of modern Liverpool. Liverpool ship-owners financed 40 percent of the European ships in the trade. The council made an "unreserved apology" for its involvement and the continual effect of slavery on Liverpool's black communities. It committed itself to programs of action "which will seek to combat all forms of racism and discrimination and will respond to the city's multicultural inheritance and celebrate the skills and talents of its people."

Lord Alton also presented to President Kerekou a maquette of Liverpool sculptor Stephen Broadbent's work *Reconciliation,* conceived by him originally as a token of reconciliation with a colleague and later used as a contribution to healing relations between Liverpool, Belfast, and Glasgow. President Kerekou indicated that he would like to have the full-scale version of this statue for Benin. Out of the conversation between the Richmonders, the Liverpudlians, and the hosts developed the idea of the *Reconciliation Triangle.* "The three statues," said the president, "would be a physical and symbolic representation of a process of bringing together in an expression of repentance, forgiveness, and reconciliation, the descendants of those that profited from the evil trade, those on the continent from which they were taken, and those now living in the place to which many slaves were taken."

A few months later, four government ministers from Benin participated in a "ceremony of racial healing" in Richmond to extend the process of reconciliation. This was building on a process in the Virginian capital that went back to a national conference in 1993, hosted by Mayor Walter Kenney under the heading "Healing the Heart of America—an Honest Conversation on Race, Reconciliation, and Responsibility." Centerpiece of the conference was a walk through the city's history, marking places of pride and of shame. It has been followed up by Hope in the Cities, a work for racial unity and community building whose approach is being increasingly adopted in other cities and countries. Hope in the Cities believes that honest conversation must include all sectors of the community, that public acknowledgment of historical wounds and sharing of stories can lead to healing and that acceptance of personal responsibility for change by people of all backgrounds can break the cycle of fear, denial, and resentment.

In the intervening years, this Southern city and the state of Virginia have come a long way. Richmond's Monument Avenue, which was marked exclusively by statues of Southern Civil War heroes, now also honors Arthur Ashe, the great African American tennis player who, as a boy, was not allowed to play on the city's courts. The Tredagar Iron Works, the former Confederate Gun Foundry, is now a museum, the first American Civil War exhibit to tell the story from all three perspectives, Confederate, Union, and African American. Richmond has had a succession of black mayors and Virginia its first black governor. Part of the story has been made permanent through a "slave trail" which is part of the city's educational resource. Author Rob Corcoran wrote in 2007 that, in a decade, the community moved from a place where race was "not discussed in polite company" to a community that is "learning to have honest conversation and to appreciate its shared history."

Two months before the statue's unveiling, the Virginia Legislature expressed "profound regret" for the state's role in sanctioning slavery, as well as in "the historic wrongs visited upon native peoples." One white legislator made headlines by first suggesting black citizens should "get over it" and then voting in favor of the resolution, which was carried unanimously. The Virginia resolution states that "even the most abject apology for past wrongs cannot right them, nor can it justly impute fault or responsibility to succeeding generations or justify the imposition of new benefits." But, as the *Washington Post* pointed out, "Expressions of repentance and remorse in public life, as in interpersonal relations, can be helpful, healing emollients. It is not just that they do no harm; they may also, as the Virginia document states, 'recall and remind so that past wrongs may never be repeated and manifest injustice may not again be overlooked.'"[1] At the later unveiling of the *Reconciliation* statue, Virginia governor Timothy Kaine said that the resolution of profound regret by the state's general assembly was appropriate since Virginia had "promoted, defended, and fought to preserve slavery."

As a part of overcoming the racial disadvantage and economic separation that is a legacy of slavery, educators in Richmond's public and private schools are exploring ways of working together with schools in Liverpool and Benin. Liverpool students, black and white, have traveled to Benin and were involved in designing panels for the base of the *Reconciliation* statue, and Richmond students came up with the inscription: "Acknowledge the past, embrace the present, shape a future of reconciliation and justice."

In August 2007, a Richmond delegation visited Liverpool to take part in celebrations marking the eight-hundredth anniversary of the city's granting of a charter by King John and the opening of the International Slavery Museum on the waterfront, which has as its theme "Remember not that we were sold but that we were strong." Dr. David Fleming, director, National Museums, Liverpool, spoke at a gala opening dinner on August 23, the anniversary of a 1791 uprising on the Island of Santo Domingo, which has been designated by UNESCO as "Slavery Remembrance Day." This uprising is regarded as a crucial factor in the fight against slavery, and the day is a reminder that enslaved Africans were themselves a significant agent of their own liberation.

Dr. Fleming said that the International Slavery Museum was needed "to help illuminate one of the darker, more shameful, and neglected areas in our history—an era in which this city played a pivotal role." It was needed also because "the consequences of that era are all around us in the shape of a rich and vibrant multinational, multiracial Atlantic world but also in inequality of opportunity, racial prejudice, ignorance, intolerance, and hatred." It was a museum with a mission: "We wish to help counter the disease of racism, and at the heart of the museum is a rage which will not be quieted while racists walk the streets of our cities and while many people in Africa, the Caribbean, and elsewhere, continue to subsist in a state of chronic poverty."

He said that the museum, through the medium of education, would provoke differing responses and emotions: "In those who believe that some races are superior to others, it will provoke doubt; in those who believe that all men and women should have equality of opportunity and who rejoice in mutual respect, it will create hope; in people of African descent—and perhaps especially in those who are descended from those who were enslaved—it will promote grief but also pride, pride in the doggedness and strength of spirit of their ancestors, which enabled them to survive the horrors of slavery and to pass on, down the centuries, that spirit which endures in many of the people in this room tonight."

Australia: National Sorry Day

I was once asked to give the invocation for the Oregon Senate. I was introduced, and the senators duly bowed their heads. As I spoke, astonished heads were slowly raised. It might have been the English accent, or perhaps it was the invocation, so unlike others they were used to. I simply told the story of a politician who I thought was a good example for politicians anywhere, anytime.

I spoke about William Wilberforce, sometimes called Britain's Abraham Lincoln and the "George Washington of humanity," who led the parliamentary battle to end the slave trade. The year 2007 was the two-hundredth anniversary of that achievement, which historian G. M. Trevelyan called "one of the turning events in the history of the world."

I was asked to give the invocation because an Australian political figure, Kim Beazley Sr., was my houseguest and had been invited to speak. He was the father of a recent leader of the opposition. His words were probably even more surprising to the senators than mine. He took as his text the words of the Prophet Micah: "What doth the Lord require of you but to do justice, love mercy, and walk humbly with your God."

Beazley went on to outline how his people had done none of those things, but had behaved cruelly, lived selfishly, and walked arrogantly, particularly in the treatment of the Aboriginal people. He described how he had devoted his political life to their cause. Like Wilberforce, Beazley may have sacrificed the chance to be prime minister in making the just treatment of Aboriginal Australians a priority of his parliamentary career.

He began a variety of initiatives to treat Aboriginal people with a dignity befitting their position as the first Australians. Early on he realized that if the Aboriginal people did not own any land, they would always negotiate from a position of weakness. So he persuaded his party to adopt a policy of Aboriginal land rights and set in motion initiatives that led to Aborigines owning an area of land larger than Great Britain.

For twenty-three years, Beazley was in political opposition, yet it was from this position that he achieved great gains for the country. When he eventually became minister for education, one of his first acts was to arrange for Aboriginal children to be taught in their own languages in primary school. An honorary doctorate awarded him by Australian National University pointed out that his two great achievements—the healing of the ulcer of sectarian bitterness as minister of education and the enhancement of the dignity of the Aboriginal people—came because he had worked irrespective of political party gain.

In the 1980s and 1990s, the Australian authorities took a searching look at Aboriginal problems. Progress was made toward creating attitudes of respect between the races, but one issue kept raising its head: the continuing effect of the policies of removing Aboriginal children from their parents. The issue was brought into focus by a national inquiry, whose thorough report on the subject issued in 1997 shook the nation. It contained fifty-four recommendations including a call for a national apology. Prime Minister John Howard was reluctant to accept its revelations or do anything substantial toward healing the wounds. Several of his ministers attempted to discredit the report.

The Australian community as a whole responded differently. Community organizations came together and organized a "Sorry Day" in 1998. I was present on that occasion. I saw the "Sorry Books," where a million people wrote messages to the Aboriginal people. All state governments held official events in their Parliaments, where they heard from Aboriginal people and offered wholehearted apologies. I wrote up the story and its background in a chapter of *Forgiveness: Breaking the Chain of Hate*. Two years later, a quarter of a million people took part in a walk across Sydney Harbour Bridge. There were similar events in all cities and many towns, and about a million people walked for reconciliation between Aboriginal and non-Aboriginal Australians. Aboriginal culture was center stage at the Olympic games that Australia hosted.

The government could not ignore so many voices. Prime Minister Howard announced that a central area in Canberra would be set aside "to perpetuate in the minds of the Australian public the importance of the reconciliation process." It would include "a memorial and depiction of the removal of children from their families." The federal government, refusing to accept responsibility for the harm caused by the removal policies, at first developed the memorial themselves, without any consultation with the stolen generations. This provoked demonstrations and even criticism from former Prime Minister Malcolm Fraser.

Members of the National Sorry Day committee, who had followed up its original campaign with a "Journey of Healing," told the minister for indigenous affairs that such a memorial could be immensely healing if it came out of genuine consultation. They offered to consult the stolen generations, former staff of the institutions, and those who fostered or adopted children, with the aim of reaching consensus on the memorial's design. This they did, listening to heartache and deeply held views until a consensus on the design and the actual wording was achieved. Months went by without a response from the government. So the committee let them know that the 2003 National Sorry Day address would be given by Malcolm Fraser. They were quickly invited for discussions on the text and because they had reached a consensus, they were able to resist the removal of words that the government found awkward.

In May 2004, the memorial was dedicated. It stands between the High Court and the National Library. Its text begins: "This place honors the people who have suffered under the removal policies and practices. It also honors those indigenous and nonindigenous people whose genuine care softened the tragic impact of what are now recognized as cruel and misguided policies." At the dedication ceremony, the National Sorry Day committee released a statement: "As South Africa's Truth and Reconciliation Commission has shown, a public acknowledgment of shameful past practices is a crucial first step in healing the wounds caused by those practices. This memorial will inform Australians from all over the country and, we hope, will inspire a new determination to overcome the continuing harmful effects of the removal policies."

The growth of the people's movement for reconciliation, in which hundreds of thousands of people got involved in the 1990s, came out of the same philosophical approach as Beazley's. Instead of confrontational political action, they appealed to the conscience of the Australian people and found a huge response. That was the way that the 1967 referendum—which gave Aboriginals the rights of all other Australians—was fought for and gained a 92 percent majority support. Beazley was at the heart of that campaign.

John Bond, for eight years secretary of the National Sorry Day, says that its work is still desperately needed: "Today thousands of

Aboriginal people struggle because their removal left them vulnerable to despair within themselves and abuse by others. Perhaps this is why Sorry Day has become a fixture on the national calendar despite the federal government's lack of support."

Kim Beazley Sr. died at the age of 90 on 12 October 2007. Three former Australian prime ministers were among mourners at his state funeral. The many obituaries paid tribute to his work for Aborigine rights. The *Guardian* wrote: "In debate and in his dealings with people, Beazley had what in the present-day parliamentary climate would be regarded as a rare fault, the desire to never hurt others personally."[2] The country's national newspaper, *The Australian*, described him as "a political rarity who put his religion and moral beliefs before his political interests." It quoted veteran political writer Mungo MacCallum, who called him "a towering and intimidating figure with something of the style of an Old Testament prophet." The article, echoing the Australian parliamentarian's words about mercy in Oregon, concluded: "He remained true to his guiding principle: 'The thoughts of God, given primacy in the life of a man, bring to the innermost motives the virtue of mercy and with it the cure for hatred that can turn the tide of history. This is the essence of intelligent statesmanship.'"[3]

A month after he died, national elections were held in which the Howard government was swept decisively out of office. When the new Parliament met in February 2008, its first action was to offer an apology to the stolen generations, hundreds of whom crowded into the Parliamentary chamber to hear it. The new prime minister, Kevin Rudd, spoke from the heart: "For the pain, suffering, and hurt of these stolen generations, their descendants and for their families left behind, we say sorry."

The response was overwhelming. Across the country, Australians gathered in hundreds and thousands to watch the speech on outdoor video screens. Polls showed that 70 percent of the population supported him. And the stolen generations were deeply moved. "Now I feel I can forgive," said one.

The apology was expressed in more than words. Mr. Rudd stated as aims of his government a transformation in the health conditions of Aboriginal Australians within a decade and vastly improved educational opportunities—a program that will demand massive resources. He invited the leader of the opposition to join him in leading a commission aimed at overcoming the desperate shortage of housing in Aboriginal Australia. His invitation was immediately accepted.

There is plenty of work still needed. But these actions have laid a foundation for a vast improvement in Aboriginal well-being. There is now a real hope that Australia's greatest shame—the degradation of the original people of this continent—will be brought to an end, and that Aboriginal people will be enabled to make their full, unique contribution to national life.

Germany: Pforzheim—After the Nightmare

At the end of World War II, Royal Air Force (RAF) ex-prisoner of war Tom Tate said to his wife, "I'm never going to Germany again in my life." Yet, fifty years later, in 1995, he returned to Germany and has gone there every March since. "I will do anything to further reconciliation and understanding," he tells me.

The story of what changed his attitude is the unfolding saga of a small community that turned a terrible crime into an opportunity to bring two countries closer together. It is a testament, whichever way you look at it, to extraordinary twists of luck or fate.

In March 1945, Flying Officer Tom Tate was one of the crew of an RAF Flying Fortress in a bomber raid over Germany. It was his forty-fifth sortie. His plane's task was not to bomb but to jam enemy radar. Hit by flak, an engine caught fire and forty minutes later, believing the plane had crossed into Allied territory, the pilot, Flight Lieutenant John Wynne, ordered the crew to bail out while he searched for an emergency airfield. Eventually, he gave up the attempt, tried unsuccessfully to bail out, and, after the fire burned out, managed to bring the plane home to England.

Tate and the others landed thirty miles west of the town of Pforzheim and were captured. After interrogation, they were moved to Pforzheim. They did not know that three weeks earlier the town had been destroyed by the RAF in a firestorm, which in twenty minutes killed eighteen thousand people, a quarter of the population. As the RAF prisoners were marched through the suburb of Huchenfeld, they were stoned. They were then locked up for the night in the boiler house of a local school.

That evening, in revenge for the attack on Pforzheim, a group of Hitler Youth teenagers, under orders from the district commandant and egged on by a mob, overpowered the guards and dragged the prisoners to a cemetery. It was clear to Tate that they were about to be killed. Somehow he broke loose in the dark and managed to get through the crowd and into the woods.

The next day Tate surrendered to the *Wehrmacht*. A soldier protected him from a second mob, shared his bread and schnapps with him, and gave him clothes and a pair of shoes in which he could walk to the station. He spent the rest of the war in a prison camp. His five fellow airmen had indeed been murdered.

The following year, Tate was asked to return to Germany to give evidence at the war crimes trials. In court, he stood before the twenty-two men and youths who had dragged them off. "I had a feeling of hatred and no compassion," he says. The commandant was executed, and the others were given prison sentences. Tate swore he would never go back to Germany.

The story might have ended there but for former German cavalry officer and prisoner of war Pastor Curt-Jürgen Heinemann-Grüder, who retired to Huchenfeld in 1989 and heard rumors of a wartime massacre. Having established what had happened, he suggested, with the backing of the local pastor, Horst Zorn, that a plaque be put up as a way of making amends.

Heinemann-Grüder was in close touch with Dr. Paul Oestreicher at Coventry Cathedral. Since the cathedral's destruction by German bombers in World War II, it has pioneered a work of reconciliation. Only six weeks after its bombing, the provost of the time, Dick Howard, made a radio broadcast from the ruins asking British people to say "No" to revenge and "Yes" to forgiveness.

Despite criticism from local people, the pastors persisted in their conviction. In November 1992, a bronze memorial was unveiled by Oestreicher with the names of the men and the words "*Vater vergib* (Father forgive)." At a special service, Heinemann-Grüder told the congregation, "Cowardice is a sin, just like fanaticism; this we confess and we seek forgiveness."

Marjorie Frost-Taylor, the widow of one of the murdered airmen, was present. She had heard about the event through an article in a British newspaper headed "German village faces its ghosts" and had been encouraged by Oestreicher to attend. For years, she had prayed to know what had happened to her husband: now she felt God was answering her.

During Communion, an older man pulled aside one of the clergy and whispered, "I was one of the Hitler Youth who shot that night. I killed them. Forgive me, but I don't have the strength to meet her." He turned and left.

Renate Beck-Ehninger, who has chronicled the Huchenfeld story in *The Plaque—Letters to My English Godson*, writes: "What a story! For forty-seven years, Marjorie had not known how her husband had died. For forty-seven years a former Hitler Youth—then perhaps sixteen years old—had borne the burden of having carried out a grown-up's command to kill. What would it have been like, had they been able to meet? To this very day, it has remained Marjorie's true but unfulfilled wish: 'I want to give my hand and say I have no bitterness any more.'"

Oestreicher presented Huchenfeld with a replica of the Cross of Nails, which was fashioned from medieval nails discovered in the ruins of Coventry Cathedral. This is an honor afforded to cities that have suffered like Dresden, which was destroyed during the war and has since worked for reconciliation.

Shortly before the plaque was put up, the pilot, John Wynne, was traced and told about the forthcoming ceremony. He had not known of the fate of the crew members. Then seventy-one and a farmer in Wales, he felt that a reciprocal gesture was called for and in 1993 commissioned a small rocking horse for the Huchenfeld kindergarten. It was named *Hoffnung* ("Hope") and was presented "on behalf of the mothers of 214 Squadron RAF." "Our future will ride upon her back," said Wynne as he handed it over to ninety-one-year-old Emilie Bohnenberger, who had lost her husband in the war but had saved another British airman from a mob and later provided a pair of her dead husband's boots for Tate's journey to prison.

A three-page spread, describing what had happened, ran in the English magazine *Saga*. Back in England, absorbed in golfing and gardening, Tom Tate received a copy of the magazine from a friend, who recommended its tours. He was about to throw it out unopened when an impulse of his "inner being," as he puts it, persuaded him to unwrap it. He read to his amazement what had happened and got in touch with Wynne, who urged him to go to Huchenfeld. Local people, he was told, had longed for years to meet a survivor so that they could express their shame and horror and ask for forgiveness. "Fate had played its trump card," says Tate.

His first visit was undertaken with some trepidation. But he reached out beyond his fears to the people of the town. He recognized, he says, that local people who had no part in the crime had lived with this ongoing stigma and realized how wrong he had been to remain an enemy for forty-eight years. He told those he met about the soldier who had helped him on the morning of his arrest: "In the hands of a lesser man, I would not have survived."

Tate met the soldier's son and has since paid public tribute to him, in German, as "a noble example of honorable behavior toward a fellow human being." Tate also met Frau Bohnenberger, who had taken a great risk in giving him her husband's boots.

Since then, Tate has regularly attended the annual commemoration ceremony. He sees the plaque as a powerful symbol of the "wonderful ties" of friendship that have been established, while the holiday exchange of children between Huchenfeld and Llanbedr, home of John Wynne, ensures that such friendships continue to be cultivated. "Friendships are most easily made between children and young parents; the relicts of war cling to their prejudices," says Wynne. "Our aim is that every primary school child in Llanbedr shall have the opportunity to visit Huchenfeld before he or she moves on to secondary school."

It is an ongoing story. In December 2002, Chris Bowlby made a program about Huchenfeld for BBC Radio, and the *Times* of London published an article by him. As a result, Glenn Hall and Richard Vinall, whose fathers had been murdered, learned more about their fates.

Are any of the murderers, like the unknown man who came forward at the service, still alive? Tate would like to meet them. "I have reached the stage to think they've suffered enough. They have had this on their conscience all these years. It is time to forgive and live in friendship and peace." He often thinks of the terror the people of Pforzheim suffered and tells them that he hopes that "in understanding and sharing your nightmare memories, you will also derive some comfort from me."

Java: Dutch POW Diary Changes Japanese Life

Nel Lindeijer lay dying in a Japanese internment camp on the island of Java in the last days of World War II. Three years of privations— shortage of food and medicines—had exhausted her. With the young Dutch mother were her four children. Her husband, E. W., whom she had not seen for three years, was a prisoner of war in Japan.

The family had been living in the Dutch East Indies when the Japanese invaded the islands in 1941–1942, and Nel and thousands of other Dutch men, women, and children were herded into internment camps. Her husband, a chemistry teacher at the Christian High School in Bandung, was a medical orderly when he was captured.

Her eldest son, Wim, then nine, was at her bedside and wanted to comfort her in her last hours. "When I am grown up," he assured her, "I will fight the Japanese." In her frailty, his mother rose up and sternly said that he should rather prepare for a time to come when he would love his enemies. "War thrives on hatred," she said, "love is the basis of peace." In her last hours, she dictated a farewell letter to her husband, which she entrusted to Wim to deliver one day. He hung it on a string around his neck.

Nearly fifty years elapsed before the full import of his mother's words, and the spirit of the letter which she had written, propelled Wim on a journey of bridge building between Dutch and Japanese.

It was some months before E. W. Lindeijer was able to return from Japan to Java, to meet with his children again and to discover that his wife had died. In the meantime, they had been living through turbulent times, with liberation from the Japanese and hostage-taking by Indonesian nationalists, all the while looked after by Adrie van der Baan, a young Dutch woman also in the camp.

When his father returned, Wim presented the letter. In it, Nel urged her husband to marry again and suggested Adrie or her sister. In January 1946, Adrie and E. W. Lindeijer were married and returned to Holland. To Adrie, then twenty-nine, it had not been an easy decision, but she felt Nel's letter was a "wonderful confirmation of God's will. It was the love of God preparing this for us."

In the years since World War II, Wim Lindeijer led a busy life working as a civil engineer all over the world. In 1980 his father died and in 1993, while working in Afghanistan, he had a breakdown. His recuperation gave him the chance to reread his father's wartime diaries, which were in the form of letters to his wife and children: twelve hundred pages written in secret while a prisoner in Japan. He reread his mother's last letter. He had taken them in superficially as a youth. Now he read with new insight and was amazed at the total absence of blame and bitterness. "There was no bad word about Japan; there seemed to be no hard feelings about the Japanese." Of his mother's last hours, he asks, "How was it possible to say farewell to four children after such a nightmare, with such a state of peace and a belief that things would come right?"

His reading brought into focus the fact that all his life he had felt guilty for his mother's death, believing that he could have prevented it had he been a better son. He had been confused by that burden and had projected it, he says, onto the Japanese. He had sworn that he would never go to Japan or meet Japanese and had boycotted Japanese products. "Deep inside me, I had misconceptions about Japan and the Japanese."

Now he told his stepmother Adrie that he wanted to go to Japan and work for reconciliation. She was supportive. In 1996 they visited Ohashi and Kama'ishi, where his father had been. This visit served to convince Lindeijer that the Japanese were human beings like him. Through their meetings, profound conversations, hospitality, and readiness to give assistance, "fear, hate, and jealousy were blown away," he said at a meeting in Delft, his hometown.

In Kyushu, there is a unique joint Japanese-Dutch monument to Dutch prisoners who died in Japan. Each year, there is a commemoration at the site. In October 1997, Lindeijer spoke there. He described this new awareness in his life and asked for forgiveness for the hatred he had felt toward the Japanese. Lindeijer had difficulty explaining to a Japanese journalist why he should ask for forgiveness when it was they, the journalist said, who did the wrong to him. "I tried to explain that I liberated myself," he says.

The following year, he wrote an article in a magazine for ex-internees in which he described how he had asked for forgiveness. Some internees objected. "How the hell can you do that?" demanded one irate reader. One of the most vocal critics went the following year to Japan and understood what Lindeijer was trying to do. They now work together. Lindeijer sympathizes with those who demand reparations but says that reparations will never be enough for a heart that has not been freed of hatred. To him, the release from hatred has been so special that he cannot stop attesting to it.

Now in his seventies, he has been on seven trips to Japan. He has given lectures in different parts of the Netherlands. He has linked up also with those in Britain working for reconciliation with the organization Agape. With the help of Takamitsu Muraoka, a Japanese professor in the Netherlands, his father's diary and mother's letter were published in Japan under the title *Kisses to Nel and the Children: From a POW Camp in Japan.* It was published for the four-hundredth anniversary of links between the Netherlands and Japan.

Wim Lindeijer sums up the three key events in his new life as the peaceful, blameless sentiments of his mother's last letter, without which he would never have gone to Japan; his father's diary, which was realistic but free of bitterness; and the wholehearted response by Japanese who showed interest, openness, and even remorse about the war. He regards it as extremely important to be open to the other person whether or not you like them or their ideas. "Respect and appreciation are key elements in reconciliation," he says. "Today it is with pride that I can call Japanese my brothers."

At the book's launching, Professor Takamitsu Muraoka, who translated it into Japanese and edited it, spoke of its effect on his own life. He said that the letters contained not a single word of accusation or denunciation of the Japanese. Every time he read them, he found it hard to control his emotions. "The authors had won an inner battle that must have raged in their hearts, a battle against natural human instincts and reactions of hate, spite, wrath, and vengeance. In the end, they were able to submit to the will of God, in which mercy and justice meet." He expressed his shame at the indescribable hardships and injustices willfully inflicted by Japanese. "I am particularly moved by the fact that some of you with whom I am personally acquainted extended your hand of forgiveness before we Japanese asked for it."

In March 2003 Professor Muraoka officially retired from Leiden University. He decided to spend one-tenth of his time, some five weeks every year, sharing his knowledge in ancient languages with scholars and students of those countries in Asia that suffered under the Japanese imperialism and militaristic aggression during the first half of the twentieth century and teaching those subjects at universities and theological seminaries there without an honorarium. "Gradually, the Lord showed us that, if you tithe your income, you could tithe your time as well, which is equally a free gift from him." In 2003 he started by giving free lectures in South Korea and the following years in Indonesia, Singapore, Hong Kong, the Philippines, and China.

In an address at Trinity Theological Seminary in Singapore, Muraoka described what he called "Facing the history of a nation: a Japanese Christian scholar's journey." Soon after taking up the post of Hebrew chair at Leiden University, he said, he had become aware of the bitter memories of many who had suffered under the Japanese. He and his wife and Dutch and Japanese friends organized a conference to which they invited about sixty Dutch returnees from Indonesia, their relatives and friends, and about twenty Japanese resident in Holland "in order to face our shared history, particularly that of the three-and-a-half years' Japanese occupation of Indonesia." In 2007 they held their eleventh conference.

In preparation for his Singapore visit, he had, he told the seminary students, studied what the Japanese had done in Southeast Asia and the "atrocious treatment" they had visited upon overseas Chinese, including many thousands of Singaporean Chinese. He quoted from a speech by the federal president of Germany, Richard von Weizsäcker, to the German Parliament on the fortieth anniversary of Germany's surrender on 8 May 1945: "Most of our German citizens today were either children or not yet born during the war. They cannot confess sins that they did not commit personally. Nobody with ordinary human sensibility could expect you to wear tattered sackcloth and sit in ashes just because you happen to be German."

Muraoka said that he agreed with von Weizsäcker. When the Pacific war ended, he was seven years old and even if he had waved a Japanese flag during the war to men departing for the front line, it would be unfair for him to be accused of complicity in the Japanese war of aggression.

But the former German president went on to say, "Our forefathers left us a stupendous legacy. Guilty or not guilty, young or old, all of us Germans must accept this past history. We are responsible for what we make of this legacy and how we relate to it. One who closes his eyes to the past becomes also blind to the present. He who refuses to register in memory past acts of inhumanity runs the risk of being infected again by the same disease."

Referring to Weizsäcker's example, Muraoka said, "First, I must fully and honestly admit that during the first half of the last century, my country inflicted an inestimable amount of damage, loss, destruction, and suffering of all descriptions, not only on POWs of the Allied forces and their civilian population, but also, and far more seriously, on the lands and people of Asia and Pacific islands. I offer no excuses; I can only belatedly express my sincere sense of sympathies for all those countless victims and their relatives and friends.

"Secondly, I must express my serious concern over the fact that my country, its successive postwar leaders, and the great majority of the population have not yet faced the modern history of Japan honestly and sincerely. For us, sixty years on, the war is not over yet. I feel responsible for this situation. I shall not remain idle or sit back on the side. I am determined to act, not just to say things."

Wim Lindeijer sees the response to his family's experiences as an affirmation of his mother's last words to him: "War thrives on hatred, love is the basis of peace."

Germany: What about Dresden?

Over many years, the biggest source of resentment in Germany toward Britain could be encapsulated in one word—*Dresden.* On 13–14 February 1945, less than three months before the ending of the war in Europe, one of its most beautiful baroque cities was destroyed by British and American bombers when they dropped forty-five hundred tons of explosives, creating a firestorm, devastating eight square miles of the city, and killing an estimated thirty-five to forty thousand men, women, and children.[4]

In a remarkable way Dresden has, through honesty, apology, and compassion, become a focal point of reconciliation between the two countries. The bombing had always been an embarrassment to the British, as the London *Times* pointed out in February 1995 on the fiftieth anniversary of the raids, but added that "it was being transmogrified into friendship and reconciliation and revitalized understanding of an older, worthier, and culturally rich Germany."

Physical expression of this transformation is the *Frauenkirche*, the city's baroque Protestant church burned in 1945. Following the Berlin Wall's collapse, Dresdeners launched a call for help in rebuilding the church. Alan Russell was one of the many in Britain who felt strongly that a positive response from Britain was imperative. He grew up during World War II and was proud of what the RAF did to achieve victory. Soon after the war, he did military service in the British Zone of Germany. While there, a German friend acknowledged to him that the persecution of the Jews had been a great wrong but added "What about Dresden?"

At the time, Alan had no answer. But as he read the first of what was to become a number of well-researched books on the subject, he found himself forced to confront the uncomfortable truth that, as one distinguished reviewer put it, "something not quite worthy of Britain" had taken place. While he felt it entirely right to honor the bravery and commitment of the more than fifty thousand British bomber command crewmen who had sacrificed their lives in the war, he felt that the victims, too, deserved a memorial since innocence, dignity, and the sacredness of life itself knows no frontiers. It wasn't wrong to bomb Dresden, he believes, since the outer reaches of the city contained both war industries and military installations, but the manner in which it was done, focusing on the historic inner city, was highly questionable. He felt that some sign of atonement and regret for the bombing should be given and that the British public should be given the opportunity to look at Britain's moral record: "Nations must be able to look critically at what has been done in their names in order to have the right to examine what other countries have done."

He worked with others to set up a trust fund for Dresden (1993) to raise money in Britain for the church's restoration. He wrote in a Dresden magazine in February 2002, "The statement of Saint Matthew about 'the [mote and the beam]' remains appropriate. It is for all members of the trust a challenge to liberate the British and the Germans from the common nightmare of self-righteousness."

The trust found a ready response around the country, and over the following years it raised around £1 million. When, in autumn 1994, it was invited to undertake the making of the new nine-meter-high baroque orb and cross that was to stand on the pinnacle of the *Frauenkirche's* dome, it enthusiastically made this the centerpiece of its actions. By a remarkable coincidence, Alan Smith, head of Silversmiths Grant Macdonald's team of skilled workers, was the son of one of the airmen who had bombed Dresden and saw his work as not only a technical challenge but as a deep spiritual fulfillment.

In February 1995, at ceremonies marking the fiftieth anniversary of Dresden's destruction, the Duke of Kent presented a drawing of the orb and cross and said, "We want this cross to be a symbol of the reconciliation between Britain and Germany. We do this in remembrance of those who died in Dresden in February 1945 and in the conviction that there will forever be peace between our two peoples. We deeply regret the suffering on all sides in the war."

The *Times* commented, "There could be no more-fitting gesture. Some Germans may interpret the present as a discreet apology. All can agree that it is a sincere act of reconciliation."

In June 2004, the orb and cross were lifted into place before a crowd of sixty thousand people. In October 2005 the *Frauenkirche* was reconsecrated, and the trust handed over a symbolic gift of Communion silver plate. To carry the message further, the trust has published books about the city's history, given scholarships for youth from Dresden and Saxony to attend schools in England and for young Britons to visit Saxony, arranged for German choirs to sing in Britain, and taken the London Bach Choir to Dresden to give two concerts in the *Frauenkirche*. Alan Russell says, "The hand of friendship that the trust sought to extend was immediately, warmly, and firmly grasped, and the feelings of deep sorrow and remorse to which the trust sought to give voice have been reciprocated in more than full measure."

In October 2006, the Duke of Kent dedicated the British–German Friendship Garden in Britain's National Memorial Arboretum in honor of all who died in World War II raids. It contains a circle of fourteen stones retrieved from the rubble of the *Frauenkirche,* each inscribed with the names of cities in Germany and Britain damaged or destroyed in the war. A plaque, in German and English, states: "Just as the city of Dresden has risen from the ashes of the firestorm which engulfed it, so has the respect that traditionally characterised British–German relations been reborn. Henceforth, may all difficulties between the two countries be resolved with patience and understanding, may their sorrows be shared, and their joys celebrated together. In the beauty of nature, as in the presence of God, we are all one."

Every morning at the National Memorial Arboretum, a silence, accompanied by the Last Post and Reveille, is observed at 11 a.m. in honor of those who sacrificed their lives in defense of freedom.

This is at the chapel, which the arboretum's founder David Childs called the "Millennium Chapel of Peace and Forgiveness" rather than of "Peace and Reconciliation" because, he told me, "Forgiveness requires a conscious act of will."

United States: Restitution to the Nisei

On 9 October 1990, the U.S. attorney general knelt at the feet of wheelchair-bound, 107-year-old Japanese-American Mamoru Eto and presented him with a check for $20,000 and an apology from the nation. "By finally admitting a wrong," said Dick Thornburgh, "a nation does not destroy its integrity but, rather, reinforces the sincerity of its commitment to the Constitution and hence to its people."

Eto was one of the 120,000 Americans of Japanese ancestry, two-thirds of them born in the United States, who at a time of anti-Japanese hysteria after the attack on Pearl Harbor were forcibly relocated to what the Japanese-American Citizens League called "concentration camps." Eto was, at the time, minister of the First Nazarene Japanese Church in Pasadena. "They were not death camps," as *Los Angeles Times* writer Betty Cuniberti put it, "but freedom, pride, and dreams died a thousand times in California, in Colorado, in Arizona, and in Wyoming, in the sprawling makeshift camps to which Japanese Americans were herded."

In 1988 Congress authorized the payment of $1.25 billion in reparations for what some lawmakers describe as "this American shame." The money was for about sixty-five thousand people: surviving internees or their descendants.

The mass relocation in 1943, moving persons of Japanese ancestry away from the West Coast because of "military necessity," followed Executive Order 9066 signed by President Franklin D. Roosevelt. So it was appropriate that accompanying each reparation check was a statement from President George Bush: "We can never fully right the wrongs of the past. But we can take a clear stand for justice and recognize that serious injustices were done to Japanese Americans during World War II."

Robert T. Matsui, a U.S. congressman from Sacramento, spent the first years of his life in a California camp. His wife, Doris, was born in a camp in Colorado. Matsui was a sponsor of the Civil Liberties Act, which authorized the apology and the restitution, along with another California representative, Norman Y. Mineta, who was interned as a ten-year-old in Wyoming, and Senators Daniel Inouye and Spark Matsunaga. Matsui saw the outcome as a major victory, not only for those who were interned but also for Congress and the country, and an end to an "arduous national march toward redemption." He did not receive any money; he waived the right so that he could vote for the bill on the floor of the House.

Twenty thousand dollars per person represented a small fraction of the funds lost by Japanese Americans through relocation or the replacement of lost property or livelihood. However, as one Japanese American said in a television interview, he was grateful for the money, but what meant most was the apology. Another framed his check and put it on the wall of his home.

What had hurt the Japanese community was the impugning of their loyalty as Americans and the persecution they suffered because of their race. Many Japanese Americans were serving in the U.S. forces while their families were forced to live in camps. Japanese-American volunteers fought in the famous 100th Infantry Battalion and in the 442nd Regimental Combat Team, which had the highest casualty rate and the most decorations of any unit of its size in all U.S. military history.

Speaking at the moving ceremony in the Justice Department, Attorney General Thornburgh said, "I am not unmindful of the historic role this Department of Justice played in the internment. It is somehow entirely fitting that it is here now we celebrate redress." Representatives Matsui and Mineta embraced, in tears, as the audience in the Great Hall sang "God Bless America." Mineta said, "Americans of Japanese ancestry now know in their hearts that the letter and the spirit of our Constitution holds true for them."

Donald W. Shriver Jr., who in his book *An Ethic for Enemies* reviews this wartime episode, writes: "Destroy democracy in war, and it may be hard to revive it in peace: Americans had a brush with that sober truth in the 1940s. But American government did revive democratic justice in relation to Japanese Americans in the 1980s. Imperfect as the repentance was, it was a great improvement on the political temptations of 'social amnesia.' Neither in personal nor political contexts is any human repentance ever quite complete. That is one of the gaps which forgiveness fills, especially the forgiveness that consists in the willingness of offended people to resume neighbourly relations with the offenders."

The Science behind Reconciliation
Joseph V. Montville

Joseph Montville is director of *Toward the Abrahamic Family Reunion,* the Esalen Institute project to promote Muslim–Christian–Jewish reconciliation. He is also senior adviser on interfaith relations at Washington National Cathedral and has appointments at American and George Mason universities. Montville founded the preventive diplomacy program at the Center for Strategic and International Studies in 1994. He spent twenty-three years with the State Department.

Michael Henderson ably and movingly conveys the rich and affecting stories of individuals who have hurt others in political conflicts and wars and found the strength to acknowledge their crimes and even ask forgiveness of their victims. The accounts of victims moved to forgive those who hurt them are similarly gripping. These are real people with authentic histories, and they become poignantly alive in the author's telling. With all this, one might ask what more is needed to persuade us of the power of acknowledgment and forgiveness as the core of reconciliation between perpetrators and victims, individuals and nations?

I suggest that a scientific support structure for the power and truth of the experiences related in these pages not only exists but is necessary to protect the psychologically delicate and necessarily vulnerable process of acknowledgment, contrition, and forgiveness. The better angels in our midst have always been and will continue to be circled and stalked by avengers who need to externalize their aggression, seek retribution, and savor total victory of their version of good over their version of evil. The more we can move the insights affirmed in these pages into the conventional wisdom, the safer our world will be. The more we succeed, fewer and fewer innocent women, children, and men will be sacrificed to the incompetence of traditional governance.

Some stories in this book refer to the resistance of governments, for example of the Australian federal government to support the popular enthusiasm of many white Australians for acknowledging their country's moral debt for its cruelty toward the Aboriginal population. There is also reference to intensely nationalistic Japanese conservatives who reject all charges of crimes against humanity and war crimes against the military regime before and during World War II. This same phenomenon can be found in more rightist Tory circles in Great Britain when the issue of England's moral debt to the Catholic Irish over the centuries is raised.

In the United States, conservatives are hounding and often terrifying Latino residents, legal and illegal. In the Roman Catholic hierarchy, conservatives doggedly resist grassroots pressures to allow priests to marry or for equal opportunity for women in the Church, including ordination into the priesthood. Extreme fundamentalist clerics in Saudi Arabia, and the more conservative Orthodox rabbis in Israel and the diaspora, are similarly steadfast in rejecting creative change in practice and dogma. There is almost no evidence of compassion in this strain of political, cultural, and religious conservatism—and fierce resistance to retrospective critical self-analysis and admission of wrongdoing and moral debt to victims.

In many ways, this "resistance to knowing" is analyzable by political psychologists and even susceptible to being worn down or even transformed into neutrality if not nascent liberality. The hard right conservatives we are discussing could be suffering from their own unarticulated sense of injustice. Or less nobly, they fear loss of power and prestige, if not retribution for past injustices they have committed. More ominously is what psychoanalyst Vamik Volkan has called "the need for enemies." This, in a sense, exists in all tribes and nations. The use of external threats real or perceived to increase internal solidarity and extend tenure for political leaders is traditional and commonplace. Of course, there are historic enemies, whose relationships are the subject of this book.

Of greater concern are the political cultures in which the enemy is cast by religious belief into the collective personification of existential evil. In the Christian tradition, but particularly conservative Protestant belief, virtue—which they possess—is under constant threat from the antichrist and his supporters. To these believers, this phenomenon is pure evil. It sometimes takes the form of foreign institutions (the United Nations is frequently accused) in the eyes of some American religious fundamentalist extremists. Or the evil can be seen in a people. Alarmingly, for many Christian conservatives, the 1.2 billion Muslims in the world, including the 7 million or so in the United States, represent the forces of the antichrist. One extreme conservative organization in the United States employs ex-Muslims and Christians and Jews to promote the idea that Muslims in America represent a vast sleeper cell awaiting the signal from abroad to rise up and overthrow the government and establish an Islamic state.

The extremist Christians align with conservative and militantly defensive Jews in Israel, the United States, and elsewhere in sharing a fear and loathing—and one might say appalling ignorance—of Islam. For Jews, the traditional tribe of Amalek, which symbolizes the Gentile urge to attack and destroy Jews for no reason, introduced to us in Genesis, has today become embodied in the Arab and Muslim people. The role of Amalek passed from the Roman Empire to Christendom, which played this role from the first century CE through the middle of the twentieth century. Today the Christian dread of the forces of the antichrist, which is deeply embedded in American political culture, has teamed up with the Jewish dread of the Muslim Amalek to threaten military attacks on Iran and other Muslim targets. This grave threat is enduring.

What does psychological science tell us we should do to prevent the battle of Armageddon predicted in the New Testament's Book of Revelation? Science tells us to do what the people in this book have done. It tells us to listen empathically to the stories and especially the fears of peoples locked in political and religious conflicts. It asks us to show respect for their humanity and their religious and cultural identity and to convey our concern for their well-being and that of their children. Then psychology instructs us to invite open and uninhibited expressions of the grievances and fears of all the parties to the conflict. An approach that involves representatives of the groups in conflict in a safe environment and with skilled facilitation almost always with requisite time begins a mutual rehumanizing process. This mitigates the inherited mutual demonization between the groups and ideally leads to a new relationship of the persons involved in such respectful engagement. Their task then is to communicate effectively with mass public opinion in their communities the information that some of the feared "others," the enemy, have begun to acknowledge moral responsibility for the hurts inflicted on their people over time. They have expressed remorse. And often, in explicit or subtle ways, they have asked for understanding and forgiveness.

There will be indirect healing processes necessary before the more obvious conflicts can be addressed successfully. The prime example in the Middle East is the need for Christian engagement with Jews to acknowledge the enormous moral debt of Christendom to the Jews of Europe. Christians must embrace Jews as a beloved people and begin to persuade them that Amalek is finally dead. To make this persuasive in the case of Islam, Christians and Jews must study and learn that the Prophet of Islam saw Judaism and Christianity as sibling religions sharing the same revelations from God but in different languages so that different tribes and nations could understand God's message. This will be a stunning surprise to the first two monotheistic traditions who know almost nothing about the third.

An even more indirect healing process must be launched between mainline and militant evangelical Christians in the United States whose antagonisms reflect mutual regional, cultural, and personal disdain and a history for many of civil war. The many methods of respectful engagement demonstrated by the better angels in this book help show the way. Popular initiatives to heal history have great impact on societies as some of the stories show. But there is nothing quite like the courage and selflessness of political leaders to accelerate a healing process between wounded peoples. Henderson gives us the example of former German President Richard von Weizsäcker who said, "Our forefathers left us a stupendous legacy. Guilty or not guilty, young or old, all Germans must accept this past history. We are responsible for what we make of this legacy and how we relate to it. One who wishes to close his eyes to the past becomes also blind to the present. He who refuses to register in memory past acts of inhumanity runs the risk of being infected again by the same disease."

History proves President Weizsäcker correct. The healing examples of the people in this book, buttressed by the science of political psychology, show us how we can make things better.

afterWORD

In September 2007, a short item tucked away in a newspaper caught my eye. It simply reported that earlier that month representatives of Iraq's Shia and Sunni Arab factions met secretly in Finland with Northern Ireland politicians to learn lessons in peace-making. Sixteen Iraqis sat down with senior representatives of the peace process in Northern Ireland and South Africa to explore the current situation in Iraq. The host was the Crisis Management Initiative (CMI) founded by the former Finnish president, Martti Ahtisaari.[1] The CMI issued a statement: "Participants committed themselves to work toward a robust framework for a lasting settlement. Those present agreed to a set of recommendations to start negotiations to reach national reconciliation. The principles of inclusivity, power-sharing, and a commitment to removing the use of violence as a means of resolving political differences were among the most urgent concerns agreed."

Martin McGuinness, Northern Ireland's deputy first minister, and Roelf Meyer, a former South African government minister, chaired the discussions. McGuinness said that while the situations in South Africa, Ireland, and Iraq differed, they shared something instructive in common. "The important lesson to learn is that if people are serious about bringing about peace in their country, that can only be done through an inclusive negotiating process," he said.

Ahtisaari, in an earlier speech on the lessons of the peace process, makes it clear that preventing the reoccurrance of violence is

193

not only about obliterating guns, but it is also about developing a healthy state and society. "I have been delighted to notice," he says, "that the issue of nonstate actors in conflict resolution has been attracting more and more researchers and academics in different parts of the world. Since there is no single way of resolving conflicts, we need much more research on the methodology and procedures of private diplomacy."[2]

This book has been less about research than about providing examples, much of it illustrating private diplomacy in action, examples which are often in short supply in books on peacemaking.

This Finnish news is not as earth shattering as the breaking down of the Berlin Wall in 1989 or South Africa's 1994 elections, but for an Englishman used to Northern Ireland being held up as a reproach to Christians for the continuing violence, it is an encouragement that we are learning from each other's mistakes and that this part of the United Kingdom has an important contribution to make. It also is a cause of celebration that we no longer have the Cold War and the awful immorality of Mutually Assured Destruction to conjure with; that old hatreds like those between France and Germany are gone, and many others are lessening; that we no longer have to worry about apartheid in South Africa, which complicated relations in all our lands.

Of course we now face new challenges—global warming and with it the coming struggle for resources, the millions of displaced people, the murderous spread of HIV/AIDS, the growing disparities of wealth and poverty, and the frightening specter of rogue terrorism. The divide between people of faith threatens us all, particularly as some Christian and Muslim groups demonize each other.

The post-Cold War uncertainties have thrown up new ways at looking at the world. The UN Human Development Report of 1994 argued that "freedom from want" and "freedom from fear" for all persons is the best path to tackle the problems of global insecurity, and "human security" has become a buzz phrase in the international community, referring to the wide range of things that cause people to feel insecure—from poverty and disease to a lack of hope. Some proponents of human security challenge the traditional notion of national security and argue that the proper reference for security should be the individual rather than the state. Certainly, we must recognize, as Cornelio Sommaruga, past president of the International

Committee of the Red Cross,[3] says, "that innovative approaches are needed to address the growing sources of global insecurity." Cooperation and building trust across fault lines are prerequisites. Could the very dangers we face become the motivation that can bring us together? It often is assumed that if we earthlings were threatened by the invasion of Martians, we would somehow join together to defend our globe. Perhaps the environmental challenges that face us all may also have a part in bringing us all together.

Dare we hope as we look forward to the coming years that innovative approaches may reduce some of the confrontations that we take for granted and continue to threaten the security of whole regions if not the whole world. I think of two countries where members of my own family have lived, like Burma, the home of Nobel Peace Prize recipient Aung San Suu Kyi, to whom I wrote asking for the contribution of a piece on forgiveness only to discover that she is not allowed to receive mail. Like Zimbabwe, where the goodwill following the words of Robert Mugabe that gave such hope when he took over as prime minister have been squandered: "The wrongs of the past must now stand forgiven and forgotten. If we look to the past, let us do so for the lesson the past has taught us, namely that oppression and racism are inequalities that must never find scope in our political and social system."

Could we dare one day to imagine North and South Korea coming together in freedom in a peninsula where two of the world's largest standing armies still face each other, ready to resume a war that was suspended but not finished fifty-five years ago? There are signs that finally a peace treaty may be signed. There have been top-level summits and bilateral agreements, growing economic cooperation, and ministers from the two countries meeting to discuss subjects such as opening their territorial waters to commercial fishing. The first rail link in half a century is being established, and thousands of people have been reunited with family members on the other side of the border.

High on the list of major longstanding international disputes is the six-decade standoff between India and Pakistan over Kashmir. Here, behind the scenes and often unnoticed by the world, serious progress is being made following the launching of a peace dialogue between governments in 2003. Indian Prime Minister Manmohan Singh said in Kashmir in July 2007 that the moment had come when people are energized to make a genuine effort "to build peace and create the conditions for a historic reconciliation of hearts and minds." He envisaged a time when the border between the two parts of Kashmir, respectively held by India and Pakistan, could become, not a line of contention, but a line of peace through which ideas, goods, and people can travel.

It is a dialogue that has continued also on unofficial levels. Sushobha Barve, about whom I write in chapter 4, tells me that a people's constituency has grown that is nudging governments to act. "Progress made by governments has been largely people driven," she says. This movement has begun to reverse "the trust deficit" accumulated over years of hatred. The first significant civil initiatives began in 1995 when two hundred Indians and Pakistanis met in Delhi for the Pakistan–India Peoples Forum for Peace and Democracy. The following year, they met in Lahore, Pakistan, and then each year since. Today, people associated with the Centre for Dialogue and Reconciliation, which Sushobha Barve directs, are in touch with the key players on all sides. Other civil society groups in India and Pakistan also are engaged with the Kashmir question. Speaking at the center's dialogue in Kashmir in April 2006,[4] Pakistan's former foreign secretary, Dr. Humayun Khan, said that the Indian prime minister's initiation of roundtable discussions was a hopeful sign and that more and more leaders from each side were visiting the other and holding talks with their respective governments. Person-to-person exchanges were also growing. "No moves toward peace and friendship will mean anything unless they rest on the support of the people in both countries," he said.

Kashmir has been Barve's toughest challenge. Going there over the past ten years has made her realize another side of the story. Kashmir is not a Hindu–Muslim question but a political issue that has never been settled. The work forces her constantly to face others' pain and suffering, she says, prompting her to look into her own heart to overcome her pride and blind spots about her country. She is not cynical because in the past eight years "what was unbelievable is actually becoming a reality. The fact that the peace process is moving forward and that so many are taking overall responsibility gives me hope."

It is just such hope that this book wants to foster in areas where disputes have gone on too long. Stories told herein offer fresh ideas as to how to reach out to "the other," perhaps giving us the impetus to act. The courage of the men and women in these pages who have forgiven after suffering terrible hurts and have been willing to ask for forgiveness for inflicting grievous hurts are a challenge to all of us. A friend from northeast India, who gave up a murderous plan of revenge for a family killing, said, "I realize I have been too sensitive to how much others have hurt me and forgotten how much I hurt others."

The most gratifying comment I ever had on one of my books was from a woman cabinet minister from East Africa. She was due to chair a session at a conference on peace building and got so engrossed in the book, she missed the session. She said to me, "If those women in the book can do it, so can I." I would like all readers, whether they see personal application or not, to gain a greater sense of reassurance that behind the alarming headlines are thousands of men and women, largely unknown, on journeys of discovery with "the other" who was once their enemy. There are many more stories out there that might help people be more optimistic about the future, a reality-based optimism that encourages greater participation. "Hope is the greatest weapon in the armory of the peacemakers," says William Morris, secretary-general of the Next Century Foundation.

Above all, my own hope with this book—and why I am particularly grateful to the distinguished personalities and academics for their contributions—is that policymakers will take more seriously the approaches outlined in these pages. A former American ambassador, John W. McDonald,[5] tells me that thirty years ago he was asked to speak on the role of forgiveness in foreign affairs. He blithely accepted but soon vowed never to do it again. For when he searched the publications and talked with the foreign policy community, he found, as he says, "Nobody had a clue. I looked and looked and looked and couldn't find anywhere forgiveness had crossed anyone's mind." Of course, he can now point to numerous places where the state departments of the world take a more serious approach to conflict resolution.

In the past, there was a tendency for some in government to hold a condescending view of "nice stories" rather than take these experiences seriously in formulating policy. But what has happened in the past fifteen years in South Africa has made even the most hardnosed purveyors of *Realpolitik* think again. Ireland, too, opened minds. American Senator George Mitchell, who was involved in the peace process, pointed out eight years ago in his book *Making Peace*, at a time when the big hurdle was the decommissioning of weapons: "If there is ever to be a durable peace and genuine reconciliation, what is really needed is the decommissioning of mindsets." In tackling mindsets, there are initiatives that private civil society can sometimes undertake that governments cannot, particularly in healing the hurts of history. And it is these unhealed leftovers from the past, the deep emotional wounds and scars at the grassroots that often frustrate the best intentions of carefully crafted diplomatic agreements. We may see more of what Kofi Annan called for in his Millennium Report to the United Nations; that is member states forming "coalitions of change well beyond the precincts of officialdom."

notes

Chapter 1

1 Irish Republican Army.

2 Non-Governmental Organization.

3 Message from archbishop's press secretary, 6 November 2007.

4 *The New York Times*, 8 October 2004.

5 World Congress of Faiths, March 1997.

6 Kaduna *Weekly Trust*, 26 July 2003.

7 PBUH is an abbreviation for "Peace and Blessings Be Upon Him" which is used by Muslims in speech and writing as a sign of respect for Muhammad and all the biblical prophets.

8 *The Pastor and the Imam* (FLT films), produced by David and Alan Channer, with Imad Karam, and narrated by Rageh Omaar. http://www.fltfilms.org.uk/imam.html.

9 28 February 2000.

10 30 October 2006.

11 Quoted in Michael Henderson, *Forgiveness: Breaking the Chain of Hate* (Portland, Ore.: Arnica, 2003), 4.

12 Martha Minow, *Between Vengeance and Forgiveness* (Boston: Beacon Press, 1998), 10.

13 Quoted in William Bole, Drew Christiansen, and Robert T. Hennemeyer, *Forgiveness in International Politics* (Washington, D.C.: U. S. Conference of Catholic Bishops, 2004), 17–18.

14 Bole et al., 15.

15 Minow, 14–24, offers a strong argument against forgiveness. But for her, forgiveness entails forgetting and amnesty rather than the kind of forgiveness that incorporates justice.

16 Geraldine Smyth, "Brokenness, Forgiveness, Healing, and Peace in Ireland," in *Forgiveness and Reconciliation*, ed. Raymond G. Helmick and Rodney L. Petersen (Philadelphia: Templeton Foundation Press, 2001), 339.

17 Smyth, 340.

18 Audrey R. Chapman, "Truth Commissions as Instruments of Forgiveness and Reconciliation," in Helmick and Petersen, 263.

19 Donald W. Shriver Jr., "Forgiveness: A Bridge across Abysses of Revenge," in Helmick and Petersen, 156.

20 Miroslav Volf, quoted in Rodney L. Peterson, "A Theology of Forgiveness," in Helmick and Petersen, 20.

21 Chapman, in Helmick and Peterson, 264.

Chapter 2

1 *The New York Times*, 28 March 1998.

2 We would be freed from foolish mistakes if we could see ourselves through others' eyes.

3 Author of *Honest Patriots* and *An Ethic for Enemies*.

4 28 January.

5 27 March 2007.

6 26 February 2007.

7 28 February 2007.

8 10 December 2001.

9 From a message to a Parents Circle concert featuring Liza Minnelli in Rome, 23 July 2005.

10 Dr. Martin Luther King Jr., 4 April 1967 at a meeting of Clergy and Laity Concerned at Riverside Church, New York City.

11 From my book, *The Power of Dignity*, which I am in the process of writing.

12 Elisabeth Kübler-Ross, *On Death and Dying* (New York: Routledge, 1973).

Chapter 3

1 They have written about their experiences in Camilla Carr and Jon James' *The Sky Is Always There* (Norwich: Canterbury Press, 2008).

2 www.theforgivenessproject.com.

3 Organization of African Unity.

4 In 2007 he became president of the International Association of Initiatives of Change.

5 "Récit d'un rescapé de la torture," 2 June 2007.

6 "Mohamed Sahnoun, la mémoire blessée d'un homme de paix," 29 May 2007.

7 2 October 2006.

8 7 October 2006.

9 8 October 2006.

10 Donald B. Kraybill, Steven M. Nolt, and David L. Weaver-Zercher, *Amish Grace: How Forgiveness Transcended Tragedy* (San Francisco: Jossey-Bass, 2007).

11 *Christian Science Monitor,* 18 October 2006.

12 18 May 2006.

13 Dr. Theodor Oberländer in 1959.

14 Gustav Heinemann in 1970.

15 Georg von Broich in 1952.

16 19 October 2006.

17 The ideologue of the Hindu right best known for his formulation that only those who regard India as both their homeland and their holy land can be trustworthy Indians, a formulation that renders Muslims and Christians suspect by definition.

18 The land or space you are called to serve, fight in, or fight for.

19 6 September 2004.

20 18 July 2002.

21 1 December 2005.

22 2 December 2006.

23 20 December 2006.

24 17 January 2007.

25 Trudy Govier and Wilhelm Verwoerd, "Forgiveness: The Victim's Prerogative," *South African Journal of Philosophy* 21.1 (2002): 97–111.

26 Miroslav Volf, *Exclusion and Embrace: A Theological Exploration of Identity, Otherness, and Reconciliation* (Nashville: Abingdon, 1996), 116.

Chapter 4

1 17 October 2006.

2 See "People Building Trust: Driving towards Peace in Sierra Leone," in *Global Update* 1 (September 2006): 4; 28 November 2006.

3 28 November 2006.

4 8 September 2003.

5 Sushobha Barve, *Healing Streams* (New Delhi: Penguin Books, 2003).

6 27 May 1998.

7 24 January 1978.

8 12 December 1998.

9 23 May 2003.

10 *Japan Times,* 15 May 2004.

Chapter 5

1 "The way of forgiveness in the ways of politics," Amman, Jordan, 24 December 1999.

2 *The Tablet,* 13 May 2006.

3   Described in my book *See You after the Duration.*
4   Scott Appleby, *The Ambivalence of the Sacred* (Lanham, Md.: Rowman & Littlefield, 1999).
5   *For the Love of Tomorrow* (FLT films), produced by David Channer, directed by Michel Sentis.
6   1960, cited in Gabriel Marcel, ed., *Fresh Hope for the World* (London: Longman, 1960).
7   Marcel.
8   Douglas Johnston and Cynthia Sampson, eds., *Religion, the Missing Dimension of Statecraft* (New York: Oxford University Press, 1994).
9   Caux Scholars Program lecture, Caux, 1997.
10 W. Wolpe, and S. McDonald, "Training Leaders for Peace," *Journal of Democracy* 17.1 (2006): 132–38.
11 Presentation and interview, Woodrow Wilson International Center for Scholars, Washington, D.C., January 2007.
12 Interview with Pierre Spoerri in Caux, August 2007.
13 Uganda gained independence from Britain in 1962.

Chapter 6

1   11 February 2007.
2   16 October 2007.
3   14 October 2007.
4   *Der Spiegel* reported in October 2007 that a commission of eminent German historians concluded that the death toll was most likely 18,000 and definitely no more than 25,000.

Afterword

1   On 10 October 2008 he was awarded the Nobel Peace Prize.
2   31 August 2007, http://www.cmi.fi.
3   Also former president of IofC.
4   "Beyond Borders—In Search of a Solution in Kashmir," Centre for Dialogue and Reconciliation, Haryana, 2007.
5   McDonald is cofounder with Dr. Louise Diamond of the Institute for Multi-Track Diplomacy (IMTD).

BIBLIOGRAPHY

Ahmed, Akbar S. *Journey into Islam: The Crisis of Globalization.* Washington, D.C.: Brookings Institution Press, 2007.

Amstutz, Mark. *The Healing of Nations: The Promise and Limits of Political Forgiveness.* Lanham, Md.: Rowman & Littlefield, 2005.

Appleby, Scott. *The Ambivalence of the Sacred.* Lanham, Md.: Rowman & Littlefield, 1999.

Arendt, Hannah. *The Human Condition: A Study of the Central Dilemmas Facing Modern Man.* Garden City, N.Y.: Doubleday, 1959.

Arnold, Johann Christoph. *Seeking Peace.* Farmington, Penn.: Plough Publishing House, 1998.

———. *Seventy Times Seven.* Farmington, Penn.: Plough Publishing House, 1997

Barve, Sushobha. *Healing Streams.* New Delhi: Penguin Books, 2003.

Biggar, Nigel, ed. *Burying the Past: Making Peace and Doing Justice after Civil Conflict.* Washington, D.C.: Georgetown University Press, 2001.

Bole, William, Drew Christiansen, and Robert T. Hennemeyer. *Forgiveness in International Politics.* Washington, D.C.: U.S. Conference of Catholic Bishops, 2004.

Borris-Dunchunstang, Eileen R. *Finding Forgiveness.* New York: McGraw-Hill, 2006.

Carr, Camilla, and Jon James. *The Sky Is Always There.* Norwich, Conn.: Canterbury Press, 2008.

Frayling, Nicholas. *Pardon and Peace: A Reflection on the Making of Peace in Ireland.* London: SPCK, 1996.

Frost, Brian. *Struggling to Forgive.* London: HarperCollins, 1998.

Gobodo-Madikizela, Pumla. *A Human Being Died that Night: A South African Woman Confronts the Legacy of Apartheid.* New York: Houghton Mifflin, 2003.

Gopin, Marc. *Between Eden and Armageddon.* New York: Oxford University Press, 2000

———. *Holy War, Holy Peace.* New York: Oxford University Press, 2002.

Govier, Trudy, and Wilhelm Verwoerd. "Forgiveness: The Victim's Prerogative." *South African Journal of Philosophy* 21.1 (2002): 97–111.

Hamber, Brandon. *How Should We Remember? Issues to Consider When Establishing Commissions and Structures for Dealing with the Past.* Johannesburg: Centre for the Study of Violence and Reconciliation, 1998.

Helmick, Raymond G., and Rodney L. Petersen, eds. *Forgiveness and Reconciliation.* Philadelphia: Templeton Foundation Press, 2001.

Henderson, Michael. *All Her Paths Are Peace.* West Hartford, Conn.: Kumarian Press, 1994.

———. *Forgiveness: Breaking the Chain of Hate.* Portland, Ore.: Arnica Publishing, 2003.

———. *The Forgiveness Factor.* London: Grosvenor Books, 1996.

Johnston Jr., Doug, and Cynthia Sampson, eds. *Religion, the Missing Dimension of Statecraft.* New York: Oxford University Press, 1994.

———. *Faith-Based Diplomacy: Trumping Realpolitik.* New York: Oxford University Press, 2003.

Kraybill, Donald B., Steven M. Nolt, and David L. Weaver-Zercher. *Amish Grace: How Forgiveness Transcended Tragedy.* San Francisco: Jossey-Bass, 2007.

Kübler-Ross, Elisabeth, *On Death and Dying.* New York: Routledge, 1973.

Lederach, John Paul. *The Journey Toward Reconciliation.* Scottsdale, Penn.: Herald Press, 1999.

Marcel, Gabriel, ed. *Fresh Hope for the World.* London: Longmans, 1960.

Minow, Martha. *Between Vengeance and Forgiveness.* Boston: Beacon Press, 1998.

Montville, Joseph, ed. *Conflict and Peacemaking in Multiethnic Societies.* Lexington, Mass.: Lexington Books, 1990.

Montville, Joseph, Julius Demetrios, and Vamik Volkan, eds. *The Psychodynamics of International Relationships.* 2 vols. Lexington, Mass.: Lexington Books, 1990–1991.

Paden, John. *Muslim Civic Cultures and Conflict Resolution.* Washington, D.C.: Brookings, 2005.

Pearl, Judea, and Ruth Pearl, eds. *I am Jewish: Personal Reflections Inspired by the Last Words of Daniel Pearl.* Woodstock, Vt.: Jewish Lights Publishing, 2004.

Pearl, Mariane. *A Mighty Heart.* New York: Scribner, 2003.

Piguet, Jacqueline. *For the Love of Tomorrow.* London: Grosvenor Books, 1986.

Ramadan, Tariq. *In the Footsteps of the Prophet.* Oxford: Oxford University Press, 2007.

Russell, Alan, and Anthony Clayton, eds. *Dresden: A City Reborn.* Oxford: Berg Publishers, 2001.

Sacks, Jonathan. *The Dignity of Difference.* London: Continuum, 2002.

———. *The Home We Build Together: Recreating Society.* London: Continuum, 2007.

Shriver Jr., Donald W. *An Ethic for Enemies.* New York: Oxford University Press, 1995.

———. *Honest Patriots.* New York: Oxford University Press, 2005.

Smedes, Lewis B. *The Art of Forgiving.* New York: Ballantine, 1996.

Staub E., L. A. Pearlman, A. Gubin, and A. Hagengimana. "Healing, Reconciliation, Forgiving, and the Prevention of Violence after Genocide or Mass Killing: An Intervention and Its Experimental Evaluation in Rwanda." *Journal of Social and Clinical Psychology* (2005).

Tutu, Desmond. *No Future without Forgiveness.* New York: Doubleday, 1999.

Volf, Miroslav. *Exclusion and Embrace: A Theological Exploration of Identity, Otherness, and Reconciliation.* Nashville: Abingdon, 1996.

Wolpe, W., and S. McDonald. "Training Leaders for Peace." *Journal of Democracy* 17.1 (2006): 132–38.

Worthington, Everett. *Forgiveness and Reconciliation: Theory and Application.* New York: Brunner/Routledge, 2006.

―――. *Forgiving and Reconciling: Bridges to Wholeness and Hope.* Downers Grove, Ill.: InterVarsity, 2003.

―――, ed. *Handbook of Forgiveness.* New York: Brunner/Routledge, 2005.

―――. *The Power of Forgiving.* Philadelphia: Templeton Foundation Press, 2005.

Yancey, Philip. *What's So Amazing about Grace?* Grand Rapids: Zondervan, 1997.

INDEX